OCT 20

THE FIVE PEOPLE YOU'LL MEET IN PRISON

A MEMOIR OF ADDICTION, MANIA & HOPE

BRANDON M. STICKNEY

bancroft
press

Cover & Interior design: Tracy Copes

Author Photo/Prison Page Illustrations: Patrick Stickney

978-1-61088-196-8—HC

978-1-61088-197-5—PB

978-1-61088-198-2—Kindle

978-1-61088-199-9--Ebook

Published by Bancroft Press "Books that Enlighten"

410-358-0658

P.O. Box 65360, Baltimore, MD 21209

www.bancroftpress.com

Printed in the United States of America

For Bruce Bortz,
who helped me get back into "The Show,"
and for Mitch Albom, who opened the gates of Heaven.

"…feeling just like this prison system wanted me to—
utterly powerless, vulnerable, alone."
—Piper Kerman, *Orange is the New Black*

"We are sent to prison *as* punishment,
not *for* punishment."
—Wayne Kramer

AUTHOR'S NOTE

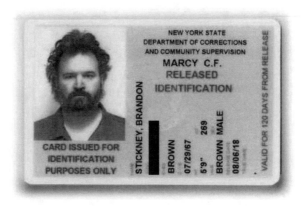

This memoir is based on my personal experiences and recollections about life in four different New York State prisons over the span of nearly two years. Due to the material's sensitive nature, I've changed most names. I've also changed some subject descriptions, some dates, and some locations of some events. Most conversations are drawn from notes I made while in prison, while some are recreated from memory afterward.

All five men alluded to in the book title knew I was a journalist and writer. And all of them urged me to write a book … with them in it. The five named characters are composites, but they are composites of real characters I lived with in prison. The five fine fellows who kept me from going crazy in prison appear here in all their ragged glory.

This book took nineteen months for me to research in prison, and nine months to write and edit after I was released. For reasons that will soon become obvious, it was a very hard book to write.

Brandon M. Stickney
Palm Beach, FL
May 2019

CONTENTS

INTRODUCTION

I first laid eyes upon Brandon M. Stickney in the local bookstore on Main Street in Lockport, New York, sometime in the very early 1990s. He recognized me as the guy who "wrote books about the Beatles," which was how all the locals knew me—"Hey, aren't you the guy?" To which I answered, "Yes."

A few days later, he showed up at our red brick Victorian manor with a copy of a book about John Lennon that I had penned with Lennon's half-sister, Julia Baird. The young man was after an autograph. After opening the front double doors of our studio at 735 East Market Street, I said to him for some reason: "You don't really want an autograph. You want a job." I then showed him into my first-floor office, and sat down behind my desk, but the job interview was no interview at all. He was hired, and I expected to see him early the next day for work on *Blackbird: The Life and Times of Paul McCartney*, among other things.

After a week or two, I said, "Look man, you might as well just move in." The house was huge, and my small family occupied only a few miserly rooms. I invited him to pick an upstairs bedroom, which he promptly did. After a while, a girlfriend of his showed up. She was nice but normal and didn't blend well with the Krishna conscious vibe going on in our artsy ashram home. Often, I could hear them making adolescent love, which I found vaguely amusing; two young kids going at it like rabbits on the second floor. It's funny the things you remember.

Brandon was an excellent worker and a very intelligent boy. I never had any expectation he was in any way adversely involved with alcohol. In fact, at some level, he seemed rather collegiate, clean cut, and hopelessly naïve about the world. A good-natured, jovial fellow, he got along well with my family and was courteous and professional with the many guests from all walks of life who flowed in and out of that beautiful big house, including everyone from the famous to the tweedy publishing drones from Toronto and New York who would come to either tweak me on some project they had already paid for or just make sure it was progressing along the lines preferred by their literary masters in midtown Manhattan.

Young Stickney was my right-hand man, a gleeful Gabby Hayes to my Roy

Rogers. He was a damn fine employee, a good and trusted friend, and professional colleague. I took him to Europe with me on a publishing tour partly because I needed him, but more because I pitied him—he hadn't really been anywhere outside the confines of the narrow-minded Western New York arena.

Together we visited classy Krishna temples in London and brothels in Belgium, and stayed in the cheapest hotels I could find—I was very money conscious (then as now) because I've often seen people from poor families who go astray when they suddenly strike it rich. Anyway, we buttoned up whatever it was I was after in Europe for, and summarily returned home. I was happy Brandon had a chance to see the world, where he always acquitted himself admirably in the discharge of his duties.

I remember going down to Florida with him in my tricked-out camper van with an automatic bed, fridge, and a crazy cool stereo system on which we played Bob Dylan's "Everything is Broken" all the way from Western New York to Key West, over and over again. Obviously, a terrific traveling song!

While we drove, I remember making love to my wife Vrnda on the bed, trying to be as quiet as possible, thinking I got away with it, only later to be nudged and winked at by Mr. Stickney about the bawdy marital adventure in the backseat of my rocking super van.

There is an incredible tale about my end times in Lockport and how everything I had built so carefully, so purposefully, so lovingly was destroyed by other people's, avarice, jealousy, and petty mindedness. Others may hold differing opinions, but now at sixty-five the way I look at the history I myself created and successfully marketed reign supreme over anyone else's views on the world of what I did or who I am.

The fact is I dropped the ball when it came to my relationships with people—trusting those I should have kept at arms-length and tossing aside those I should've embraced. Being wealthy is hard work and it doesn't come with an instruction manual. Anyway, I fucked up and lost, or rather, had it stolen away, piece by piece by persons—who here shall remain nameless. But, as they say, you know well who you are!

As for Brandon, I never knew anything about his savage substance-abuse. I think I recall him doing a bit of cocaine back in the day and not thinking too much about it (even though it wasn't my cup of tea). I was a pretty much a live-and-let-live kind of enlightened dude. Fifteen years and about five lifetimes later, I heard that Brandon had become a hopeless addict and was in and out of jail on various offenses in that insular, close-minded, know-nothing town of Lockport. That black hole of blue-collar colloquialisms would be enough to make anybody a junkie. I blame Lockport—don't blame him, say I!

Brandon's a lovely man with a good heart whom for quite a time, ended up the worst kind of unsalvageable human wreckage, stomping around that one-horse town making one monumentally stupid mistake after another until now, after a decade plus of complete and ardently dedicated self-destruction, he has finally come to his senses, or so I hope!

There is an interesting parallel here: I too went crazy for approximately the same period of time, but my drug of choice was beautiful young Thai women. Now that I have quietly fucked my way from one end of Southeast Asia to another, I've pretty much had my fill and now live quietly and contentedly with my ten-year-old son, Eden.

To be honest, I do regret all those years of my devotional practice lost, my beautiful home decimated by those closest to me, my career in ruins by the glut of crappy free content on the Internet, which prevents people from getting in their cars, going to a decent bookstore, and plopping down $35 for a copy of one of my thirty-two books.

Strangely, while all this was happening, pretty much the same kind of soul-sucking monster was eating away at my man Brandon. As a highly productive and responsible reprobate, however, I still managed to turn up in about twenty-five Z movies, start a hip T-shirt design company, resurrect my audiobook business, and push out an angelic little boy who sits across the room from me now as I fiddle with this crummy iPad while talking about a guy Eden never knew and long ago, a life he never lived.

In many ways, this introduction is as much about me as Brandon because we were, and are, kindred spirits, brothers in arms, lovers of the literary life walking together now (even without seeing each other for decades) as colleagues and the closest of friends. Which of us enters first the yawning grave over in Lockport's historic Cold Springs Cemetery, just around the corner from my old manor, time will tell. But from the moment he showed up at my grand front door seeking an autograph—perhaps three decades or so—I have had nothing but love, respect, admiration, and compassion for this exceptionally talented, big-hearted, terminally scattered soul.

Read this book carefully because I promise you it will contain wonderful words, unparalleled insight, stalwart cautionary tales, and honesty plumbed from the very marrow of his now fifty-something bones. Brandon sees the world like a yogi, though he never practiced. His clarity of vision was never compromised in any way. Even at the height of the oddly self-chosen destruction that he embraced, he knew what the fuck he was doing. He knew it was wrong and he knew how it was hurting himself and everyone he loved. All of which, of course, made it all the more horrific for the hero of our story—poor, poor boy.

The measure of the man in this epic, one-man, Shakespearean tragedy is of a soul, who while unable to control the onslaught of his own life, knew perfectly well everything going down. Just like Macbeth, Brandon was cursed with a vision in which he witnessed his lower self beating the shit out of this wonderful man on an almost daily basis—no, hourly basis—for years.

Being relatively new to the art of being an old man, I've learned we tend to prattle on (especially about the ever-present past, which is still so close behind). I am, to be honest, morbidly bitter about everything I accomplished and then lost by the avaricious, evil reach out of both the people closest to me and the American government, who for some strange reason, saw me as an existential threat and helped reduce my elegant self-made Krishna temple into what it is today, a second-rate imitation of what Martha Stewart could do to a house if she didn't have any fucking money or taste.

Yes, I'm old, poor, bitter, and spent, but like my little brother Brandon, I still can see clearly, and speak frankly. By the way, I have (after a twenty-year sabbatical) once again picked up my Krishna conscious devotional yoga aspirations. I'm hedging my bets in case there is a God at the end of this long torturous life.

Good luck to you, Brandon! I love you, now and forever, and when at last we pass through the portals of this temporary material world, as Jimi Hendrix once sang, "Then I'll see you in the next one. Don't be late."

Geoffrey Giuliano (Jagannatha Dasa)
Pattaya, Chonburi
Thailand

PREFACE

I'd like you to meet five individuals who affected my life in a profound way. One found me when I was lost. Another worked to save my soul. A third guarded me through a difficult time. Still another helped me realize this was just an experience, just a temporary nightmare that would soon end. The fifth was a man of authority who got to know me best and gave me the most important gift—laughter.

After I went behind bars—a university-educated journalist convicted of a drug offense—I learned that most of my brethren were there for their second or third time. They knew jail life and thug life. I knew neither. It was only through the friendships of these five men that I was able to survive, mentally and physically, behind the razor wire.

The first of the five was named Big Bear. He said he was of rare descent—part Indian, part Italian. I met him in a superstorm of prison chaos, and he guided me so I could put my prison world in order.

Then there was "Pastor" Mark, whose background was questionable, but he served as a guide as well during my incarceration. Pastor Mark proudly urged me to look at his stack of Bibles and "find the way."

Gummy was named for the fact that he had no teeth but ate like a normal man. He was like a bodyguard to me. Though he dealt drugs on the outside, he was, on the inside, a wise soul, passing his homespun wisdom on to me whenever he could.

Highway drifter and Robo-Tripper Gandhi served as a best friend and mystical guru during our time together. We talked of Kerouac, space, the tarot, the zodiac, his distant family, and the compelling topic of life on the road.

Valefor was different altogether. He was a corrections officer, one of those ill-tempered monsters we were supposed to avoid because they made prison hell. Valefor was one in a million. He talked to us as equals and got to know our histories. He protected my mind, often giving me a dose of his intelligence, emphasizing that "prison isn't forever."

These were the five who generously protected me through their friendship and advice. Prison makes you forget the difference between right and wrong. So, I never thought there'd be anything positive about the prison experience, but they helped me learn how not to wind up a homeless alcoholic after prison.

We were together for a lot: the biting shackles and leg cuffs; the mess hall running out of food; interrogations by the corrections officers (some of which turned violent); the apathetic treatment at the Infirmary; the officers watching our every move; the school classes that taught us nothing; the dodging of officers' speeding vans; witnessing the guard attacks on other inmates; and much more.

We had our share of agony from prison life, but our friendships were transcendent, so much so that we felt free, floating out of the prison into the sun, the vast land, the roads that led home. Together we talked, acted, and thought without restraint.

We all had leave dates and we prayed (thanks to Pastor Mark) that we would make it. To be free, out in the world, again.

This is our story.

THE PARTY'S END

"Punishment is frightening, and confinement;
the modern punishment of choice,
frightens in a particular way. ...

Our response to crime remains a blunt
and expensive instrument that more often seems to
scar the criminal than reform him."

– Ted Conover, *Newjack: Guarding Sing Sing*

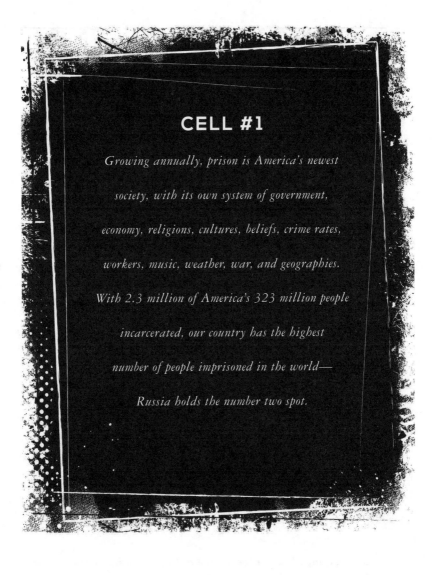

CELL #1

Growing annually, prison is America's newest

society, with its own system of government,

economy, religions, cultures, beliefs, crime rates,

workers, music, weather, war, and geographies.

With 2.3 million of America's 323 million people

incarcerated, our country has the highest

number of people imprisoned in the world—

Russia holds the number two spot.

CHAPTER 1

AMERICA JAILS JOURNALISTS TOO

"There is always some madness going on,
and whether you like it or not, you're involved."
—Eldridge Cleaver

I had spent over four months at the Niagara County Jail, a place I thought I'd never visit much less stay. The jail became intertwined with my life after criminal justice caught up with me on the road to hell; today, I was leaving … for *prison*. I'd soon learn that prison made jail look like summer camp, that I'd actually long for the halcyon days in the county jail.

We did not know, but soon found out, that an hour-long bus ride to the maximum security Wende Correctional Facility was going to take something like four hours. Why? Why four straight hours in shackles and biting handcuffs? The longer the ride, the more overtime pay for the unionized corrections officers.

I was leaving my hometown of Lockport, New York, in the spring, my favorite time of year. My neighbor at the county jail was Max, a young guy from nearby Niagara Falls. His charge was murder. He and another fellow, a bean pole named BK Jim, had lured a "friend" to a wooded area near the Falls casino and stabbed him to death (thirty-two times) for $80 so they could buy pot. Max told people the cops didn't know who did the deed until they got a tip about BK's cell phone. He had talked to someone about "this guy we stabbed and ripped off." A couple of geniuses.

It was springtime. But not for us. We had been waiting in the jail's tank for hours, listening to a few inmates pontificate about a Niagara Falls gang. It's been said that gangs did not originate in the ghettos and rough streets of our cities. The gangs started in jails as inmates sought protection, brotherhood, drugs, and, most importantly, identity.

One of the dudes said to me, "O.G., you got a smoke?"

I said, "I don't smoke, sorry. What's O.G. mean?"

"Old Gangsta, dawg," he said, blinking. "You the Original Gangsta, O.G., my nigga," he said. "Don't ever 'Sorry.' Mad respect, O.G." I was mildly flattered. I know I did a lot of bad, underhanded, and unforgiveable shit, but this was the first time I'd ever been called a gangster.

The county jailors took us out of the tank to prepare us for the state prison bus. I listened to the boys in blue as they handcuffed us, then wrapped a long chain around the waist to connect to the handcuffs and leg cuffs. As they ordered us about, they heckled us as if we were on a playground: "dickwad," "asshole," "fucker," "motherfucker," "jerkoff," and others, while female C.O.s stood there chuckling. I was called "Fucker," by one, for no reason. Not always a friendly jail. I liked being the O.G. better.

As if that wasn't enough, they locked a black box around our wrists to reduce hand and arm movement. I was lucky. I got an old man C.O. who'd administered the psychological survey to me (months ago) and had put me safely away in the SHU (Security Housing Unit) for crazies. Today, he was cordial to me and didn't lock the cuffs too tight. Other officers cuffing convicts across the state weren't so nice. They put Stun-Cuffs around inmates' wrists or ankles, using electric bursts via a wireless transmitter to keep prisoners in line.

There was a warning from the county guards that the state corrections officers would be abusive. We were told we'd be taking a van to get to the prison. They put us in shackles, threw our personal items in the garbage, and loaded us onto the bus.

State prison. I'd be spending my summer behind bars, with no end in sight. To men in county, state was the big time. "Going upstate."

It's nearly impossible to climb bus steps in shackles. On the state prison bus, there were unusable windows—they were near the ceiling, so no one outside could see us. As the big bus moved, all we could see was the sky and the tops of trees.

Fellow inmate riders had more to offer. If you don't have your indictment or other court paperwork, they said, you were a "rapo" or sex offender, trying to hide. I saw other inmates at the county jail being needled and called "rapo." But I knew I wasn't one. "I sold suboxone to a cop," I said, to blank stares and accusatory looks. "I'm no rapo."

Behind bars, sex offenders are viewed as the lowest form of convict. Next to narcs. Once discovered among the others, they are vulnerable to all kinds of abuse, from inmates and from C.O.s. I learned that for inmates, I fit the sex offender profile: no tattoos, beer belly, glasses, short hair. The other, normal inmates might have had one or more items from the list, especially tattoos. This is the first subject inmates discuss whenever they see someone new (Rapo!), especially someone without paperwork. My denials made their case even stronger.

"This yo firs bid? Every dog got they paperwork," said a black guy in the seat in front of me.

"I don't," I said. "No one told me to bring it." I was suddenly very mad at my defense attorney, Katy Mock, the public pretender, for not schooling me on what I needed to be ready for state prison. I knew people at the county jail—why didn't *they* clue me in? I was going into this shit blind. What else didn't I know?

I learned a "bid" is your prison sentence. I learned that prisoners who've had multiple bids and have their arms coated in tattoos are highly regarded. Committing murder and carrying guns, or selling guns, were also cool. First-timers have a lot to learn, too much for some others to bother with. It was almost certain that those with multiple bids had relatives who were also in prison, generation to generation. Pride was taken in this fact. Rites of passage for the young O.G.s. They were part of America's secret society, populating our prisons.

It seemed as if everyone on the bus eased a few inches away from me and stopped looking in my direction. Light desperation hit—*must prove my innocence.* I held up my arms, still shackled, pulling up my sleeve with my teeth, and uttered, "See my track marks?" I struck up conversations about being a writer, news reporter, author, and the groovy stuff I knew about big crime cases.

Most of it fell on deaf ears, except for the two convicts who questioned me—interrogated me, really—trying to prove I was not an author.

- How much money you make?
- Who published you?
- Where'd you get your information for the book?

They couldn't prove anything against me because I am an author. I answered the rather obvious questions with ease.

For years, I had been a police reporter for the *Union-Sun & Journal* in Lockport (north of Buffalo), often visiting the jail's communications office to gather reports of arrests, fires, deaths, and the general mayhem that occurred overnight in my small General Motors town. It was a gossipy, stuffed-shirt job, yet I thought I was following in the footsteps of Hemingway, Burroughs, and Hunter S. Thompson. Any anti-establishment scribe's example suited me. No one told me you wind up in trouble when you try to be someone you're not.

I eventually went from the US&J to the Associated Press and A&E. I even wrote a book about America's deadliest act of domestic terrorism, the Oklahoma City bombing—perpetrated by a man from my hometown area. James Collins wrote of it, and me, in *Time* magazine. Court TV broadcast a documentary with me as the main talking head. I covered McVeigh's trial in Denver, sitting between Jeffrey Toobin and Greta Van Susteren. I talked about McVeigh's methamphetamine use in *Time*. That was my scoop, and it was picked up by many news outlets. I was even quoted in the tabloid *Star*.

I had a career then. Also a serious drinking problem. Cocaine too, on weekends. Okay, whenever it was available. Cocaine was my "can't stop" drug. I'd be drunk and say, "I'll just sniff this little bag and I'll be done." One line and I was bar hopping all night, looking for more.

My pride took a serious hit. In 1997, I did not win the Pulitzer Prize. But *All-American Monster* was plagiarized by a member of the *Los Angeles Times* Pulitzer Prize-winning team. His book, *One of Ours*, copied nearly three chapters of my book. Reading my unattributed words, I considered his plagiarism an honor, certainly, but it was also a punch in the face. His publisher, W.W. Norton, could have published my book instead of stealing it from me. The *Buffalo News* and the *Columbia Journalism Review* both took him to task for the blatant theft. The *Village Voice* interviewed me but didn't want to poke the bear, Norton. I didn't file a lawsuit. I did use Norton as an excuse to drink more heavily.

Raised a small-town but well-read boy, I took a writing course at Skidmore College's New York State Writers Institute. My teacher was Jay McInerney, the author of *Bright Lights, Big City*. Jay and I talked a few times after class. Drank beer together in the rathskeller. He invited me to downtown Saratoga Springs for an old-fashioned pub crawl with friends Candace Bushnell and William Kennedy. Bushnell's then husband, city ballet dancer Charles Askegard, told Jay that half of the NYC ballet dancers were gay. Jay got everyone within hearing distance laughing when he quipped, "Which half?"

Author Joyce Carol Oates attended the institute both summers I was there. We spoke at length about Lockport, where we were both born, thirty years apart.

We shared a twenty-year correspondence, which culminated in a short story I'd publish with Oates's *Ontario Review*. I was starstruck—John Updike appeared in the same issue, Summer 2006, number 64.

And old N. Frank Daniels, whom I met at Skidmore, was there, just before HarperPerennial published his novel, *Futureproof*. Daniels came to stay at my house in Lockport in 2004, when I was still married. He was writing a new book and wanted to get away from Atlanta and his heroin habit. I was no AA sponsor; I obtained cocaine and Vicodin for each of us, which we used with Jamaican rum after a good day of sitting at the typers. We enjoyed plenty of rum and Sprite to wash the Vicodin down. We really thought we were getting somewhere.

CELL #2

Judges seem to dole out harsher sentences to African

Americans and Latinos. Our prisons are also

more ethnically diverse than some states in our

nation. And they are exceptional examples of

the American police state, alive and well in the

Prison Industrial Complex. How did we get here?

Decades of "tough on crime" prosecutors, prepping

themselves for higher office, pushing for overlong

sentences and conviction of innocents.

CHAPTER 2

AFTER THE FLOOD

"End-stage addiction is mostly about waiting for the police,
or someone, to come and bury you in your shame."
—David Carr, *The Night of the Gun*

A decade earlier, the Timothy McVeigh/Oklahoma City biography and
related documentaries I made opened doors for me. McVeigh was
from my hometown area, Lockport, and I had covered the terrorist
attack and bombing trial for the newspaper. I eventually left full-time journalism for higher pay and made it to a management position at Mercedes-Benz
Financial Corporation. Finally, the drinking took over and I washed out with a
series of ad agency jobs, performed while sniffing a lot of opiate pills.

All it took was a 2003 operation by Dr. Dettoo, followed by a script of hydrocodone, and my fate was sealed. Alcohol and opiates allowed me to live in a daily
heaven, even when I was finally on welfare and shooting heroin. I loved it, sniffing
a pink Opana 10 milligram, and feeling that slow gathering of euphoria. All my
pain—mental and physical—was gone. I was filled with ignoble happiness and
energy, my mind in a spectacular fireworks show. Today, I can still feel the pill as I
crushed it, the wonderful powder as it went into my nostril, employing a playing
card I used to cut lines.

When someone said I should start sniffing, I didn't know that I had quite an
affinity for inhalants. I learned that hydrocodone was in the same family as heroin;
both were opiate-based. It got to where I'd sniff ten or more "hydros" in a sitting.
Then hydros weren't enough, so I told my old coke dealers, who switched me
to Oxycodone. Then I snorted Opanas (Oxymorphone), dilaudid, Roxycodone. I
chewed fentanyl patches. And when the local scene was out of pills, I got dope sick
and resorted to heroin. Heroin didn't hook me the way Opanas did.

History lesson: Opana, or Oxymorphone, was invented in 1914 in Germany
for injured World War 1 soldiers who became amputees. It had a special "happy"

ingredient. The cool kids called the drug "14-Hydroxydihydro." I started sniffing it in 2008—I only needed one pill every five hours, daytime, and I got happy and slept great at night. About that time, my dealer, Danny, said his coke sales had all but ceased. "Now everyone's buying pills." At first, I paid $8 per pill; that went up to $60 a pill.

Elation. Strength. Energy. Intelligence. Charm. These are just some of the feelings one had under the influence of Opanas. As well as a sense of charity/philanthropy. Me and thousands of other addicts across the country were buying opiates from cancer patients, who'd obtained prescriptions. The cancer folks gave their prescriptions to our drug dealers, and then paid their mortgage, gas, electric, and other bills from our drug money. Small-town dealers were handling thousands of dollars a day. Their bills were paid too.

When the opioid epidemic broke (sixteen-year-olds with clueless parents injecting themselves), Oxymorphone was one of the biggest killers in overdose, heart attack, and respiratory depression. In 2017, for the first time in the FDA's history, the agency issued a request to pull Oxymorphone, a "currently marketed" product, from the shelves. The request was granted on July 6. Only generic forms of Opana were available as of winter 2018.

It seemed there was no way to stop, even after losing my wife, house, cars, book collection, artwork, *everything*. I didn't care because "the high me" said I wasn't materialistic. Because love had been lost. Opiates became my religion, making me feel closer to God. I even joined a born-again church on the outskirts of Lockport and was baptized. Told people I was recovering from alcohol, though I was borrowing money and drinking harder than ever. Mixing alcohol with opiates was Hendrix/Morrisonland—you wouldn't live long. I made my home in Barone's, a long-abandoned music store. I called my life denial, or part of it anyway. Barone's was in such an advanced state of deterioration, I felt as if I was living in a condemned warehouse. That didn't matter. I was in a near-constant state of euphoria.

Was that what I was really looking for, deep down—God? Being high is heavenly. For some, drugs become God. Allison Moore wrote in *Shards* that, "I didn't know what to do without it. Ice (meth) was the only thing worth living for—I had felt that from the second it entered my body. I needed it to survive the world. Regardless of the fact that it had begun to kill me, ice was now my savior."

My wife and I separated in October 2005, when Hurricane Katrina flooded New Orleans, our honeymoon spot in 1993. It wasn't until March 2015, nearly ten years later, that we signed our divorce papers. I was in and out of AA then, but only because friends had asked me to seek help.

I loved drinking more than life itself and was convinced it would transport me to literary nirvana, just as it had for Cheever and Kerouac. I thought I could live as an intellectual while regularly exploring the dark taverns and drug houses where fate took me. I had a university education but was more comfortable around prostitutes and dealers than I was with the scholars in my circle, like feminist author Joyce Carol Oates, celebrity biographer Geoffrey Giuliano, and philosopher Paul Kurtz.

AA bothered me from the start. My first meeting was after a night of hard drinking. I was anxiety-ridden, paranoid, and jittery. They said I was "white knuckling it" and laughed it off. I didn't think it was funny at all. Neither AA, nor my doctor, who knew I was drinking too much, listened to me closely enough to realize I was going through an anxiety attack, which originated in anger and had a mental component.

I distrusted AA and its facile "Let Go and Let God" clichés. After a few meetings, which I only endured because of the comradery and coffee, I knew the formula. Individuals would "share" that they boozed up and did nasty things to others. Then, like AA founder Bill Wilson, people said they had an "awakening" with AA's help, "put the plug in the jug," were transformed into sobriety forever, and now had the gift of serving other people in the community. What a whopper! According to *The Guardian*, Wilson's awakening was the result of an acid trip, and the man died of complications from his other addiction/disease—smoking. Nevertheless, AA devotees forgave those character flaws and still journey annually to Bill's grave in an East Hampton, Vermont cemetery. To them, he is more than a minor savior.

They taught me Step Nine of the Twelve Steps: make "direct amends ... except when to do so would injure them or others." Imagine if a priest was asked to do this, because you know they made some people happy, some sad, and others angry. Imagine anyone who did not have a drinking problem doing it. They'd find it impossible; they might even get killed. After so long, guiltily setting things straight just doesn't resonate.

As a journalist, there were thousands of people I made happy and, likely, just as many who I hurt. As Brandon M. Stickney, there were many in my drunken, drug-using days I made happy or infuriated. I wanted to say "sorry" to some, leave some alone, and tell others where to go. *Shards* author Allison Moore got sober and found she didn't feel she "had the right to enter their lives and selfishly apologize. The more I faced my past in therapy, the more I realized my actions inflicted irrevocable pain and damage not only on those I loved but also on myself."

Memories, for some, might make them drink again, bring them down and finish them off, but not me. If "all" alcoholics and all intoxicants are the same, according to AA/NA ("A drunk is a drunk is a drunk"), I stand among the different. Someday, the recovery world will realize that all drugs and all people are different, requiring individualized treatment to initially succeed, then remain sober, no matter how expensive.

Addiction treatment expert Anne M. Fletcher said, "Despite the fact that group counseling is the predominant format, its use for addiction has not been well-researched, and there is no evidence that it is critical to the recovery process. Some people benefit more from a one-on-one approach."

The old-timers in AA told me to surrender my pride. Writers need their pride to go on. I sarcastically said I needed to raise $30,000 for Passages Malibu, an upscale rehab facility, because there were no legitimate places in my area that dealt with drinking problems. They all followed the AA creed. I told AA I wasn't sure about its God thing. They said it was not a religious program but a spiritual one. If you look up "spiritual" in the dictionary, it says, "having to do with religion." AA people always split hairs with me, with the skeptics, over words, manipulating the meanings to suit their own purposes. Just like addicts. So, the drinking has to stop for the AA member, but the addiction is still strong.

Drunks were accused by AA of being controlled by "ego" (not Freud's definition), selfishness, and narcissism. Then the same folks uttered praise to God for keeping them sober and getting them to AA meetings. If anyone was narcissistic, it was these people, imagining that God is so involved in their lives, that there are no accidents, and that God will also prevent mosquito bites.

When I made it to a psychiatrist, she diagnosed anxiety and manic depression. I was prescribed medication that turned me around. The AA folks told me to drop the pills or I wasn't going to get sober. I told them they were not psychiatric doctors and had no idea how to treat mental illness. That shut up one pushy old-timer.

The divorce paperwork seemed to spike my desire to rebel against convention. I had a clean record, other than a 1996 DUI. In 2015 and 2016, I was arrested three times for shoplifting alcohol, trespassing at an old apartment, and committing another minor, intoxication-related infraction. Taking beer from stores became a habit and, because I knew them, several store owners let me off with a warning. Mine was a small town—turning a blind eye was good business, sometimes.

Alcohol had been part of my life since high school. That's what we did back then—used fake I.D.s, drank and drove around, walked the small town, visited friends whose parents were away, or went to nearby Niagara Falls, Canada, where the legal drinking age was eighteen. There was drinking in college and many Buffalo bars to visit. My normal life was punctuated by hard-drinking weekends.

In the 1990s, I settled down a bit for marriage. A reporter at the local newspaper, I covered state politics, the county legislature, the school board, and sometimes local crime. My wife worked with "at risk" kids in North Tonawanda. These were sad cases: unemployed parents who ignored them, no money ... marginalized, like some of the inmates I'd meet years later.

The newspaper had an 11 a.m. deadline. It was a high-stress job but rewarding. Getting in the paper satisfied my early need for instant gratification. Though my wife and I had our own friends, we seemed to identify more strongly with my parents' friends—the rebels, hippies, and philosophers who had witnessed the revolution of the 1960s. Thirty years later, they still viewed "The Man" and cops as the enemy.

While I worked on an early novel, we made our marriage about the good times. We weren't going to be like others—traditionalists, conservatives, and those who gave in to divorce. I had periods of incredible energy at the paper, followed by days of sadness and lethargy. My internal mood was often on a roller coaster. The sooner in the day I got drunk, the better. My extreme emotions, either high or low, were killing me. I could not find a safe middle ground.

Since junior high, I'd experienced high anxiety. As trauma physician Gabor Mate wrote, "The denizens of the hell realm are trapped in states of unbearable rage and anxiety." I hid it from everyone, even the sadness. I thought God was mad at me. As a young man, I felt I had lost something. I sensed a crippling nostalgia—but for what?

When I was sixteen, I had my first blackout from alcohol. Not remembering four hours of what I'd done made me feel embarrassed, but not sure about what.

The blackouts stopped in my twenties, after more drinking practice.

My friend B.E. Chamberlain and I were guests at my older cousin's graduation party in Lyndonville. My parents were there too. After wandering around bored, greeting my cousins, aunt, uncle, grandparents, staring at the pool, telling jokes, the two of us wandered into the house. In the kitchen, we found a fresh, unopened bottle of Jamaican white rum, which my aunt or uncle must have left out on the counter. We exchanged glances and nodded. Chamberlain stood watch at the door while I poured us five or six shots into two tumbler glasses. We sat at the kitchen table and drank the rum as if it was water; we made twisted-taste faces because of the hot, invisible sugar juice and enjoying our find.

The door opened, and my grandpa came in and spoke with us: "Are you having a good time?" "Eat any cake?" "Go see your grandmother." Grandpa walked away, toward the bathroom. Maybe he thought we were drinking water. On the other hand, Grandpa probably smelled the booze on us, maybe thinking "Boys will be boys. Let them experiment and they'll see what happens." Chamberlain and I downed what remained in our glasses (it almost came right back up for me) and walked outside. The day was awash in bright silver and gold, and things felt a little topsy-turvy, but I was holding my own 154 pounds upright. No one had detected us yet, though I had to be acting peculiarly.

The rest of the event turned into alternating invisible and lucid moments: flashes of standing under a tent, kissing a girl I'd met, and her kissing me back, on my cousin's canopy bed, wanting more from her, talking to Chamberlain and the girl he'd met, hiding in a clothes closet in my cousin's bedroom so we could be alone (the girl saying, "Not another closet"), my mother telling us to get out of the closet, and me not wanting to leave the arms of this beautiful blonde.

Next, Mom and Dad up front, me and Chamberlain in the back seat of the Firebird. The Who on the radio, us singing "Pinball Wizard," "Won't Get Fooled Again," and "Who Are You" while Mom kept saying "Shut up," but laughing as well. We thought we were harmonizing, but Chamberlain and I couldn't sing at all. Going to bed, throwing up in the bathtub. Waking to vomit on my pillow. The sun up on a new day.

It may seem like I remember quite a lot of this blackout, though I estimate at least four missing hours from that day. I did not remember what my girl looked like. Or her name. I didn't see my cousin all day, not that I recall. My cousins made fun of me the next time we saw each other, at Christmas. At my grandparents' house, my cousins told me "Mary" was a fat chick and kept talking about me at school.

At the time, Chamberlain was fifteen and I was sixteen. At the party, the two of us had gotten very drunk. I loved the feeling, thinking I'll do this more often. My father talked to me a few days later, admonishing me, and giving me a box of condoms to avoid having sex without protection. He was wrong (I never got to third base), but I didn't challenge him.

Years later, at the newspaper, I had episodes where I couldn't breathe normally. My wife and I went to the ER at Lockport Memorial Hospital. When I tried to breathe, it felt like my lungs were exceeding the capacity of my rib cage. Extreme pain. Racing thoughts, rapid heartbeat. The ER doctor said there was nothing wrong with me.

Paranoia haunted me, at home and at work. Alcohol made the paranoia and the anxiety cease. So that was my self-prescribed solution. My career moved forward, so I became an alcoholic workaholic. I wrote a non-fiction book and enjoyed all the perks of a first-time author. I was just twenty-nine.

Then, one day, I was making great money at Mercedes-Benz Financial, attending conferences and trade shows and fraternizing with attractive PR women from other parts of the world. There were five-hundred people at my office, and I directed all communications. My job, that of marketing manager, was one of the top ten in the company. I controlled internal and external communications, reporting directly to our two CEOs. We sought banking contracts, accounts worth up to $20 million. I managed four people in the marketing department—two graphic artists and two project managers. We were a valuable team until about 2003, when the fallout from Sept. 11, 2001 hit the industry. I drank out of fear, slipped up in just about all my responsibilities, and left Mercedes (my branch of the company) by mutual decision.

We bought our Lockport house on Morrow Avenue back in 1999. I worked full time, and my boss said he would pay for me to obtain my MBA. My wife became a full-time mother and domestic goddess. Things were good. We had friends over every weekend, my daughter played soccer, and my folks took us to the country club for dinners. I reviewed books for *Publishers Weekly* and *Foreword Magazine*. I got to know ABC President Ben Sherwood and corresponded with Michael Chabon and Rick Moody. I went to Saratoga Springs for writing conferences. My new book, about the Seven Sutherland sisters, was sure to be a monumental success. I became a talented and generous masseuse, for one person—my wife.

No matter where you go, though, your character defects come along. They sneak up on you. We bought cases of rum, and I hid coke in my desk. Being poor at math, I insisted that my wife do all the Stickney accounting. Any discussions of money were avoided. We were bankrupt by 2005.

By 2005, I was also useless and unemployed. We lost the house. My wife and I separated, and I figured since I was on my own, I was going to party until the end. I obtained a low-paying job in mental health of all places. My customers had a variety of mental illnesses, and I realized that I was just like them. A brief return to marketing and advertising as a copywriter proved a failure. I lost three jobs in two years. Then I decided I'd live until my unemployment money ran out.

On a typical day during this lost period, I woke up around 11 a.m. to sniff lines of a crushed Opana. Then, comfortably high, I'd head to the corner gas station to beg for change near the door. I needed $2.80 for a grape Four Loko drink, which was twelve percent alcohol. I'd find some ghetto friends and drink in the sunshine near the Erie Canal, while they participated in the summer fishing derby. If it was a weekday, I'd visit an attorney or businessman I'd known and borrow twenty dollars for drinks for the rest of the day. The alcohol increased the strength of the opiate pill by seventy percent.

Whenever I needed money, I could count on my close friend Jim Kane, the son of my old boss, Dan Kane, from the newspaper. Jim ran a house-painting business and hired me intermittently for cleanup. He gave me $20 here and there, and it kept me going. I visited his cottage on Lake Ontario and soaked up the positive energies from the waves. Jim never failed to tell me to "slow down on the alcohol."

My friend Brett Garcia, a pool installer, was in town by 5 p.m. at the Niagara Hotel, a Kingsmen biker bar. After we had a few rum and Sprite drinks, he'd cash his check and we'd go to my dealer's house to score some opiates. The dealer had three kids, six cats, and two ferrets running around. Lockport had a free Friday night concert series that we attended. Acts such as Kim Mitchell, Kansas, Burton Cummings, and Eddie Money were booked every year and 20,000 people flooded downtown. Beer drinking went on until midnight, after which I'd wander back to my apartment. Since my divorce, I'd lived alone. It was an incredibly lonely and unproductive existence, except when I was high. Then I was a proud hedonist.

I lived and loitered at the "drunk houses" of Lockport. With unemployment money in my pocket and time on my hands (I still applied for jobs), I visited Dan Hazlett's house on Evans Street every day. The cast of characters there were people who appeared frequently in the newspaper's Police Report. Hazlett lived to drink and smoke but hated drugs, so the junkies and crackheads hung out in his kitchen and bathroom. It was the only place I could go at 9 a.m. and drink with others.

Brett Garcia and I went to Sean Parker's house across town and drank with him—then Sean started spending all his beer money on crack, so I ceased my visits. Nappo's house on Spalding Street had a festive crowd, especially in the summer for horseshoes. The police were at Nappo's house so much one summer that City Council members demanded an investigation of the landlord and property. I bought Opanas and cocaine and shared with these dime-store outlaws.

I visited Nappo on a day when I was junk sick—runny nose, stomach ruined, and muscles twitching all over. He let me in and said he had a little morphine, if I wanted it, no charge. I didn't like morphine (no euphoria), but knew it would cure me. Nappo said he only had a used needle. I wanted instant relief, so I cleaned it with Clorox, then water, and he shot me up. It hurt like the devil because the needle was bent. After an initial rush, I was well again.

It had been a mistake (not just morally). The needle started an infection in my left arm that grew to the size of a golf ball. I hid the injury while I couchsurfed at Hazlett's, wrapping a t-shirt around my arm. When it finally popped, it stunk like rotted food. After two weeks, it shrank and went away, but left a scar the size of a dime on my forearm.

I had read years earlier that the great writers and painters of another age had, like Jesus, hung out with prostitutes and criminals. I thought I knew what I was doing.

Then there was my Washburn Street apartment. I was unemployed but still writing and occasionally publishing an op-ed. My roommate, Brett, was a junkie. I let him live with me for free, as long as he shared pills and an occasional shot of dope. I never learned how to shoot up—he did it for me, reluctantly.

When my drug life got to be too much, I called 911. Before I got hit by the car, I didn't pay for ambulances and ER visits. Bills sent to my apartment went to the round file. As I sat in Erie County Medical Center three days after my alleged suicide attempt (death by car), the social worker came to me with an application for Medicaid, which was approved. New York used to be called "the Cadillac of welfare states" by Republicans who hoped the poor would move away or die. Even though I was addicted and mentally ill, Medicaid made sure I had health care; not so in some other states.

You'd think getting run down by a car would have woken me up. After being on and off the wagon, I drunkenly stepped out in front of a Buick on Walnut Street after a local Kenny Wayne Shepherd concert. The car hit me in the knees at about 40 and I pinwheeled over the vehicle, landing on my head in the road. The first cop to see me told his cohorts on the scene, "Investigate this as a fatality." I looked dead.

The pain and confusion of recovery at ECMC were numbed by all the opiates the medical staff provided. Through all of it, though, I kept writing, keeping notes on the madness. I wanted to tell stories like Charles Bukowski. Another anti-establishment author.

Our street became too much for Lockport City Hall, which enacted a bill that made Washburn and surrounding streets into an "Impact Zone." I felt like Scarface, standing on the porch of my dealer's house, watching an officer in an unmarked car taking photos of me. Lockport was an example of what was happening in towns across the country. The American Friends Service Committee noted in its 2012 report that, "while drug use occurs throughout society, low-income, urban communities are more heavily policed, in part because more daily life occurs in public spaces, and illegal activities are (easier) to find."

For the record, I was the worst drug dealer in our country, maybe on the planet. After watching some of my friend drug dealers, I figured I could do it with my suboxone. After all, I had purchased drugs ever since those $5 bags of pot. From age seventeen to forty-nine, I must have witnessed hundreds of deals. Couldn't be that tough. And I'd have money! Israel, a Latino guy with a thick accent who was in rehab with me, actually gave me the idea and encouraged me to sell to him.

How many times did I sell suboxone? Twice, both times to Israel. I may have had plans to widen my network, eventually. Drunken fantasies. At no time during any of this did I think about investigators. I was drinking heavily at the time, and

I recall that Israel had asked me six or seven times to sell. But he was hot. In fact, when I mentioned the drug to Israel, he felt *my* chest for a wire. That meant he was definitely not a cop, right?

Over a four-year period, I attended ten addiction rehabs, and had eleven visits to the Niagara Falls Hospital psychiatric ward for alcoholic suicidal ideation. It was half my fault I failed my treatments, and half their fault. Rehab reception was with a nurse at each place. The nurse asked questions like how many drinks per day, estimated, but I couldn't do that—the number of drinks and pills I took per day was always different. I wasn't trying to achieve a number. I remembered reading a memoir by Papa's granddaughter, Lorian Hemingway, who said she was drinking a case of beer a day. At that time in my life, thirties, I was fascinated. How could anyone drink that much? And yet I got to that number sometimes as well—later, in my forties.

Alcoholism crept up on me, as it did others. Musician Alice Cooper said in *The Harder They Fall* that, "It took about four or five years to get to that point. It was a very slow creep. It wasn't like all of a sudden I was there drinking that much. I wasn't aware it was happening and no one else was."

Some might say the billion-dollar Twelve Step-based rehab system was broken, unable to deliver on its promises. "…We have a treatment industry that relies on the justice apparatus to keep feeding the treatment system, which is less about good medical care and rehabilitation than about enforced abstinence," said Ethan Nadelmann, executive director of the Drug Policy Alliance. No wonder I always had the feeling at rehab that something was wrong. We wound up victims of "treatment," instead of recovered.

My outpatient providers and the courts placed me in Reflections at Lockport Memorial Hospital, Mount St. Mary's in Lewiston, Terrace House and ECMC in Buffalo three different times, First Step, and Sundram Manor halfway house in Niagara Falls, Conifer Park, near Saratoga, Clifton Springs, outside Rochester. The most useful rehab placement was White Deer Run in Allenwood, Pennsylvania. At none of those places did anyone ever tell me my addictions were worse because of mental illness.

Sundram Manor in April 2015 was a memorable halfway house, but not for its recovery program. Sundram had a hypocritical director, Olivia Bun, who loved to scream as if she was fightin' with a sista. Apparently, she was fired after I left. Sundram had a stipulation that we had to give them our food stamp benefit for the meals we prepared. But the staff ate with us all the time. Something was wrong at Sundram. Actually, more than one thing. My brethren at the facility hid in their rooms and smoked crack. Also, we had to clean the restroom marked "Staff". We were not allowed to use it, but we were forced to clean it. The curriculum was the same as two other facilities I attended. I knew the only way I'd stop drugs was if I made the decision to do it. And I did—I quit it. But Four Loko and lines of an opiate were shadows haunting my mind.

As Elizabeth Vargas wrote in *Between Breaths*, "… Thoughts played over and over in my insecure, anxious psyche. The only thing that could hold back the bad feelings for a while was alcohol. For a few hours each night, things would be alright. The anxiety and resentment would soften and recede just enough to make it bearable. But the cocoon of a white wine buzz can only take you so far."

School anxiety had started my drinking career at sixteen. I learned this at White Deer Run, where I met the psychiatrist who finally diagnosed me with co-morbidity (having two chronic illnesses at once, such as, in my case, bipolar syndrome and alcoholism), and prescribed life-saving Lithium. All those 28-day programs preached was abstinence, which might have worked for some. But if I was going to stop, I'd have done it when my wife asked. And 28 days in any group program would not get to the heart of the mental health issue causing and exacerbating the drug abuse—anything from childhood trauma to PTSD. Programs didn't go that deep.

Before the addiction rehabs, I had been a guest of the Niagara County Jail. I found that rehab and jail had a lot in common:

- You can't go outside, or leave, without permission
- Those in charge are always right
- There's nothing to do
- You get three meals a day
- They don't cure addiction
- Each has plenty of legal and illegal drugs
- Each has its share of the "insane"
- Each involves petty rules and maximum punishments

- There's a human response from AA and other organizations that says we have "The Answer" to addiction. The answer, courtesy of journalist Benoit Denizet-Lewis, is, "Ask for help, help others, stay honest, and try like hell to feel (your) feelings. If I do those things, the odds are pretty good that I won't relapse."

Then there was the God response. I tried to find God. The sober types in my life did not understand my needs and desires.

A neighbor, Pastor Michael, knew I had a drinking problem and started visiting my apartment regularly. I really liked him; we had long philosophical and spiritual discussions. Hollywood makes the mistake of portraying alcoholics and opiate users as being out of it, unable to function. I was quite lucid. In fact, when I was high, and conversing with Michael, I felt we were getting somewhere, transcendentally. He said that when I was married with family, had a house, two cars, great job, money, summers at the beach—in fact, nearly everything a man could want—I was still miserable. Yes, I said, I felt a cosmic hole in my life, in myself. Jesus, he said, was supposed to fill that hole. Michael explained "faith" in ways I had not heard it described before.

He urged me to come to his church and "meet some new people and find inspiration." Church was Sundays at 10:30. After waking with a hangover and sniffing a pink Opana 10, I'd feel happy. Superhuman, Mr. Personality. Michael took me to church in his van with his wife and six kids. Suddenly, I had a family again. I was part of a family. The church called it our "Forever Family." During the ceremony, I started feeling that the Bible passages were about me and I was making a connection, for the first time, with Christ.

And I did meet new people. Even though they said things like abortion was murder, that Islamics were going to cut our heads off and martyr us, and that the world was coming to an end, I still believed this was the way. I even participated in Bible study group. The new problem arose on the Sundays when I did not have opiates. I had to substitute suboxone, alcohol, Ativan, and/or Adderall. The suboxone, which contained an opiate, was the only medication to help me in connecting with God. I was baptized at the church. Interestingly, the car "accident" (or was it on purpose?) happened four months after my baptism. That would have brought me much closer to God. But it was not "The Answer."

It was 2014 when I met Israel who lived on Washburn Street, near my welfare apartment. We were attending outpatient rehab, in the same program. I was waiting for my suboxone script, a drug that helps people get off heroin. Israel sold me some of his suboxone. When I finally received my script, I sold him some of mine. And that was it. My name was on the District Attorney's list. Israel was a narc and got me on tape, twice, selling him suboxone. Though the indictment was sealed, an old newspaper contact got me the grand jury minutes. Israel was the culprit alright. I could tell by the way the grand jury stenographer quoted his thick Spanish accent. Israel brought down nine others who were dealing.

I was charged with two suboxone sales—a total of four wafers priced at $20 each. And I was charged with two counts of possession, which was silly because it was my own prescription. I pled guilty to one felony sale and entered drug court, a kind of probation where, if you stay clean and do what the judge says, they drop the felony. If they find you using any intoxicants, you go to jail.

I couldn't believe my situation. The same person who once appeared on MSNBC with host Jack Ford was now broke, stealing vanilla extract from stores (it's forty percent alcohol). Begging for money at the gas station, stealing beer and pills from friends' houses, stealthily grabbing liquor bottles from my lawyer's stash. The same guy who went to Hollywood (twice for my first book), who sat next to Jack Black, was now high most of the time. It seemed like the friends I lost each day were replaced by even more people who would help me get in trouble.

My ex-wife called me one day, yelling at me to take her name as "emergency contact" off all my medical records. I laughed and laughed.

I used a lot. Tried to fake the urine tests, diluting samples with water. Went to county jail six times for "violations," each involving two-week stays. Finally, the judge, William Watson, kicked me out of drug court. The Supreme Court judge, Richard Kloch, gave me two years in state prison and two on parole. I waited in the county jail to be sent to state prison.

Now, why would a university-educated author, documentarian, and business marketer sell drugs to a narc in Lockport, New York? I wanted money and beer, sure. But maybe there was something else going on. According to theorist Gary Becker, people break the law because they make calculations about the probability and likely cost of getting caught. Then they determine if the crime is worth it. To an addict, a crime is almost always worth it if it leads to more substances.

Before all this chaos, I had lived an almost normal life. I was born in 1967 in Lockport, a town of 30,000 north of Buffalo. My father worked at Bell Aerospace as a designer while attending art classes at the University at Buffalo. My mother attended Bryant & Stratton Business School. They were married on a Sunday.

We were poor, living at Grandma's house until Dad secured a better job. After graduation, he got into advertising and, by 1971, we had a nice place of our own, with a pool, in the Lockport countryside.

Though my parents were of age to be hippies, they were right on the edge. They did use pot and speed now and then, hung love beads, and had a sizeable rock record collection. They didn't protest, sit-in, or support causes and candidates. Dad played guitar and painted with acrylics, and Mom read tarot cards and analyzed dreams. Since they were only in their twenties, all their friends were young. I was the first kid in the circle—I got to know these older folks as I grew, and they became my friends along with their public-school children. My uncle, Mason, was in the adult friends group too, encouraging my love of reading. But my world of Matchbox cars, KISS, and water guns was about to change.

When I was ten, we moved to Charlotte, North Carolina and Dad opened a new satellite ad agency office for Faller, Klenk & Quinlan of Buffalo. Because we were in an affluent neighborhood of East Mecklenberg, I was bussed to a school in the poorest black neighborhood of Charlotte. The state's "bussing" program. Kids came to school without shoes. I made friends with all the black kids; the whites just called me "Yankee."

Doug Stankey and Andrea Jordan were my friends from the Crest Hill Drive neighborhood. We went roller skating and to the cinema on Saturdays to see "Grease," "Smokey & the Bandit," and "Every Which Way but Loose."

Around Christmas 1979, my grandfather died. After that, Grandma couldn't bear to be alone. Within months, we were packing to go back to Lockport. We started all over again on Regent Street and I attended middle school. Every Sunday in the fall, thirty of us from Regent and Grant streets and Morrow Avenue played football on the front yard of the Lockport Board of Education building.

I was obsessed with The Who, discovering the band the year it broke up,

1982. I felt the alienation in Pete Townshend's songs because, though I had friends in my neighborhood, I was shy in eleventh grade, until I discovered LaBatt's beer at a seniors' party at Ray Patenaude's house. Beer tasted terrible, but it helped me break out of my shell. I went from blending into the lockers to starring in two Shakespeare plays, and as Chief Sitting Bull in "Annie Get Your Gun." I joined the American Field Service and the church Interfaith group.

Suddenly, I had an opinion on everything, and Holden Caufield was my hero. My fear of people disappeared. I became friends with my English teachers, Rosanna Sandell and John Koplas, and I dated a beautiful and oddly interesting girl named Joan. I started having house parties when my folks were out. My school friends commented on our house—I never realized it, but original artworks by my father and my uncle decorated the living room, dining area, and staircase. The Stickneys were different, a step above without the conceit, and that made me interesting. But somewhere in those drinks and friends, I was getting sick with panic. At times, I couldn't concentrate on school, had a new girlfriend every week, and couldn't have fun with friends unless I had a six-pack of Canadian beer.

Like my father, I graduated from the University at Buffalo. My degree was in English Literature. I was trying to write a first book. At the time, I lived with five friends above a bar called Stan's Home Plate. Nights, I was a banquet waiter at the Best Western, and days I went to classes and worked at the Lockport Buffalo Bookstore on Main Street. Every night was Mardi Gras above Stan's, and I became a daily drinker, chasing away the hangovers.

After founding his own ad agency, Dad became successful with such clients as Dunlop, Blue Cross, and Lockport Savings Bank (now First Niagara). My father and I often had long conversations about the arts and the books we read. My favorite professor was Joseph Conte, a man who taught "alternative" literature: Beckett, Mathews, DeLillo, Calvino, and Hawkes.

At the bookstore, I met Beatles biographer Geoffrey Giuliano. I quit the hotel and the bookstore and became his literary intern. We toured America, visited Soho Street in London and Brussels to interview Paul McCartney's "Wings" band, and wound up in Key West at Ernest Hemingway's house. While my friends were taking jobs in landscaping, roofing, and insurance, I was doing something completely different, meeting women, and taking a boat across Lake Ontario to see Giuliano's Canadian publishers.

Throughout my ten-month internship, Giuliano offered sage advice—give up drinking. I didn't listen, and when I left him, I got a job working for editor Dan Kane at the *Lockport Union-Sun & Journal*. I closed bars with politicians and school board members. Kane never allowed me to call in sick, saying, "Call in when you're healthy and you can enjoy yourself out there."

When the Oklahoma City bombing happened in April 1995, perpetrator Timothy McVeigh wasn't talking. It was the largest act of domestic terrorism in American history. The international media came to our newspaper to interview us for information on McVeigh's hometown area. I helped CNN, NBC, A&E, and Court TV when they were creating documentaries on McVeigh and wound up being the featured reporter in the interviews, the star of the show. I obtained a deal with Prometheus Books, eventually took a PR job with Mercedes-Benz Financial, and bought my own house.

With every year that passed, I was drinking and using more drugs. Though a highly functioning addict, I was surprised I'd made it as long as I had without more trouble. It wasn't until I left a few ad agency jobs and signed my divorce papers that the end came—with the indictment. It may have seemed so for a while, but I don't think my life had ever been normal.

I'd thought of suicide since the age of sixteen, either a result of school trauma, my early experiments with rum, or both. What makes a basically positive, outgoing kid start thinking of suicide? Inner darkness, movies, news? Hidden memories? A voice in my head was saying, *Brandon's dead. He killed himself.* But there was never a question to go with that answer, just the statement, in my mind, about that forthcoming evil tragedy.

I still hear that voice today, though it's a nearly forgotten echo, acted on just once, and then fading into the background. Starting around 2010 (when I lost my last job), when I had no one left but drunks in my life, I began to use 911 frequently. The police and ambulance drivers were used to me, giving me that trip to Niagara Falls Hospital. The guy who wanted to die by his own hand. The easiest way would have been jumping from the overlook to the canal bank, a 200-foot drop onto hard rocks at the canal wall.

I didn't really hate myself, like many other addicts and suicides. I hated this life, this American system of "screw everyone over for profit," from Apple to

Congress. Steinbeckian. And I hated workplaces, where everyone acts like someone they're not. It became impossible to get anything done at Mercedes-Benz Financial because there were so many people who wanted to take credit for any kind of success.

All businesses operated the same way. There was the boss, the boss' best friend, the guy who did nothing, the office slut, the manager druggie (me), my nemesis, who was also the boss' friend, the guys who wanted the boss' job, and those who wanted my job. Every job was the same—great for the first year, I was the hero, and then, once I learned what was really going on, I became paralyzed. And drank every night. I thought I'd retire from Mercedes. Paranoia knocked me down, and out of the job. It seems the same would have happened whether I was using or not. That voice was self-defeating—*"Oh, Brandon."*

How long ago had it been when I felt nervous about what my wife might think or say about me having a drink at 10 or 11 a.m. on a Saturday? Saturday was my favorite day of the week. I snuck around our Morrow Avenue house, wondering if she'd stay upstairs, if she wouldn't hear me open that beer in the cellar. I never realized how loud a pop top on a beer can was until I tried to hide it from my wife. I got the evil eye. But just a few years later, as a divorced man, I felt free to open a beer or pour a drink at 8 a.m. and then drink all day. Now I wondered why I had ever been afraid of her or her judgment.

What had been missing from my life since we split? The mean faces and concerned speeches were gone, along with an ulcer that cured itself. Opiates had filled my life, so I no longer needed love, or other people. I was on a death bus driving into a land of strangers, without my booze and pills, and I had no idea what I needed.

"I'd like you to leave. This isn't working." The words a hungover husband hears just before he gets a divorce. My wife decided I was the monster and needed to be kicked out. She had me go to rehab, AA, and kiss her ass with apologies, but nothing worked. I did not want to change—why should I? I still don't want to blame the alcohol—AA folks always blame the alcohol. Then there was that voice in my head telling me I was w.r.o.n.g.

My wife shocked me with her declaration. My father said, "Don't leave. Stick it out." Clinical depression. Bipolar. Anxiety. Disorders controlled me. I self-medicated with rum, cocaine, and opiates. The first rum drinks I had were samples from the dark bottle my parents kept in the kitchen. From age sixteen onward, it had been around, not every day, but there in the background. When we bought the house on Morrow Avenue (it was my grandmother's), I found a yellow- and tan-striped rocks glass in their old cupboard.

Grandpa Joe Arrigo drank highballs from that glass. He was my hero, a World War II vet, Army captain, paratrooper. He'd sit in the living room with his glass each night, watching TV. I started drinking rum and Sprite (no caffeine) from his glass. Grandpa Joe died when I was thirteen; I missed him. The drinks brought back my memories of fishing with him on Long Point Beach, Canada. That little glass became a close friend. A nightly companion. It battled my enemies: panic, paranoia, and depression. Alcohol gave me a myriad of feelings that I enjoyed: peace, energy, excitement. Who wouldn't want to feel that way each day?

News personality Elizabeth Vargas smartly described her love of wine in the confessional memoir, *Between Breaths*. "I liked alcohol. I liked the way it made me feel. There's a sweet feeling that you get from those first few glasses of wine. The world is softer, smoother, more golden … I could finally breathe." Vargas notes that people in her life became "smarter" and "more interesting."

That little glass was, for me, a comfort until 2001. My wife demanded that I stop drinking. Go to AA and make it stick this time. I was clean for a month. Then September 11th arrived. I was at Mercedes-Benz Financial in Amherst. The new building had TVs everywhere for corporate presentations. Watching the towers burn was like looking at all the TVs in a Walmart. Management sent us home at 10:30 a.m., all 500 of us. Trying to drive was difficult, looking at the blue sky, trying to interpret street signs, avoiding other dazed drivers.

I made it home and stood outside 45 Morrow Avenue, talking to my wife while our four-year-old little girl played on our front porch. We didn't want anyone watching TV. I told my wife I wanted a drink—the stress was too much. She found ten different ways to say no, but I left anyway, to buy some rum. The glass was back out. I couldn't sleep that night; I kept drinking.

I didn't like alcohol. I LOVED it. It tasted like sugary chemicals, and speedy medicine. If I got drunk before ten, I'd sneak out of the house, hitting the Lockport bars in search of cocaine, keeping the drunk going longer, turning into "Alert Brandon." Respected businessman by day, high-flying wreck by night.

I did not know I was sick, but I did know I was running off the rails. If I say it was fun, do you agree? Or do you say, "only for a while?" If you were the voice of reason, I mean.

The AA book has the broad generalization, "Those who do not recover ... seem to have been born that way. They are naturally incapable of grasping and developing a manner of living which demands rigorous honesty. Their chances are less than average." Since I fit into that category, the statement felt like an indictment. I could gain acceptance nowhere.

AA went on to say, "There are those too who suffer from grave emotional and mental disorders..." Honesty, it continued, was also the key for this group, of which I was a member. I did not know until reading the Big Book that my disability was "grave." There was no way to go home, and seemingly no way to recover.

Looking back, I realize my wife had said it. She said she had cried for two years about me and my problem. She told me in our Morrow Avenue kitchen that she wanted me to leave, for six months. And we could see about things then. These are all her words. Once I was out of the house, that six months turned into a year. Then I figured out that the day she shoved me out, it was forever.

A few years earlier, my wife handed me the name and number of a psychiatrist in Amherst. I knew I had a problem, so I went to this woman on a Saturday at noon. I thought I had a drinking problem, not anxiety and depression. When my wife handed me the scrap piece of paper, I looked at her name—June Stein. I imagined a leggy brunette a la "The Sopranos."

I was instructed to go to the back of the house. She and her husband lived in front and she saw patients in the back room, an elegant and warm space. I was disappointed when I saw June—she was an overweight, frizzy-haired grandmother of four. Not sexy at all unless you're into granny porn.

The outcome of our five $100 hypnosis meetings was that I counted how many drinks I had at night, and I realized why my mother cried so much when I was in the womb. I was not born out of wedlock, yet two of my grandparents wanted Mom to get an abortion. If you could meet my daughter and see how intelligent and creative she is, you'd understand why my mother made the transcendental decision of keeping me.

I decided to stop talking to June. I felt, in too-real memory, I actually heard my mother weeping when she found out she was pregnant with me. Before the shotgun wedding. It freaked me out, having a glimpse of something I never should have seen or heard.

Sometimes I blamed my wife, sometimes me, and other times, no one. I also understood my mind was broken. I needed help, though finding it seemed so elusive. Finding out about my mother's tears was just as bad as finding out my wife was seeing other men, right under my evicted nose. I should have been smarter, especially when she started up with her own psychiatrist, who sent my wife home with a free copy of *Codependent No More* by Melody Beattie. My wife knew then that we were done.

My initial drinking was to meet girls. Journalist Pete Hamill wrote that drink "has so many rewards: confidence for the shy, clarity for the uncertain, solace to the wounded and lonely, and above all, the elusive promises of friendship and love."

I was in the bottle all day long, some days, when my wife told me she'd had enough. I suppose she figured that if she booted me out, I'd wise up, sober up, and fly straight. I chose the opposite. For the next ten years, I'd see my daughter if I was sober, on alternating weekends, but I'd always have a few drinks and some pills once she'd gone to bed for the night. Weekends stopped in 2010 when I lost my ad agency job and my apartment.

Losing everything is romantically American, written about by hundreds of authors. Nic Sheff is the author of two memoirs on addiction. In *We All Fall Down*, Sheff muses, "I start using, and the whole world just closes down on me. There are never new opportunities; no callbacks ever come. My car gets towed, and I end up losing everything all over again."

People say today, as they did then, "I never in my life hoped I'd become a

_____."

Fill in the blank with: Drunk, Junkie, Prostitute. All three. Overeater. Compulsively angry. Compulsively compulsive. Truthfully, after I knew I was drinking too much, I wasn't worried that I'd become an alcoholic. Alcoholism was cool. My heroes were alcoholics—artists, writers, actors. There had to be something there, including William Blake.

Nobody I knew dealt in that particular platitude. My parents' friends liked wine, weed, and song. None of these people ever got in a fight or arrested for liking to drink and smoke. Or taking a pill now and then.

Then there was me and my wife, and our drinking friends. Snacks, drinks, and weed brought us together. The couples who survived didn't turn into what we never wanted to be. Depending on the person, that might have happened anyway.

November began my period of couch-surfing, staying at various friends' houses and paying rent from my unemployment checks. This lasted about two years as I drank and used every day. I gave up on everything and let intoxicants make me happy, though it was hell when I ran out of money for the week. Sick and weak, in withdrawal.

The sickness from the opiates and alcohol was like having every orifice in my body bleeding as I walked to find some relief. The muscle aches, flu symptoms, diarrhea, insomnia, racing thoughts, panic, agony. I had been in a maze, walking into walls, looking for the way out to get money and the pills I needed to make the body superstorm cease.

Then I had to borrow. That was easy—I was a published author who'd worked from 1990 to 1995 at the local newspaper. I knew everybody who was anybody in town. It was a matter of pride for local developers, lawyers, and anybody in business to open their wallets and hand me a few twenties. Some saw a friend in need. Some saw a man on his way down. Some were saying goodbye.

I figured if life just didn't work out this way, then I'd end it. I thought of no one else but myself—me was all I had left. My daughter had her mother, and the whole family was on her mother's side. I had no one, and I had had enough.

I worked for a drug dealer, cleaning the house and watching the kids. I was with him through two girlfriends and the birth of two children. I never "ran" any drugs. That was not my job. My job was the yard and the house, the reward for which would be money for drinks and an opiate pill. One pill cost between $20 and $100. For 40 ml. of Opana. I once paid $175. I was in withdrawal, and this chick who was my other dealer happened to need all the cash she could get. The best description I have of withdrawal is like staring at the sun, with each inch of your body, while being force-fed waste: unbearable muscle pain, inability to think or "do," gagging, falling down, but having to get right back up because the world hurts. And you know your suffering will continue because no one will ever give you an opiate drug again. So, is it time to end it?

Then my unemployment money ran out. I didn't care that much because I had the dealer and a slum landlord to support me. I cared enough to jump in front of a car on August 17, 2012. My self-destruction was nearly complete. A Mercy Flight helicopter picked me up and took me to Erie County Medical Center, where I lived on free painkillers—dilaudid injections and Roxycodone pills—for a month and learned how to walk again. Then I was sent to an old folks' home in Middleport with a script for Roxycodone. The home had a rehabilitation program and I stayed there for a month, cheeking my Roxys so I could snort them in my little bathroom. I watched VH1 and was visited by the chick drug dealer and by Pastor Michael. By the time I left to go home, I had been high for two months straight. I was also given a month's script for Roxys.

Mental illness. I self-medicated to cover the symptoms and live my life. My thoughts of death and suicide began around sixteen and hovered in my mind until I was forty-five. Arrested for shoplifting booze while highly intoxicated, I told the policeman I was suicidal. I was put in the county jail's Special Housing Unit (SHU), isolated in my own cinderblock cell with a wide metal door. The SHU at Niagara was for female inmates who came in bellowing because they were coming down from meth or crack; escape artists and wrist slashers with suicide claims, inmates ill with strange ailments, and those who were a danger to others.

According to the Department of Justice, more than half of all jail inmates had a mental health problem, from major depression and mania to psychotic disorders and high anxiety. The department's study noted the totals: 705,600 in jails and 479,900 in prisons.

After a day of recovery and clonidine-induced sleep, I took a look around my 8x12-foot cell. There was my bed, bolted to the wall, my seat-less metal toilet, and a small sink. Deputy Tim Blackley, my former Regent Street neighbor, was the SHU supervisor that day. He opened my door and said, "Stickney. You used to be a hell of a writer." Blackley wondered why I was here, and I told him. He wheeled the book cart over so I could select a few titles. He also gave me five sheets of paper and a pen. "Get back to work," the deputy said.

I was in the jail several more times as a result of drug court violations. Each time, a deputy asked "mental state" questions. I got to know the routine. And when he said, "Do you have anything to live for?" I said no. That was my ticket back to the usually peaceful SHU.

There were seven or eight other inmates in the SHU. Being locked in, alone, wasn't so bad. I'm a writer and an only child, so I was used to being alone. All I did was read, sleep, talk to my inmate neighbors through the walls, and count the wet toilet paper balls stuck to the ceiling. I didn't have to deal with inmates or C.O.s. I got to talk about my mental state with a counselor once a week. I also knew that once I was out, I'd go back to drinking.

Solitary confinement causes inmates to get creative in finding things to do. Edward Bunker wrote in *Education of a Felon*, "You meditate on everything you know. You sing all the songs you might recall, in whole or in part. ... You think about God—is there one or many?—and why does he allow so much pain and injustice?"

A surprise roommate suddenly ended my solitude and took up more of my time. One day I heard the keys in the thick metal cell door. An officer I didn't recognize slid a long metal bed into the room, next to me. The bed was covered in rust. Following the bed was a handcuffed inmate who reminded me a little of Neil Patrick Harris. By the time the C.O. took off the handcuffs, Doogie had asked him three times to use the phone. Those of us in the SHU cell made calls from a pay phone the officers wheeled to our door on a long black chord.

The officer said "maybe," and locked the door. I introduced myself, but he did not. Doogie was clearly agitated, yearning to get on the phone with his girlfriend. He stared out of the window. I asked what had happened, even though inmates aren't supposed to inquire; they are supposed to wait until they get told.

Doogie said he had dropped their baby down the stairs. "She was slippery because she had just been in the bath." Then he whispered, "I was drunk." But he had not told the police about the alcohol.

The phone arrived at the metal door and Doogie got on. For the next forty-five minutes, he begged the baby's mother to tell him she still loved him. I doubted it since Doogie had also confided to me that in the fall, the baby had broken an arm and a leg. "Say it," said Doogie, "Say it."

To me, it sounded more like Doogie was a liar, that he and his girl were fighting, and the baby was injured. He had already lied to me once, saying he worked as a military policeman. He was sloppy in word, thought, and deed; he wouldn't make five minutes in the armed forces.

We were locked in twenty-three hours a day, with an hour for recreation. I usually skipped recreation because I never liked playing or watching basketball. I certainly didn't like Doogie. He would have won top honors in a national worst

SHU roommate.

At the time, the SHU was my second home. It was a getaway. No contact with other inmates, unless we spoke through the wall. No jail noises, except C.O. keys. Reading. Writing. Sleeping. My medication, which was brought to me. I only cried once, staring at the sun through my window, hearing "Free Bird" on the C.O.'s radio. After several SHU years, I suppose I wanted something more.

After twenty-four hours with Doogie, I was moved from the SHU. Psychiatric cleared me to go back into the general population. I was moved to the old part of the jail to a big room separated by wire fence. I dropped my stuff at my new bed and saw Amp, a guy I knew from Washburn Street. He asked me if I'd heard about the baby abuser. I said he had been my last roommate.

"He's gonna get his ass kicked if he comes in here," said Amp. A few inmates gathered around us. We bumped fists "hello" and the discussion stayed on Doogie.

"It'll be on the news tonight," said Amp. "Piece of shit."

Doogie came into the dorm and all eyes were focused on him as the 5 p.m. TV news started. Was it a coincidence or fate? The crowd of inmates, who had read of this crime in the Lockport newspaper, began chanting, "Chance, Chance, Chance." Doogie's real name was Chance.

It was an inmate assumption that C.O.s, when they dealt with a piece of shit, would arrange something like this—move the child abuser into a dangerous dorm right when the local news was coming on. The bubble officer told him to take bed ten. As the news of the crime began on the TV, inmates moved toward him. He looked as if he woke up without his testicles—he was that terrified.

"You almost killed that baby," Amp said to Chance. Then it was on. Amp and another inmate took fast, wide, sweeping swings that connected, and Chance ran to the bubble to ask to be put into Protective Custody (PC), which was packed with child abusers, sex offenders, narcs, and those who feared the angry mob.

A minute or two later, Chance walked out of our lives and into Protective Custody.

That night I had a dream about walking a dog, a yellow lab, near a baseball diamond. It was a warm spring evening. Then the dog, which I knew as God, was walking me.

The dog angled its head toward my wrist and bit very gently, so as not to hurt me or break the skin. There the dog led me to a place of peace, of relaxation. Then I awoke, in jail, but with great satisfaction that at age forty-nine, I had had my first dream of God.

A year earlier, at the Niagara County Jail, I was sprung from the SHU for good behavior. First, they put me in H Block, which was hell. It was in the old, mold-coated part of the jail, reopened when the new sections of the jail filled up. It was all young kids, ghetto-speak, and barred cells. I had a toilet and sink, circa 1950. My walls were coated in two decades' worth of graffiti. There was a detailed pencil drawing of a Spanish woman in doggy-style pose, her genitals exposed for all to see. Unable to communicate to the ghetto talkers, I spent my time erasing her crotch with soap and water.

I was in that cell about four hours when the psych nurse visited and asked if I felt comfortable about being released to the general population (GP) in the "pods." The Niagara County Jail had a reputation as a "nice jail," meaning the staff and correction officers were actually friendly. I don't think there's another jail like it on Earth.

I told the nurse I could handle GP. Deputy Shanley and another C.O. walked me over to Pod 2. The four pods were arranged in a circle, with a communications desk at the center. Entry was through an electronic outside door to a sally port that led to the other electronic entry. There was a bottom floor, two TVs, a library room, the C.O. bubble, and stairs. Two officers were on duty. There were sixty cells total on two floors. Bunks were for new inmates and single rooms for long-timers.

I was let into Pod 2 and spoke with Ricci, the officer on duty. The county jail is in Lockport, so I knew many of the jail employees, both from childhood and from the newspaper. Ricci told me to bunk in cell 4. "Tell your bunky you get the bottom," he said.

I got to the cell with my bag and was shocked to see Osama bin Laden. Right on my bunk! He was actually a tall man from Trinidad, soon to be deported. Same weird hat, same hair, same beard, same height. Bin Laden refused to speak English or to give me the bottom bunk. I didn't fight him. That would be unwise—he had brought down the Twin Towers.

"Stickney!"

Outside the cell was Mark Morgan, a mutual friend of Danny, our main dealer. He was in for eight counts of robbery. I now knew where he got all that money that went into his and his wife's pockets for drugs. His well-built arms were peppered with track marks.

I sat at a card table with Morgan and another friend from my dealer's house, Stoli, who was in for burglary. Stoli's fingers were so sticky, he even stole a baby ferret from a pet store for the dealer, whose friend wanted his other ferret. I didn't know people shoplifted pets. Thanks to Morgan and Stoli, our dealer had new ipads, laptops, iphones, jewelry, and other precious items that were hot on the streets.

This was my fifth time in jail. Now, I was here with friends. And wasn't I feeling at home? I was still a writer, but I was no longer the guy who had a family, the guy who worked at Mercedes, the guy who went to Hollywood.

I reflected on my relationship with Bill Holly, a friend from 12th grade. He wound up graduating from Cornell, and getting engaged to a beautiful doctor with a home in Westchester.

Bill's bachelor party was in New York City in September 2002, lit by the imposing and unforgettable twin beams of light. We took in a New York Rangers game, stayed in the Chelsea, and bar-hopped for two evenings.

He worked for Scribman Associates, reputedly a Manhattan gangster organization involved in construction. We joked that Bill was "the undertaker." Bill's other friends were executives or directors at Bank of America, Moog, Apple, Firestone, Mobil, and the list went on. Bill's brother Charlie was there. Charlie was a lobbyist in D.C. And I was the guy from Mercedes. It was a buttoned-down crowd.

Now, at the county jail, I was with friends who had robbed people from Bank of America and Moog. I had so much to write down. This was going to make a good book someday. Maybe.

Morgan said, "So, getting along with Osama?" Nothing good comes from jail, except when a pal makes you laugh out loud.

WENDE
CORRECTIONAL
FACILITY

MAXIMUM SECURITY

CELL #3

This mainly invisible society, costing taxpayers $80 billion annually, adds more people every day, expelling a much smaller number. Prison government, which is glaringly un-American, where men lose their rights, seems to have no leadership while its bureaucracy grows in relation to the increasing number of incarcerated. In addition to lifers, and hardened, more experienced criminals, the new, right-of-passage generation of 18 to 21-year-olds are flooding prisons across the country, and many have been convicted of gang violence. They have been labeled "hard to manage."

CHAPTER 3

CRASHING THE RECEPTION

"Ideally, prisoners should fill each correctional institution's
educational classes until they are bursting at the seams…
If we, as prisoners, were working with sober mental clarity, our prison
environment could be transformed into universities of higher learning."
—From a prison circulated essay, "The Upside-Down Kingdom," Anonymous

After hours of handcuff agony, we finally reach Wende Correctional Facility, our next stop from the Niagara County Jail. The cuffs hurt more and more the longer they are on. New York State was thrilled. With each prison we'd visit, the prison would get paid by the federal government because we counted as inmates, even if we were only there for a day. Wende was the first of a four-stop state-prison journey for me.

They hauled us out of the bus, and we were marched in shackles to "intake." They finally took the shackles off, which felt good as we tried to get our wrist and ankle circulation going again.

At intake, the C.O.s do their best to embarrass the hell out of you, from getting your jail mug shot to the old anal probe. I don't think they were really looking for drugs or weapons in my rear-end. They just wanted to hurt me, and they did. Taking off all my clothes before armed officers was bad enough.

Sample of how state C.O.s talk to new inmates:

- Stand the fuck over there.
- What the fuck are you looking at?
- Are you fucking stupid?
- Are you from fucking Mars?
- Do you know where the fuck you are?
- I'll ask the questions, fuckhead.

I listened to this for about three hours while the seven of us were processed and violated. So, I knew that I was in state prison, and that it was nothing like county jail. And that the C.O.s weren't model citizens for the prisoners to look up to and emulate. This was 2017. And yet they acted like it was 1817. And got away with it. But this, for me, was just a preview.

While we were being processed, my fellow inmates created a low buzz. It was secretive chatter about whether I was a rapist. It was like junior high, when you know the other kids are talking about you, but you can't do anything about it. I was highly paranoid, the panic creeping into my rapid heartbeat. Rapos did not fare well in state prison. How was I going to prove to them that I had sold drugs? How could I get my paperwork?

The C.O.s ushered us to cells somewhere in Wende. We could look out and see a gray-yellow wall. We could not see outside, each other, or the guards. We could hear the guards talking, but they told us nothing. Not how long we'd be there, when we'd eat. Anything. Isolation as punishment.

Then the noise started. Inmates talking to each other in, what I began to call "ghetto speak," but which has also been viewed as a minority art form. The conversations like this were all the same:

- Kick it with him 'bout the shit.
- Where you at? (Where do you live?) 716? (Area code)
- You know Mookie? Or Shine?
- They on some bullshit.
- How many bids you done?
- What's it for? Work (crack)? Got a Body? (Killed someone?)

The conversations were loud, as if broadcast. Places, people, and things they had in common kept the inmates busy. As Muhammad Ali said, "Ghetto is not a place where you live. It's a mentality." It reminded me of a passage in *The Catcher in the Rye*, where Holden observes a new friend meet an old acquaintance of his: "Then he and old Sally started talking about a lot of people they both knew. It was the phoniest conversation you ever heard in your life. They both kept thinking of places as fast as they could, then they'd think of somebody that lived there and mention their name. I was all set to puke…"

The new prison language, so foreign to me, seemed to be spoken by all races behind bars. *Figures in Black* author Henry Louis Gates, Jr., wrote: "…The black rhetorical (routines) include marking, loud talking, testifying, calling out of one's name, sounding, rapping, and so on ..."

For the first time in my life, I knew what it felt like to be in prison. Like being stopped in traffic by a cop. That feeling you get as he leaves his cruiser and walks up to your driver's side window. That's the feeling you have in prison, and it never fades. It's anticipatory, it's anxiety. Let's hurry up and get this over with, yet you know it'll take the afternoon to process you. And then you'll be behind bars. This circling shark is going to take a bite.

It was the beginning of May, so it was warm in the jail. The air was thick and stale. The C.O. put an industrial fan on and, thank God, it was louder than the inmate noise boxes. The conversation was covered up and the noise boxes didn't like that. They shouted to the C.O. up the hall, but he ignored them.

There was only about a dozen of us stuck in there, but the auditory assault sounded more like rioting fans at a Jay Z concert. They were talking—no, shouting—so loud and spitting out words so fast I plummeted into confusion and terror. My breathing was off, my heart ready to detonate. I sat on the lower bunk, alone in my two-man cell, and began breathing exercises; my lungs hurt. This was not just a panic attack.

It was my catastrophe. My doom.

After nearly two hours of suffering, sweating, and feeling ready to die, the noise remained just as loud, and I was covered in sweat. I couldn't cry out—I had already learned my lesson that those officers up the hall were not here for me. Eventually, the nurse came around with medication. Surprisingly, she and the officer let me stutter through my story. The nurse said she'd come back with something. Her attention alone was nearly enough to reduce my fear and my symptoms.

Deciding to keep nervously busy, I searched my cell for something to read. First, I read the graffiti. My walls were chipped, the bars black, my little sink and toilet dirty. Then I lifted the mattress up and found a magazine. Flipping it over to the cover, I saw it was a recent issue of *Harper's*. How something this smart made it into my dingy cell in the middle of nowhere, I'll never know.

There was an article on Michigan's water crisis and another on suicide. "Suicide Notes" was by Daphne Merkin, a well-respected literary critic. The first sentence was, "Self-inflicted death has always held an allure for me." My kinda gal! Diving into the article, I fantasized about how to do it. I could not last through two years of this shit. I wanted to leave my dead body to the state as a burnt offering. The article was pro-suicide in a way that made me get serious. I didn't have to take the heartache and pain for existence anymore. "Rapo!" My God. I was going to be surrounded by morons on both sides of the law until 2019.

We got no recreation time at Wende, and no showers. I was there for four days, including a weekend. A few of the other inmates from the bus were taken away Friday, to go to other prisons. We were fed, but the C.O.s ignored our calls and requests. Isolation, again.

Then those paint-chipped metal bars squeaked open. We were given the opportunity to make a phone call. I spoke with my mother in Palm Beach and asked her to contact my good-for-nothing public defender and send me a copy of my indictment.

Once back at the cell, I found I had gifts! Inside a package were three green slacks, three short-sleeve shirts, three t-shirts, three pairs of underwear, three pairs of athletic socks, a winter coat, and big, black stovepipe boots.

"This is your state prison outfit from now on," said a C.O. walking by as we sifted through the clothes. I forgot they had taken our sizes when I was getting the anal probe by that overly friendly officer.

On Monday, we wore our new clothes, making it official that we were owned by the state.

Then we were shackled again and tossed on another bus.

ELMIRA CORRECTIONAL FACILITY

MAXIMUM SECURITY

CELL #4

The increase in prisoners has been governed by many factors, dating to the 1960s, according to the American Friends Service Committee. A committee report stated, "Incarceration became the default setting rather than the backstop of the criminal justice system... Contributing factors to the prison boom included fears of crime and unrest, (ongoing) political hysteria regarding drugs, a backlash against the gains of the civil rights movement, widening economic inequality, and a decline in demand for low skilled labor." This report from 2012 is prophetic. The exact same issues face our nation today.

CHAPTER 4

BAD BOYS, BAD BOYS

"Nothing, absolutely nothing happens in God's world by mistake."
—*AA Big Book*

Those four days at Wende were followed by a day-long bus ride to Elmira. Handcuffs, leg cuffs, chains, yelling. Oh, lots of yelling. This second bus was bigger—a Greyhound-type. The faces of the men going to be put away? Lips like lines, eyes staring straight ahead. Few people talking. The radio up front playing "Still the One" by Orleans.

I got weird looks. Somehow, everyone on the bus "knew." Those who concentrated on other matters were young men caught between youth and adulthood, waiting to hip-hop and carry the gun. But too inexperienced, with no solid gangsta record or 'hood cool.

Arriving at the Elmira facility, we all commented on how ugly the place was. A metal and brick mausoleum with a Tower of Babel in the middle of a woodland. We sat, still shackled, outside in the parking lot for over an hour.

I've read the Bible, but the only passage I memorized years back, the one that really hit home now, went like this, because in prison, I would be surrounded by those the Bible described:

"Listen, my son, and be wise
And set your heart on the right path
Do not join those who drink too much wine
Or gorge themselves on meat
For drunkards and gluttons become poor,
And drowsiness clothes them in rags."

We debussed at maximum-security Elmira's "reception center," which sounded like we were going to a cocktail party. This two-hour trip had turned out to be a nearly six-hour trip. "Cha-Ching" for the C.O.s. For me, the ride meant struggling with my handcuffs, fear, anger, racing thoughts, and anxiety. The rapo accusation had not yet been beaten down. I was boiling over at Katy Mock, my public defender, who should have told me something, anything, when I was led away from the courtroom on sentencing day. She just didn't care.

Her head never seemed to be in the game. It must have simply been laziness. If I wasn't wasted all the time, I would have fought for myself in court. My first attorney quit my case twice. Mock was a substitute. She could have helped me in some way but chose not to. Folks talk about reforming our justice system; the public defender needs a new job description.

"Enjoy your shave," one inmate said to me.

I looked at his black teeth. "I don't shave," I responded. I looked up front to see the road beyond the driver.

"They're gonna shave you—beard, mustache, and head," said Black Teeth. He laughed.

Ponytail, behind me, said, "Unless you're Jewish, Muslim, or Rasta, you get a close shave."

I looked at the bald guy next to me, whom I had met on the way to Wende. "I don't have much further to go," he said.

Ponytail said he was Jewish and had "the papers to prove it."

I was raised Catholic. Yet I was never that religious. I sat there, horrified, thinking: Will I look like Baldy here—a victim of Auschwitz?

I looked at the bald guy and had an idea. I said to him, quietly, "I'm half Jewish. On my mother's side." He just nodded. I struggled against my shackles, thinking, "But I don't have the papers to prove it." Then I thought, "Who carries papers around saying they're Jewish just to avoid a haircut?"

So, at that strange time in my life, I officially became a half-son of Israel, my father being Irish Catholic. My mother was a little girl whose parents were stationed in Austria during World War II. In fact, she was born in Linz, Austria. And has the papers to prove it.

A small piece of my story was true. Mom's father, Joe Arrigo, was part Jewish, but it was a family secret, for reasons unknown. Joe's father, Lester Arrigo, was half-Spanish, half-Jewish. And to hell with you, New York State! I wasn't getting a haircut!

With a heart-rattling thump, the bus doors finally opened. A fat C.O. with a night stick told us to "fall out and line up next to the fucking bus," one by one. I was in a daze, my thoughts and imaginings out of control and panic setting in.

The walkway entrance to Elmira Correctional's first floor flats was castle-like, similar to Tim Robbins' entry to the prison in "Shawshank Redemption" (film-makers used the Ohio State Reformatory.) A large hall, a parade of new inmates, walls as high as the sky, with prisoners in cages as far as the eye can see. The prisoners threw insults and debris, including burning toilet rolls, at us. The place smelled of fire, the ghetto, and urine. Trails of smoke eased around us like a slow tornado. I had imagined this moment because the prisoners had chatted about it on the bus.

I decided I'd walk proud with an ironic grin, so no one would know if the ribbing was getting to me. And that's what I did. Luckily, I was not set on fire. "Rapo" was shouted all along the way. I said to myself, "It's not me. I'm the drug-dealing writer."

We were strip-searched by officers, a process the Elmira staff calls "Nuts and Butts." We lined up in a series of rooms the size of closets, with black curtains serving as doors. Four-at-a-time we entered the four rooms. We each had an officer (mine was my height, and soft-spoken actually) who told us where to stand and to clean out our pockets. I had nothing. As ordered, I handed the officer my boots, shirt, shorts, socks, and underwear, in that order. Strip-searches were the only time I'd been naked before another man and I began to shake when I took my shorts off. Soft Spoken asked me to lift up my testicles, nodded, then said, "Turn around and spread your cheeks, then cough." I did as told and he said, "Get dressed." I left the little room disoriented, as if I'd been violated both psychologically and physically.

After the searches, the officers gruffly marched us to a cage with a TV. We sat close together in this black cage—for two hours! I felt as if I had half a seat. In the newspaper, I'd once read of a guy who helped stop POWs from being put in tiger cages during Vietnam. Why was it okay here and now?

An older guy across from me was introducing himself to a neighbor. "I'm Joey Buttafuoco," he said. Since I had been a reporter in the early 1990s, I knew that name. I looked; Was it him? Was he the big Italian dude who seduced the Long Island Lolita? It had been more than twenty years. The guy was old, and if the famous/infamous Joey had not taken care of himself, it might have been him. Stupidly, I was like, *Wow, I'm near a famous guy. Jesus. I was more famous than him.* (A check of the Internet post-incarceration proved my Joey was not *the* Joey; mine was too old and stooped.) I also learned that there are many Joey Buttafuoco's in the New York-New Jersey area—the name is almost as popular as Smith.

Some inmates got loud with their ghetto talk, and a giant white monkey man in uniform screamed, "Shut up!" Another C.O. opened the cage door and handed a tray inside. It was bags of lunch for all of us. I was afraid to eat because, in my heightened, panicked state, I might have to go to the restroom, a request that had been turned down for others.

The lunch consisted of two slices of bread, bologna, and American cheese in wax paper, two sugar cookies, and a tiny juice cup. It was just enough food for a seven-year-old. The caged men began trading juice for cookies, baloney for cheese, and more. I tried to start up a conversation but was met only with nasty looks. They could see I was not one of them: no tattoos, overweight, glasses, and proper diction. I was something else—something they didn't like.

The TV broadcast a ridiculous movie with The Rock. It was unwatchable, though the others were enthralled. Those who were talking spoke of how many fights they had won and how "no matter how many women you got, they all bitches." I kept flashing back to a memory—these caged men reminded me of something, the lot of them. The ugly tattoo parlor. Then I thought of it: I was in the middle of a Narcotics Anonymous meeting.

I kept waiting for a fight to break out. There were four other cages in this big room, stuffed full of uncomfortable men. C.O.s' walled offices surrounded us, officers inside shooting the breeze. I wasn't nervous. I was tired and pissed. Making us wait here was pointless. This prison had plenty of dirty cells we could be in now.

I had covered the Gov. Pataki administration for the newspaper. Not much had changed between then and now with Andrew Cuomo Jr. as governor. The state had a bottomless budget, and debt, and there was almost enough room in our fifty-four prisons for all of Manhattan. But Pataki somehow found time to make life worse for felons.

Sometime after the cage but during the dizziness of this zoo, we were taken for those haircuts. The guards had us wait in another caged room—I felt like an ape, staring out at the people walking by, insulting us, staring at us. And I watched as victim after victim came away bleeding from the black man with the clippers. This guy was languidly cutting the hair so close he was slicing into their scalps.

Well, *this* Jewish gentleman wasn't going to tolerate it. The rule was, for the religious, like me, either cut the hair or the beard/mustache. Of course, I chose beard/mustache. The "barber" went easier on me than the others. And no one tried to check my papers.

A C.O. (we'll call him Booby) in the I.D. photograph room gave me shit. "No haircut, Milquetoast?"

"I'm Jewish. On my mother's side."

"Do you practice? If you don't practice, you're a jailhouse Jew."

I said nothing. He was trying to get me riled. Bet he thought the word was spelled "Milk Toast."

He was supposed to take my fingerprints, and when he did, he yelled at me the whole time and wasn't gentle or patient. The C.O. was either acting or had no idea what he was doing. Did he need me to tell him how to do his job? He told me, "Turn your hand." I thought he meant to the left. Booby went absolutely crazy, shrieking, and wandering around the room. Total psycho. He grabbed my hand and flipped it over, called me a moron, etc. (Takes one to know one.) When he finally completed the task, he locked eyes with me and said, "Get out of here before I punch you in the face."

After photos were taken, they told us we had to pay $2 for the I.D. It would be charged to our commissary accounts. A few days later, Booby showed up at my cell door to tell me my beard had grown too long so I needed a new I.D. I thought: *That's state-run extortion, stealing money from inmates every time they "need" an I.D.* Booby was hitting me with a 110.31 infraction from the *Standards of Inmate Behavior*: "An inmate shall pay the cost of a replacement I.D. card whenever the inmate's appearance has changed as the result of a beard, mustache, or change in hair length or color. Refusal to voluntarily pay for replacement cost may result in restitution being imposed through the disciplinary process." Meeting with Booby alone was a disciplinary process.

I was thinking then, "C.O.s are not here to protect. They are here to provoke." Former inmate Jimmy Lerner said, in *You Got Nothing Coming,* that in prison, a lot of the officers sound just like inmates with their cursing, ghetto speak, and outright threats. Lerner: "Must be some kind of reverse Stockholm syndrome."

Luckily, I was on Lithium for bipolar. The drug dulls emotion. Without it, I'd be at maximum anxiety and worry over this asshole who chose to antagonize me the entire time at Elmira.

We were given cell assignments after seeing a psychiatrist. I told him about my bipolar depression, anxiety*, paranoia, and my medications. I was in the "severe" category of mental illness, according to the doc. He secured me a cell on the first floor, the lowest level in the reception area of the prison castle. If I tried to kill myself, help could get to me faster. That's how they think. The walls of this place oozed Kafka's blood. As he said, "The first sign to the beginning of understanding is the wish to die." The great thing about death was it would get me out of here. [1]

In reality, if I tried to kill myself, the C.O.s would take their sweet time coming to me. Wouldn't care whether I was alive or dead. And the ambulance would take hours. If they called one. Reception's infirmary was on the 7th floor. Anyway, my floor was the best place to be—easy access to chow, recreation, and activities. And cigarette smoke rises.

As we stood getting our cell numbers, a C.O. looked at me and said, "What're you looking at, you fat fuck?" Again, I said nothing. Betrayed no emotion. So, he grabbed the night stick on his belt and waved it at me as a warning of sorts.

Inmates often discussed beatings in New York State prisons. There is a case still apparently in the courts, about an inmate who lost an eyeball. (A quick, post-prison check of Internet news revealed an eye injury at an inmate work site, an Arizona inmate who ate his own eyeball, and a former inmate who won a $3.9 million settlement after being beaten by a gang of officers, including a chief and a captain.)

Convicts at Elmira also spoke of an inmate beaten so badly by a C.O. that the night stick got stuck in his dented head. I learned then that both inmates and C.O.s lie. It was unholy how guards could kill convicts and get away with it. The notorious story was Gowanda Correctional, near Buffalo, where a C.O. pushed a handcuffed inmate down a cement staircase, breaking the victim's neck. Apparently, it was a rather routine practice there. The man, scheduled for release, was supposedly mentally challenged and had scuffled with officers in the past. On

1 Forty million Americans are affected by panic and anxiety. Over twenty-one million suffer from some type of depressive disorder.

this day, the victim's sister was waiting to pick him up. At the gate, she was turned away—he was "still being held," she was told. She didn't find out her brother was dead for about two days. Certain types of C.O.s made it easy, and quick, to go from inmate, to victim, to dead.

The Human Rights Watch released a grim 127-page report detailing incidents from across the nation in which corrections officers have "deluged prisoners with painful chemical sprays, shocked them with powerful electric stun weapons, and strapped them for days in restraining chairs or beds." And prisoners have suffered broken jaws, noses, and ribs at the hands of their captors. A laundry list of additional, purposeful torture, and murder, was included.

These victims were mentally ill prisoners, in facilities *with* psychiatric personnel. Either the psych staff was too scared to speak up, or their complaints were ignored, according to a 2016 piece in the *New Yorker*. The Human Rights Watch report cited the examples of a number of inmates, including one purposely killed by a scalding hot shower (for two hours), and another dosed with pepper spray forty times. Nationally, a majority of officers are virtually untrained in mental health and react with force when sick inmates act up, like schoolyard bullies who pick on slow kids.

Jamie Fellner of Human Rights Watch said, "In badly run facilities, officers control inmates, including those with mental illness, through punitive violence."

It seems as if the institutions that "rehabilitated" convicts have become mini-cities inside a police state, ruling with an iron fist. H. Bruce Franklin is the editor of *Prison Writing in Twentieth Century America*. It's like an American prison system revolution, in favor of evil. "Central to this counter-movement has been unrestrained growth of the system, harsh mandatory sentences, a 'lock 'em up and throw away the key' media campaign, 'three strikes and you're out' laws ... the creation of 'supermax' penitentiaries, and abandonment of all pretense that prison should be designed for rehabilitation."

Officers' prevailing attitude about the mentally ill was as bad as their dislike of addicts. C.O.s received minimal training in how to manage the mentally ill, and absolutely none in overseeing addicts. It was easier just to label all prisoners "the scum of the earth." To trauma physician Gabor Mate, author of *In the Realm of Hungry Ghosts*, drug rehabilitation and law enforcement would need years of training to change attitudes and truly correct or rehabilitate addict inmates. "Those we dismiss as 'junkies' are not creatures from a different world, only men and women mired in the extreme end of a continuum on which, here or there, all of us must locate ourselves. ...The discoveries of science, the teachings of the heart, and the revelations of the soul all assure us that no human being is ever beyond redemption."

It's just like anything and everything in the U.S. One side has Republicans, God, AA/NA, faith-based 28-day rehabs, group care, the War on Drugs, fanaticism, and prison. The GOP has a one-size-fits-all approach.

On the other side are the Democrats; Science, psychiatric hospitals, individual care, rehabs based in science, and new theories on treating addiction. In fact, the Democrats want prisoners to find recovery through one-on-one treatment, no matter the cost.

Addicts and the mentally ill are caught in the middle. And the government makes billions annually in the War on Drugs, courts, jails, prisons, dated rehab programs, and putting the recovering poor in prison.

The drugs are also caught in the middle, especially prescription painkillers. Gabor Mate said in his book: "Drugs do not make the addict into a criminal; the law does." Supply and demand is not just economic theory. It's a law as powerful as life itself. Dr. Mate wrote: "When alcohol was prohibited, drinkers were breaking the law. If cigarettes were illegal, there would be a huge underground market for tobacco products. Gangs would form, criminal business empires would flourish..."

And each decade, it seemed, a new drug was demonized across the country. Those shouting the loudest about the epidemic didn't care that much about the people—there were other, more profitable reasons. Benoit Denizet-Lewis is the author of *America Anonymous*. Denizet-Lewis explained, "Occasionally, there was a scientific basis for why we stigmatized a particular drug, but just as often it was based on political or economic interests."

We filed out of our new cells (mine, cell 38, ground floor) after being called to dinner. The C.O.s had us marching in line, double-time. I thanked God that I avoided the lead position in line. If you were there, you were fodder for the C.O.'s criticisms, as in "Don't you fucking know your left from your right?" I didn't. I never have, especially under pressure. No wonder I hadn't driven in a decade. As we marched in our hideous, humiliating green uniforms, we were now part of the New

York State inmate army, expected to behave as if we were in boot camp.

I am an addict. As an addict, I do not like being told what to do. And I wasn't buying this shit. I wasn't walking double time, wasn't kissing ass, wasn't working for The Man. And I was not going to crack under the pressure of the audio assault from the noise boxes. Some inmates immediately went to work for The Man, painting walls, running items from one cell to another, cleaning floors. I kept my attitude in check; I was not completely insane. I was not looking for a beating. I kept to myself, hearing the following from the C.O.s of reception: "What the hell's wrong with you?"; "Are you stupid?", and, my favorite, "Ya want a slap in da head?"

The mess hall was packed. The staff gave us meatloaf, potatoes, and beans on a tray, and then, at the lines' end, they gave us a spoon. My neighbor at the table said, "Hold onto that spoon or they'll beat your head in." I held onto it, ate, returned my tray, and took the spoon to the exit. I admit, I was frightened. What about the spoon? Then I saw inmates putting their spoons in a bucket as a C.O. watched. On the way back to my cell, an inmate told me that a spoon "makes a gnarly shank" when filed down.

With the noise level, the cigarette smoke, the Medusa-like C.O.s, and the unknown menace lurking in the hallways, I was happy to get back to cell 38. I often confused my cell with cell 38 across the hall. One side was A and one was B; I didn't know which was which. Lost, I got some mean looks from the guards, as if they thought I was screwing around. Finally, one day I saw a mark on my wall that was not on the other side, so I let the mark guide me.

Inside cell 38, I felt like a prisoner in the Civil War. That's how old the room and its utilities looked. Elmira's whole complex also looked as if it had gone unwashed all that time. It was built in 1876, about one hundred miles outside Buffalo, and had a warden named Zebulon Brockway who called for strict discipline and a military atmosphere. Always the trailblazer, Brockway was praised for his policy of corporal punishment, which was adopted by other eastern states.

Little white mice came to my cell at about 3 a.m., scratching the locker and startling me out of my sleep. I chased one out. Another had grabbed a sugar packet from somewhere and came into my cell though the doorway. It looked as if the tiny creature was bringing sugar to me.

It was cute, but only for a few seconds. There were mice, bugs, and disgusting garbage strewn about the hallway ... Where were the inspectors? Jail administration?

"Permitting insect and pest infestations" and "unsanitary conditions" were against the United Nations' Convention Against Torture (CAT), Article 16, which I did not know at the time. Each of the four prisons I stayed at had its own level of filth, no matter how many porters they had pushing brooms and buffers. And just who was going to enforce the U.N.'s C.A.T.? Especially when Barak Obama himself said the conditions I experienced did not exist. "I can stand here today, as President of the United States, and say without exception or equivocation that we do not torture …" The forty-five inmates brave enough to testify for the "Survivors Speak" report, issued by the Committee Against Torture, would certainly disagree.**

Each morning we were awakened by a bone-rattling fire-hall bell. Eight floors of guys thudded down the stairs to "chow." It was a Tuesday, after breakfast, when all our cell doors opened, electronically. When that happened, it meant we were going somewhere. But prison is not like county jail. In prison, those in charge tell you nothing. So, I had to guess what to put on: boots (inside) or sneakers (rec time)? The wrong cell doors opened often. And if the door closed and you hadn't left your cell, you were in deep trouble.

Luckily an inmate named Bear was on my side. At a meal, he just started talking to me. Part Italian, part American Indian, Bear asked my name, my crime, if this was my first bid, and then said he believed me—I was a journalist caught in a drug deal. "Rapo?" he said. "Fuck them. You're not." His cell was near mine and he knew other inmates were trying to label me. I still told my parents during calls that I desperately needed those court papers.[2]

We gathered outside our cells, single file, me safely third in line. We marched up seven flights of cement stairs to a hideously ugly "hospital" room. It was ugly because the designations naming the rooms had been painted, by an amateur or a child, on the walls. The room where a nurse took blood had a gigantic, blood-filled syringe above the doorway (what a message to junkies). The dentist's room had a big set of teeth. The psychiatric nurse practitioner's wall had large blue pills. *Wow*, I said to myself, *this is Moronland.* The doctors and nurses I saw had that PTSD look on their faces and I thought they couldn't possibly provide good care here. There were also American flags and U.S. soldiers in action poses on other walls. Maybe the artist was the son of a staff member or C.O. There needed to be two worlds; one for

---

2. The Committee Against Torture report was published by the American Friends Service Committee, a Quaker faith-based organization, dating to the 17th century, that supported friends imprisoned for their beliefs. The report was created "in response to thousands of calls and letters of testimony from prisoners and their families about conditions in prison." Forty-five testimonies were presented in the report, each bloodier and more disturbing than the first.

this "art" and one for Norman Rockwell.

Loudly, we were ordered to get in three lines—lines that went from the office all the way down the stairwell on the second floor. And then we began visiting stations, being yelled at every five minutes to "shut up." I went to six or so offices and wound up at the bloody syringe. Some staff were civil, some rather unfriendly. The "nurse" took my blood, taped my arm with a cotton ball, and then said, "Get out of my office." *Gladly, bitch. This was an infirmary. They were supposed to be helping. What good is a dead prisoner when the state can't make money from them anymore?* They wanted to know if we had AIDS, MRSA, hepatitis, or any other easily transmitted afflictions.

Then I was off to the psychiatric office. I didn't know what to expect because I had just seen the psychiatrist a few days earlier, scoring the bottom floor cell. Now, a brunette who smelled like cigarettes was there to meet me. She had a desk and I had a small chair. Questions were lobbed in my direction:

- Do you have anything to live for?
- Have you ever attempted suicide?
- Do you have any plan to harm yourself?
- To harm others?
- Whom do you have as a support system?

Per New York State law, these questions must be asked at every jail or prison when a new inmate arrives. The answers determine whether the inmate will be housed in general population or in an infirmary cell such as the SHU. The successful suicide rate at some facilities is rather high, so prevention has been increased. Of course, not all facilities in the state report accurately to the Albany bosses (a suicide may be recorded by a C.O. as a "disturbance"), but that's a different story.

Unlike her cohorts, the psychiatric nurse was kind. Despite my being overwhelmed by these surroundings, which she sensed, I was comfortable with her. She made me feel as if there might be an end to prison, for me, someday. This was just a weigh station. A brief stop, for me (two years), in this journey through our legal system.

There was a sticky moment, though. "Have you ever attempted suicide?" The word always made me think of Ernest Hemingway, and a point I'd researched in a number of his biographies. My answer to the brown-haired psych, as it is with the others, "Yes, that car accident in 2012."

"What happened?"

"I stepped in front of a moving vehicle. A Buick. A blue Buick." I almost smiled when I said it. An outdoor rock concert in Lockport. I was drunk on Four Loko. On coke and suboxone.

She wrote on a small pad of paper, making check marks. She nodded and really made me think she cared.

"Then I must ask once more," she said. "Do you have any plan to hurt yourself or others?"

"Absolutely not," I said, though I did think of suicide all the time (in my dreams, the top of Kurt Cobain's head was always missing.) This could not be healthy, but I couldn't tell anyone this truth, or I'd be in an institution, for a while. I thought of Sylvia Plath's *The Bell Jar*, when she wrote, "It was as if what I wanted to kill wasn't in that skin or the thin blue pulse that jumped under my thumb, but somewhere else, deeper, more secret, and a whole lot harder to get at."

As we were wrapping up our medical exams, we talked and got away with it. We exchanged treatment stories and an inmate named Doug said, "We had a medical field office like this in Iraq."

"Was the staff, the nurses, at least nice?"

"Not at all, no," Doug said. "But these fools are worse. I mean unprofessional."

My mental image was of the "nurse" in the syringe room. As a few of us looked through the room's bay window, the last inmate in our group was in the patient chair when, suddenly, blood squirted out of a tube in the kid's arm, onto the window. Instead of attending to the kid, who yelled "Help!" the nurse shouted at the voyeurs and slammed her door.

As if nothing out of the ordinary had happened, a C.O. said, "Line up." While the kid screamed behind the door, we all left.

⸻

Then it was lunchtime. I never caught on to walking in a line with others, or marching. It's like my feet were programmed to go in the other direction. "Turn right," inmates would shout at me while C.O.s yelled, "What the fuck are you doing?" They were all very helpful to the lost guy.

We marched to the lunch line. From inmates in white smocks, we received trays of chili with rice and squares of cornbread. We picked up cups of "orange drink," and plastic sporks, and marched to our table. There were about 100 inmates eating at metal tables. They ogled us, and we stared back at them.

In my literary career, I had befriended or interviewed people like Jay McInerney, Joyce Carol Oates, and Geoffrey Giuliano over dinner in Saratoga Springs, Manhattan, and London, and now I was having a "meal" with one-tenth of New York's underworld. I had a new set of associates.

Bear would wind up being my friend through half my bid, one of the five important people I met in prison. He had thick dark hair and brown eyes, and was in shape without bulging. He talked to me as if we'd known each other for a decade. It gave me hope, though I was worried he was crackhead crazy.

"If you want to read, I'm the book guy," Bear said. "Two cells down from you." Though paranoia was eating at me, I was paying attention—a fight could break out between anyone, plunging the cafeteria into an Attica riot. I was in the prison system that included Attica, Rikers, and Sing Sing.

"Okay," I said, "I need a few books." I hoped there wasn't a charge.

"After lunch," Bear said. "By the way, do you always walk around in a daze?"

Never heard this before. Or maybe I did. People had dropped hints over the years. Now, I was on Lithium for bipolar and Haldol to stop racing thoughts, which interrupted sleep. I did feel dreamy, and not intensely sad from the manic depression. It was a dreamy peacefulness even though I was in prison.

"I guess," I agreed. "But I never really noticed before."

"Ever wonder why you get yelled at so much? It's like you're in your own dream world."

Yes, I was clueless when it came to finding my cell. And people did yell at me for calling the first floor "the first floor" or "bottom floor," when everyone knew the floor as "the flats." The C.O.s yelled when I could not find my cell (38), before I discovered the mark on the wall. I was distracted by the fishliners, the noise, and my own paranoia. The C.O.s were always hurrying us … to go nowhere. It, along with everything else at Elmira, amounted to brainwashing to get us ready for our own, individual prisons, which we would soon see.

"Must be my medication," I said to Bear.

"What?"

"Lithium."

"Why?" said Bear. By now, five or six people at the table were listening. Prisoners are terrible gossips.

"Suicidal. You know the drug rehab in Pennsylvania called White Deer Run?"

"I'm an addict," Bear said. "I've heard of most of them."

"White Deer Run. I was wandering the grounds and the woods last year, my mind set on my own death. I couldn't live without drugs—rehab wasn't working. Replacing heroin with prayer? Jesus Christ. My mind was all bent, man. I wept. Wept. I was irrationally sad, not knowing why I wanted to die. I had written 'cut here' on my wrists."

Bear and I shared more about our rehab pasts. Then a C.O. yelled that it was time for Table 5 (ours) to go back to our cells. We hadn't eaten much, but I was excited to have met someone with similar interests. Bear promised to get me a book or two in the next hour.

We all filed out of the mess hall, dropping our sporks into the empty bucket. Not only were the sporks saved, cleaned, and used for the next meal, we had to be sure they weren't made into shanks. I was going to do my part to prevent jailhouse violence when I saw the C.O.s staring at me. I discovered my hand was empty—I had left my spork on the table. A punishable offense, especially if I couldn't find it! I turned around and walked against the flow of fifty bodies going the other way. But that's the way I did things, I couldn't wait for everyone to pass and risk getting caught. Nearly back to my seat, I saw a black kitchen helper standing there, holding the spork. "Looking for this?" I thanked him, took the spork, and got back in the exit line. I got lucky, getting it back and not being screamed at or hit by the C.O.s.

Back at the cells, Bear met me just before the bars closed. He gave me *Armageddon Dawn*, a book from the "Left Behind" series. It would be the first Christian book I'd ever read, beside the Bible. The barred door closed, and I realized I had everything I needed: a room to myself, a bed, a book, some bread (wrapped in clean toilet paper to stay fresh,) and a little toilet nearby. After being in County, I was used to prison cells. Since I wasn't much of a discipline problem, the Elmira C.O.s left me alone.

One problem was brewing, though. Whispers about me being a rapo were increasing thanks to a blond-haired kid in a cell near me. I knew. I could hear the tale traveling from one cell on the flats to another. I was afraid. I was a drug dealer, not a rapo. Last night at bedtime, when the lights went out, the whole crowd in here started up. Someone bellowed a kid's name and then said he had touched an eight-year-old and an eleven-year-old girl—the two of them sisters.

Then they all got in on it. The inmate crowd sound was deafening, raining down on the lower cells on Elmira's flats, voices funneling through:

"He was with an eight-year-old, and an eleven-year-old. Rapo! Rapo! Raaaaaaaaaaaaaapoooooo."

"Touched a kid."

"Kill yourself, rapo."

"You gonna get castrated. Cut you dick off, rapo."

Like an ocean wave, the word "rapo" moved from one end of the hall to the other, a thousand angry shouts, and then the wave would go back the other way. The rapo was invited out of his cell to meet his taunters. "I'll cut your ass, rapo." I thanked God they were not talking about me. The Greek chorus went on for about an hour, then died down as inmates drifted off to sleep. I could only imagine the young inmate they were talking about, shaking in his cell. During my time at Elmira, four new pedophiles came in, so I got to witness the ocean of yelling several nights. I felt the sticky swarm, the dark quiver of confusion that is fear.

I spoke with Bear the next day through the wall, saying I knew my day of reckoning was afoot. I woke up scared. "I got it," said Bear. "Don't worry, dude." Later, Bear talked to the blond kid, and I was happy for that. However, the kid had told a bunch of people, so I'd have to get to them soon, with proof. It was agony to know the truth and be surrounded by people I couldn't convince. Many an inmate had felt this way, in history.

I stood watching the inmates fishlining, tossing weighted shoe strings to each other, moving items from one cell to another, as if they were fishing. We did not have personal garbage cans. When an inmate had garbage, like an empty coffee sleeve, candy wrapper, dead mouse, or newspaper, they threw them out of their cell bars to the flat's floor. Detritus piled up and inmate porters came with large brooms to gather it up.

Some pimp across the flats from me would sit on a paint bucket at his cell bars and address a pal on the upper floor. I could not figure out if the name of the man upstairs was Brett, Brick, or Brock. The bucket guy did not speak English. I wasn't being a bigot—he engaged deeply in the unrecognized art form of ghetto speak.

Bucket: "That shit stupid funny, Brett. They on some bullshit, man. I'm axin' you, do you feebee?"

I wondered what had happened to "bro"? There was "man," "dude," "Brett," "Brick," and "Brock." Brett seemed to stick with the ghetto speak as the others faded from the backstreet lexicon.

The old white-haired black dude in the cell across from me, the other Cell 38, asked me where I was from, what the area code was there, where I worked, what my crime was—all to try to trip me up. The guy next to him said loudly, "No one goes to state prison for selling four suboxone." Another inmate disagreed. "Shit, dawg. They'll send you up for sellin' one."

I should have bragged about all the cocaine I was moving between Rochester and Buffalo—it would have enhanced my prison reputation. Society's values are inverted in prison. Inmates involved in organized crime and major drug trafficking were the upper echelon, while college-educated folks with legitimate employment were at the bottom. But the coke story wasn't real, and in here I had to tell the truth.

The tension was building. Tonight was my night, I knew. I brooded, my mind in a storm. I felt the electric menace in the air, the capacity for lethal violence on the part of inmates and C.O.s. I didn't know what they did to rapos in the yard, at meals, in hallways—all prime spots of attack, Bear said. I could imagine.

Then the mail came. A passing C.O. dropped a May 15 letter from Inmate Accounts through my door bars. I opened it to find a list of fees that I had to pay—court surcharge, crime victims (everyone who is convicted must pay this), and other charges. I was never so happy to get a bill because, on the list of such billing charges was a "sex offender registry fee." My court surcharge fee totaled $300. My sex offender fee was zero. Why? Because I am not a sex offender. Of course, I knew I was not a sex offender, but the thousand gossipy old women who make rumors up out of nothing were coming to a boil about me. I held the paper and danced around my cell—I was going to stuff them.

Bear told me I was next to the cell (on the other side) of Bill, who was the main gossip—he had even asked me for my indictment, which I did not yet have. "Ooooh, Billy," I said to his cell bars. He appeared, and I told him to hold out his hand. "You can stop gossiping." Then I thought better of saying any more. I did not need a fistfight to go with this. You never forget your first day in state prison or your first fight. So, I went with, "Take a look at this."

He took the paper from me and was quiet. "Okay," he said. Then he called out across the great hall, to three cells. "Stickney is straight," was all he said. That was it. I had made peace with Elmira, thanks to a bill from New York State.

I would hear "rapo" again at a place where sex offenders outnumbered other inmates by three to one—Collins Correctional—which, it turned out, was the next destination on my journey. Technically, we were still on the bus, just interrupted by a two-week layover at Elmira.

I took another look at my surcharge bill from the state, wondering how I was going to pay it. And the government had a plan for that—what my father called "a regular racket." Extortion and graft.

The state creates prison programming and hires officers to give inmates an experience that will make them never come back, and think they've died and gone to hell. But today's designer drugs and opiates have stronger control over the mind than the threat of state prison. At Elmira, after conversations with other inmates, it appeared to me that the never-come-back system had failed. It's time for change because, here in 2019, inmates are coming out bigger addicts and better criminals, which creates job security for the whole justice system.

It took only a few days for me to figure out that it's all about money, not corrections, or rehabilitation. It was also about misery. B.M. Dolarman described lockup thusly in *Prison Noir*:

"... the place where man's dignity goes to die. ... To recreate it, move into your broom closet. Give the key to the guy who was the biggest bully at your school. Have him feed you only cheap, starchy, flavorless food. Only take a shit in full view of strangers. ... You'll never be able to fully account for all the factors that make it miserable."

That same day, I was called to see a guidance counselor. Waiting outside her office, I was seated next to a black man with a white cloud of hair and train-track facial wrinkles. He said hello to me. He asked how long I was down. "Two years," I told him. He said he was in jail for life. He was a professional house thief/cat burglar, he said, convicted of raping one of his victims.

"Don't believe what you may hear about Nappy J. Ain't no rapo, Nappy J. No rapo. Some crackers pulled a faster one."

I was amazed. How could he do *life*? If I were him, I'd take myself out—hang it up. He said he "end denured," (endured). Also that a few minutes before the Parole Board might change everything for him. I doubted it.

The guidance counselor yelled "Stickney" and I wished the man luck.

Mrs. Kiff introduced herself and motioned for me to have a seat. Her desk was a mess of folders and papers. She handed me a paper of dates. Mrs. Kiff was looking at her computer and said, "You're eligible for Shock." She was clearly confused. Shock was an early release program with military-style living and six months of drill sergeant-type direction.

"No," I said respectfully. "I have a mental illness."

"Oh, I see," she said. I wasn't getting Shock. I wasn't getting out early.

She focused on the paper, which said my maximum term would end on December 12, 2018. My Conditional Release (CR) date was August 28, and my merit eligibility date was May 14, 2018. That last one was nice. It was only eleven months away.

The maximum date in December was if I got in trouble a lot, breaking the *Standards of Inmate Behavior* and winding up in The Box. The CR date was if I didn't take each of the prison's programming recommendations. The merit date was if I could be the ideal inmate.

I left Mrs. Kiff with a smile on my face—I was going home in May because I would be the model prisoner. I had to call my parents. But May was much further away than I thought.

The cell doors squeaked open one morning. No one told us anything but "line up." You had to be psychic to know it was shower/phone time. Bear apparently was, and he yelled "grab your towel," and I did. The C.O.s marched us up three flights to the gym and we waited on the bleachers for our turn in the showers, ten at a time. It was the first time in my life that I showered in my underwear. And showered with inmates. I did not know what to do, so I followed the lead of the others. I had prison shower clichés on my mind: *Was someone going to get raped? Gang raped? Knifed? Would there be a shower fight? A riot?* I worked to keep my eyes on the wall, on my body, the floor, so I didn't look at another man's face, or anywhere else. I was almost disappointed when no one did anything absurd. After showering, I had to go "commando" in my state greens, my wet underwear hidden inside my towel.

Then it was phone time. At my turn, I called my parents in Florida. They were retired and had been living in Palm Beach for a decade.

My mother said, "We wanted to tell you that, after this is over, we'd like you to come stay with us for a while."

That was a jolt. They had stood by me throughout this felony charge and my drug court/ jail stints. Palm Beach meant leaving Lockport, New York. Lockport was where I had no home and the parole officers would be on my back because there weren't that many parolees in Niagara County. Lockport also meant temptation. I had been drunk on every corner of that town, and Danny, my main drug dealer, lived right there.

I had moved out of my parents' house when I was eighteen and went to live above a bar with my old high school friends. Moving back in at fifty?

"I don't know what to say," I said. I was happy—Florida, the beach, leave jail, and go retire at the beach.

"Think about it," my mother said. "And we'll discuss it more as the months pass."

Bear was next to me and asked if my parents would call his mother and tell her to put money on his phone account. My mother did call Mrs. Bear and the transaction was a success.

Bear was put on "draft," meaning that he'd leave Elmira tomorrow, leaving me all alone in my first bid, my first time in state prison. "Make the first time the last time," he said. The thousands of strangers, living right next to me, living in my mind, a 24/7 riot that chills under my skin. Bear was excited to be going to another prison, getting out of this hell. He gave away all his books. The next morning, he was gone.

Medicine was given after dinner. My cell bars would open, and I'd walk the flats to the tiny office where the med nurse handed out the stuff that kept me going. Preventing me from being emotional, a coat of armor in this environment, lessening fear, stopping the tears.

The nurse—a guy—was very nice. He was the first truly friendly person I'd met here beside the lady in the Infirmary who smelled like cigarettes. I wanted to tell the nurse that my anxiety was worsening. Bear advised me one day, "Never ask an officer for anything." The C.O. you tell can't be expected to grasp your mind's issues. He'd either purposely misunderstand, laugh, or offer to give you a beating. At the med line, three officers stood by, socializing about union matters more than observing inmates.

There was a tall black guy in line who cheeked his meds, so he could sell them later. Sleep meds, and Wellbutrin, the jailhouse cocaine. I'd walk back to my cell with him and he'd hold a pill between his teeth, drying it out. Pills got wet and started to disintegrate when you "cheeked" them.

After meds, the cheekers, robbers, murderers, n'er-do-wells, and the others met outside in state greens for recreation. The rec yards in Elmira were stark, football field-sized voids of cement and sky. Nowhere to sit, nothing to exercise with, lots of nothing except other prisoners and C.O.s. So, we walked in circles. Others stood, watching inmates walk in circles. Drug dealing and fight planning went on as well.

The other prisoners seemed to accept this landscape as if it was normal, the way it was everywhere. I couldn't accept it at all.

A guy named John distracted me from my doldrums. I'd met him at lunch, I'm sure. He wore glasses, and all I could think of was "Breaking Bad." John resembled the actor, Bryan Cranston. Bald, gregarious, nervous, warm, even in prison. We hit it off, talking crazy about everything, as we walked the hot pavement.

I asked John what he did. "A lot of crack," he said. "I had this sexy girl, 23, and I was always getting her more crack. See?" He held up an unfolded photocopy of a 7-11 security camera shot. John was at the center, arm extended, holding a big black gun to the clerk's head. The register was right there, waiting to be opened. The image was very exciting and alive, very wild west, kept handy in his sock. There were other robberies.

On that night, the girl, Jill, waited in a Chevy two parking lots away. Inside the store, John demanded, "Give me the money," to the clerk while the cameras recorded it all. But none of that mattered—they had crack money, $300-plus. As he was about to get into the car with Jill, he dropped his glasses in the parking lot. Unaware of this, they left the scene.

Asked why so much crack, John said, "How else is a guy like me going to get a fox like her?"

I countered, "If I may say, she's a crackhead. She won't be sexy for long."

As John and I spoke in the rec yard, fellow inmates, organized by races, walked by. Many have said it, and the stories are true: The races hang around their own kind. Some say, "If you're not racist when you get to prison, you will be when you leave." The audio assault was what got me. Some races, it seemed, vocalized hundreds of decibels louder than the others. Culture clash. Blacks turning into Muslims. Latinos, Dominicans, and Puerto Ricans speaking rapid Spanish. Whites and their White Power. Very few Asians. Only a couple Eastern Indians. No Chinese. Some American Indians—the most respectful of all. I was a small-town boy, a WASP. It was culture shock to me. This was the first time I'd ever shared a dorm (bedroom) with so many races. I had a lot to learn.

"Breaking Bad" John said he saw a buddy of his killed in Iraq. He had PTSD. Anyway, John said Jill wanted to go back and get his glasses. She demanded it, in fact. Said they wouldn't get caught. But they did. She got four years and John got seven. He lost all his possessions as well as his Army pension.

We stared at the sunset, and the C.O.s had us line up military style. It was like we were training to be Nazis, or victims. John spoke of a book he was reading, something about a battle, God vs. Darwin. He didn't know the title. "It's a little too technical. It's all I have."

"My book guy left this morning."

He changed the subject. "What do you think of the Ebonics?"

"I call it ghetto lingo," I said. "I have no idea what they are saying. Does being raised in the ghetto make them deaf? They are always asking each other, 'You hear me?' 'I'm down for another six.' 'You hear?' It's after every sentence. And 'You feel me?' They all do it—black, white, Latino, and the lot."

John was laughing. He used another oft-repeated line from the ghetto: "That's a fact."

We were learning that prisoners have their own way of speaking, imitated in big city ghettos. It was all gibberish. In state prison, I could tell I was going to have a problem with communications. These guys also said, "My nigga," after every sentence. I concluded that many of these people were talking but not listening. They were talking to pass the time, to hear themselves talk, to get loud.

Former inmate Michael G. Santos wrote in *Inside: Life Behind Bars in America* that one ghetto voice he heard went thusly:

"I started out as a young G. Know what I'm sayin'? I be crawlin' out the window when my moms was asleep. I just went out. Know what I'm sayin'? I be robbin', stealin', just takin' shit up of a muthafucka. I got mad squabbles, good hands, I can fuck a nigga up. I be like goin' to the Church's Chicken. Know what I'm sayin'? I orders some food, and when the muthafucka axes me for some money, I whip out the burna. Know what I'm sayin'? I just point the pistol in a nigga's face and say, 'Let me get dat out da register, bitch, befo' I pop a cap in yo muthafuckin' skull.' Word! Dat's wuzz up."

"My nigga." "That's a fact." "Know what I'm saying?" "Dawg." These words and phrases were repeated endlessly in inmate conversation. Jimmy Lerner served time and wrote *You Got Nothing Comin'*. Lerner explained, "I'm starting to figure out that all this 'know what I'm sayin' stuff is not really a question, or even a rhetorical device—it's just white noise designed to fill in conversational gaps."

The 8th edition of the college textbook *Communication* seemed to bear witness to my dilemma. "The average person in the U.S. spends 50 to 80% a day listening but actively hears only half of what's said, understands only a quarter of that, and remembers even less. Most people use only 25% of their capacity to listen."

Back at my cell, I plugged my headphones into the wall radio. I could not change the pop station, but it was nice to have anyway. There was a song, "Sign of the Times" by Harry Styles, which struck me. There was also audio of some cable TV station. I made a cold cup of coffee (no hot water) and plugged the holes in the wall to keep the mice out. I was told that roaches came out of the sink. I plugged that as well.

It had been days, but the time came when I had to use my seat-less metal toilet. There was no door, just bars. I looked out from different angles to see if any felons would get a show. I had no idea how to cover up. Should I put a sheet over my seated body?

Well, I "went," and it was quick, then I flushed many times, trying in vain to dispatch the odor. And then the flats started complaining. "Put yo sheet up when you do that. No one want to see you."

I asked, "How do I put a sheet on bars?" I found out that I was supposed to tie the sheet corners to the top of the bars. Then I thought: *If they didn't want to see me on the toilet, why were they looking?* I learned that, like prison chess and basketball, inmates stare at each other all day—it's a regular activity, inmate watching.

How was any of this nonsense going to correct me? Jack Henry Abbott's *In the Belly of the Beast* explained: "…No one, not the wardens or the pigs or the government, can control that power, that force, in such a way as to change a man to become what we consider a fair version of 'Rehabilitated Man,' i.e., the good citizen."

The next day, I met my nemesis. About 10 a.m., our cell doors opened, and we all walked out to the flats. A giant balding C.O., the guy who took my fingerprints, came along and ordered us into two lines. Then we marched—one line at a time—outside to the prison parking lots. I made sure I was not a line leader since I didn't want to get screamed at for not being able to march or lead a line.

We got yelled at when we marched too slow. We got yelled at when we marched too fast. We got yelled at when we went too far left or too far right, under a hot sun on what otherwise would have been a beautiful morning.

What were all my friends doing out there? My judge? My useless public defender? God? I stood among the state's criminals, the convicted, the doomed. Because not only did we have sentences to serve, we also had parole, the government watching us after our bids, waiting to pounce.

We went to the I.D. room to get our photos taken. They make new I.D.s at every prison—a total waste of time and money. My nemesis, the big mean C.O., was in there. He looked up at me and told his C.O. buddies, "I hate him. I don't know why. I just hate him." Now I didn't hate that C.O., I just mentally assessed his level of intelligence as low and knew I was better than him and that I always would be. I'll be creating and living a great life while he is out hunting squirrel for dinner.

The author of *Newjack: Guarding Sing Sing*, Ted Conover, wrote that officers are trained to keep their facility secure, not safe. And training includes not caring about the prisoners and blatantly denigrating them, because inmates are "inanimate objects." Due to workplace frustrations, Conover wrote, C.O.s may achieve satisfaction and even mirth by belittling and hurting prisoners. He quoted one officer in an Albany training facility that the use of a baton is preferred torture. "I've heard those ribs crack," the officer said. Some inmates do present a danger to officers, of course. Yet well-behaved and cooperative inmates seem to get painted with the same broad brush.

Sing Sing officers break ribs and arms as if it's part of the job. A facility inmate testified for the American Friends Service Committee's "Survivors Speak" report that another inmate was being physically abused by an officer. The inmate resisted the abusive officer and was then jumped on by twelve other C.O.s, who handcuffed him. While the sergeant yelled "Break his arm," the C.O.s beat the inmate into a coma.

The same inmate testified that he witnessed two deaths. One was refused heart medication. The other was beaten to death for looking at a nurse. As the years pass, C.O.s seem better at killing people than the gun-crazed ghetto cops. Maybe there should be a question on the state C.O. exam: "Do you mind killing innocent, defenseless inmates?"

Granted, Sing Sing officers, Conover wrote, often have to dodge urine, shit, and dangerous objects hurled at them by prisoners. C.O.s have died in surprise inmate attacks, fights, and riots. An officer's safety is constantly at risk. But why the game of one for one? Shouldn't guards content themselves with professionalism? Something that lets the prison administrators or local courts dole out punishments? As it is now, C.O. versus inmate is a war with no end. The same goes for mentally ill inmates. Why would a C.O. work with them without full training? The current, three-hour course isn't enough.

The training for officers overseeing "inmates with special needs" provides definitions, needs, possibilities, and safety information. Officers are expected to memorize the seven types of mental illness they might see: schizophrenia, depression, bipolar disorder, PTSD, antisocial personality disorder, and adjustment disorder. Symptoms and suggested actions are discussed.

What are officers supposed to do if an inmate is experiencing severe, obvious symptoms?

1) Keep it simple

2) Do not argue

3) Keep the inmate calm and focused

And contact the facility's OMH to take over and place the inmate in a safer environment. The document did not say that if the inmate begins screaming and shits his pants, guards should place the subject in handcuffs and beat him to death. According to American Friends Service Committee, this kind of thing happens often, all across the country.

The course handouts said, "As a correction officer, your job involves care, custody, and control." The class also covered the seriously disabled and the mentally retarded. Learning was fostered by memorization and role play.

One officer I interviewed at Marcy, Clive, was a ballbreaker for years but changed his ways when he got married and had kids. Clive said his anger on the job was lessened due to a solid family life. He even stopped drinking. And he'd become one of the more popular officers at the prison, with fellow C.O.s and with inmates.

Clive said that in his early C.O. days, he was known to take down inmates, handcuff them, and place a boot on their necks, all while laughing his head off. "And I learned that when you beat them, they gotta be handcuffed," he said. "I don't do that anymore. I developed a conscience."

After my run-ins with Booby, I thought about how, as a corrections officer, Booby not only represents the prison, he represents the whole state, and the 62,000 other unionized correctional officers. In fact, all C.O.s should be setting a standard of respect and understanding among themselves and with the prisoners, at least with nonviolent convicts. The "fatherless" prisoners (the youngest inmates in American prisons number about 800,000) need authority figures they can look up to and respect. In fact, they are prisoners now because they've never had anyone to look up to, much less respect.

Instead, C.O.s are told they are "$40,000 babysitters," and have been known to say that inmates are "the lowest of the low" and the "scum of the earth," these thoughts even justifying the use of unreasonable force. No wonder there's a warped relationship between the inmates and officers.

I decided I would think more about this as my bid continued. I knew I was a bit naïve, though I also knew people had been asking for change for a century. Why didn't they get it? "Because this is punishment," Booby would say. "You're lucky it ain't fucking worse." But punishment does not rehabilitate. Also, I knew, Booby would be here dealing with the manure long after I left.

After two weeks at Elmira, it was time to jump into the shackles again for another bus ride. I had stayed at the Niagara County Jail, then Wende, then Elmira, and now was going to a new place. Anticipation and anxiety were confronted by relief, I was happy to be leaving Booby's headquarters. Inmates talked about how during their last time at Elmira, they had to stay there for a month or more. I feared a similar fate.

The latest destination, Collins Correctional, was 150 miles away, near Buffalo. I braced myself for a four- to six-hour trip, and I wasn't disappointed. The driver used country roads rather than the much faster thruway.

We all had to wait on the bus for the passenger C.O. to retrieve a briefcase and a gun—the gun just in case we had a Houdini on board who'd escape his shackles, set all of us free, and incapacitate the two guards. A real renegade. So, we could, what? Go running around the countryside in our jail greens? I guess stranger things have happened in action films, the Clinton Correctional escape notwithstanding. Maybe that was the problem at Clinton—they all thought this was a movie.

The guards told us not to talk during the trip. There was some grumbling. On the road, I tried to sleep. It's really difficult with handcuffs shackled to your chest. The black box securing the handcuffs (for minimum movement) was overly confining and made the silver handcuffs bite into my skin. They gave us bag lunches, which were impossible to eat while in shackles. I was, however, able to manipulate a vanilla cookie from the bag.

And there was no way to use the bus restroom. *These are human rights abuse*s, I thought. They go unnoticed because our society dislikes inmates. C.O.s love the handcuffs; it's easier to beat someone to death when they can't fight back. I'd only been in prison two weeks and I was already angry and paranoid.

And for good reason. During my bid, I would have five shackled bus trips in which drivers took the longest way to get there, to get the most overtime pay. The black box over the handcuffs had been widely criticized. According to the American Friends Service Committee, "Being shackled for excessive periods of time" went against U.S. law, which defined the practice as "torture," not only because of the physical pain but because it profoundly disrupted the "senses or the personality."

COLLINS

CORRECTIONAL

FACILITY

MEDIUM SECURITY*

*Just as mean and nasty as maximum security.

CELL #5

The prison economy is supported by the United States'

individual regional governments, with major financial

awards for prisons that meet certain criteria or milestones.

For example, a prison will be rewarded money for

management of an educational program (where outcomes

are not measured) or for the number of prisoners it has, even

if a prisoner is in transition to another facility and only

on-site for one evening.

CHAPTER 5

A SHORT FUSE

"106.10 - An inmate shall obey all orders of department
personnel promptly and without argument."
—NYS *Standards of Inmate Behavior – All Institutions*

Arriving at Collins Correctional, I realized I would be living merely forty-five minutes away from my hometown. Think of it: Six hours of driving to get back practically to where I started. Someone got money, and if you're a taxpayer, you paid for it. American prisons cost $80 billion annually.

A former mental institution from the 1890s, the Collins campus was similar to that of a New England prep school with a spread of stately, dark-red brick-buildings.

The property borders Ellicottville, Buffalo's ski country. In a winter storm, Collins resembles *The Shining*'s Overlook Hotel. During the spring and summer, it's like Knowles' Devon School. It looked more famous than it was; the only well-known inmate was Lindsey Lohan's father a few years back.

Collins housed a number of the mentally ill, including me. My diagnosis was level two on a one-to-five scale, one being the most dangerous. Level two meant: "Expresses suicidal ideation and behavior is somewhat dependent on the stress in the environment. History of impulsive and violent behavior but no current signs." I wasn't violent. Never had been.

New York State prisons hold more than 10,000 inmates who have a psychiatric diagnosis. Some 38,000 are housed in the few psychiatric hospitals that still exist. Nationwide, the number is at 500,000. Prison writer John J. Lennon (no relation to the late rock star) commented in *Esquire*: "The financial toll is enormous: treating prisoners with mental illness costs twice as much as providing community-based care ... Ten out of every eleven psychiatric patients housed by the government are behind bars."

Reportedly, $5 billion is spent annually to imprison nonviolent offenders with a mental health disorder. Lennon: "Jails and prisons have become our de facto asylums." In an emergency, a mentally ill man will see handcuffs before he sees a stethoscope.

Part of the blame goes to Ronald Reagan, who repealed a Carter bill in 1981 to grow federal-community mental health programs.

The enforced culture in a prison today is that of officers in charge of facility security, not inmate safety. The officers run the show—it's the law's house. This point was illustrated by Eyal Press in the *New Yorker* article "Madness" dated May 2, 2016. Knowing next to nothing about treatment, psychiatric or otherwise, Press wrote that the C.O.s in at least one Florida prison, intimidated and manipulated psych workers (trying to address symptoms and improve lives of the mentally ill). Officers tortured, encouraged suicide, and killed inmates as routinely as making rounds. The same officers created an environment of full-scale retribution if any of the counselors or prisoners reveal the truth to investigative bodies. So the truth is buried.

Press noted: "…Prison counselors and psychologists often feel a 'dual loyalty'—a tension between the impulse to defer to corrections and the duty to care for inmates." Also, "…Security staff might retaliate if heath staff reported abuse." And they did.

Gazing at the grazing geese and ducks near the Collins administration building, if you ignored the razor wire fences and marching corrections officers (who might stop and harass or frisk you, or worse, mid-walk), you could almost forget that you're in a prison: the inmate-tended grass was green, the bushes were trimmed, and there were various flowers in spectacular bloom.

It was the third prison on my journey. Because I was a new prisoner, I could not see how nice it was, so I saw the bad in just about everything. I saw only that I had a little less than two years of this staring me in the face. Thirty-seven years after their onset, my illness and addiction finally put me on the conveyor belt so many others had ridden: emergency hospitalization, homelessness, jail, and then prison. The district attorney who prosecuted me told my judge that I should remain in jail longer due to my disorders.

A resident of Collins, I was now caught in a contentious relationship between

DOCCS and the Office of Mental Health (OMH). OMH was my metaphorical shrink, renting space from Collins to care for me. But when there was an emergency, who had the authority to care for me? Collins first, OMH second. They were only working together because of the asylum closures of the 1980s.

At my first Collins mess hall meals, I thought I was attending a circus. Loud voices echoing and exchanging ghetto speak, all eyes engaged in suspicious glances, broken men eating the slop. It was simply a big room with no art, just a sign telling us the rules on what not to do during our "20 minutes" of eating. There were long tables with seats too close to each other so inmates couldn't help but rub arms. Officers demanded assigned seating. The inmate kitchen staff wiped down tables and swept the floor.

My attention was caught by a burn victim. It was as if we could see under his skin, his veins, muscles, everything in motion as he entered the mess hall and joined the others in line.

It appeared to be a white man, yet 80 percent of his skin had been burned away. He had no hair, no ears, a nub for a nose, and transparent hands. I stared. He appeared to be smiling. *My God*, I thought, *what has this man been through? And to be in prison on top of all that.*

It looked as if some of his skin had been taken from other parts of his body to replace what was lost. I'm surprised he was allowed in public, he seemed so dainty and helpless. I couldn't get his unholy image out of my mind. I asked around about the skinless man. I got bits and pieces of the story from different people: He was a Korean with a family and a house. He may have been gay. He wanted money, so he burned the house down with his family inside. They were all dead. To be convincing, he had also set himself alight as well, but the fire got out of control. He had been charged with murder, yet was still awaiting the insurance settlement.

Now I knew the entire story could have been true. Or false. The journalist in me wanted to interview him, but I never got close enough. Then, after thinking about it, I doubted the whole tale. If the skinless man had committed such a crime, he'd likely be in a mental institution for inmates, rather than an honor dorm here.

When I was at the C3 dorm, all I wanted to do was sleep. You'd think that prison would be a nice respite from life. No responsibilities, free meals, a bed. But it's not that way at all. It's standing in long lines, mandatory gym time, violence, housecleaning, and other mandatory busy work. Getting frisked and yelled at, dealing with hundreds of inmates who are crazy and never graduated high school. Asking C.O.s if you can use the bathroom, and enough little contradictory rules to make you insane.

At Collins, I began attending AA meetings again, just for a break from the daily death march. AA has a stipulation that during meetings, the conversation be kept to one's problems with alcohol. Unfortunately, folks act as if they're seeing a shrink or are there to tell tales of woe about their girlfriends and families.

Collins AA was no exception. And no group could be further from a drink than us, or so I thought. The group facilitator was a spry black man with glasses and reddish hair. He explained that he had a problem with beer and crack cocaine.

"When I was running," he said, "my family had no food, no clean clothes. I beat my wife." He kept drinking and getting high. His teenage son wrote of the situation in his diary: "no clean clothes for school and no love in the house." He was very sensitive and wrote that his life would be better if he "was with Aunty in Heaven." He hung himself at seventeen. His father kept getting high.

He tried to kill his wife by slitting her throat with an emery board. She lived, of course. "You're lucky," a cop laughingly told her in the front yard.

I left that AA meeting ten minutes early. I had heard enough.

When I first arrived at Collins, a bunch of us were forced to endure an administrative orientation. It was an hour of obvious rules, "behavior standards," and bureaucratic doubletalk. Superintendent Thompson was there to "welcome" us and make sure we'd "have a pleasant stay." I visited the restroom, with C.O. approval, so I missed most of Thompson's grinning, five-minute speech.

We were given a small yellow book that had eighty "Institutional Rules of Conduct," from "no fighting" to "sunglasses only when outside." There was also the "106.10" rule that allowed any prison staff to make up a rule and demand punishment. Those would likely be for inmates singing too loudly or defecating on the infirmary lawn.

I saw Thompson only one other time. He visited the dorm and wandered through with a C.O., pointing out things that were wrong with inmate cubes. My cube was near 49, where Thompson stopped and told the inmate to take his map of Quebec off the wall. Thompson confiscated the map.

Had he been thinking of the infamous Clinton Correctional escape of two years back, and fearing that if someone here got out, they'd head for Quebec because they'd studied the map? A 595-mile walk, or drive if they had help? I shook my head and thought: *This prison, like any other, has cuttings, suicides, and overdoses, and Thompson, the superintendent, is worried about a map from Canada?*

Interestingly, a TV series was made about the two escapees and the female staff member who set them free. "Escape from Dannemora" was broadcast on Showtime in 2018.

I was also welcomed to my new home at Collins by a C.O. named Hubbard, whom I would get to know better as the days passed. I was just happy he didn't bark at me like the others. He told me I was in cubicle 15 and pointed in the direction of a window.

As I made it to 15 with my clothing bag, I met a kid who looked like Urkel from the '80s TV show. He said, "Uh, you're not one of those guys who, uh—"

"No," I said, "I'm not a rapo."

"Let me see your papers."

In the time when I was in Elmira, a package arrived with my indictment and other court papers. I kept it at the top of my garment bag. I handed him the papers, saying, "I sold suboxone."

I met him and my other neighbors, Heat and Cougar da Admiral (usually just called Cougar). Like a gang banger, Cougar wore a do-rag, his pants sagging, displaying the back of his underwear. I would see this fashion statement often.

Then, standing there like an angel sent from heaven, was Bear. The man who had showed me the ropes and protected me at Elmira. I was already in his debt. I didn't think I could ever be happy in jail, but when I saw Bear again here at Collins, I was. Two cubicles away from me he stood there, smiling.

Bear showed me around C3, as our floor and dorm were called. He pointed out the phone room, kitchen area, restroom, showers, and the TV room. Surprisingly, there was no designated area for cards, dominoes, or chess as there had been at the county jail. Instead, inmates here played inside their cubes, often loudly.

Of course, Bear noticed that after my long bus rides, I needed a shower. He lent me a man-sized towel, three times the size of the hand towel the jail provides. Also, he provided me good shampoo and a Dove soap bar. I showered—no one else was in there, though I did fear shower-rape—and then went back to see Bear.

He surveyed the floor and pointed out which inmates were cool and which weren't. As the days passed, Bear revealed he was "good at jailin" because he had been in and out of prison for twenty-three years. He loved cocaine. And he stole from major stores, selling the merchandise, to get his coke money.

Bear pointed out Cougar da Admiral, a large black man who looked like Shug Knight. He obviously had money because his cube was well-stocked with supplies, from notebooks to foods.

"Cougar's all set," said Bear. "He doesn't need anything from anybody. He's a writer too. He's written five 'hood books so far."

I didn't believe Bear because I was jealous, but it was the truth. He did write all those novels, they were just inside a pile of his black marble notebooks.

Bear talked about Heat. Heat made model cars, planes, and caskets out of popsicle sticks. He was also a tattoo artist, offering to give me my first tattoo for free. I declined. I've never liked tattoos: dirty, ugly, and permanent. Who'd want that? Only every prisoner and cool-wannabe on the planet. The more tattoos, the longer you been down!

A quick check of the handy *Standards of Inmate Behavior*, half in English and half in Spanish, noted that inmates were not allowed to create "a fire, health, or safety hazard." Arson was listed as the first no-no, followed by tattooing. It stated, "An inmate shall not tattoo or otherwise permanently mark his or her body or allow his or her body to be tattooed or permanently marked by another. An inmate shall not be in possession of an instrument or device used for the purpose of making tattoos."

Considering standard 118.20, Heat could have received a Tier Three ticket to The Box for thirty days. He possessed a tattoo pen, and gave tattoos to others and to himself. I would not be prosecuted because, eventually, I would supply Heat with Bic pens I had brought with me. The ball was useful to him somehow. He would keep our pens-for-cookies agreement secret.

I'd seen arms covered from wrist to shoulder—a veritable sleeve of tattoos. I saw neck dragons and neck crowns of thorns. I saw teardrops indicating that Bear had killed someone—maybe a cop. There were spiders, webs, exotic women, cupcakes, witches, lightning bolts, infernos, names of children and of "bitches," team logos, fierce dogs, jungle cats, dice, cash, pirates, scrawl poems, Biblical passages, swastikas, and even a jar of Planters nuts. Writer and former inmate Jimmy Lerner said the "full sleeve is the badge of the recidivist."

Heat said he gave one customer green skulls with black snakes on his forearms and an Indian woman's face. A Chinese inmate told me once that his back was covered in dragons, and they'd cost him $6,000!

Bear said I looked like a combination of *"The Hangover* guy" (Zak Galifianakis) and some professional wrestler named Mankind. "Get a tattoo. Add to your badass look," said Bear.

After a week or so had passed, Bear showed up at my cube. "I want to write a book," he said. He already knew practically everything about me and all my recommendations on how to write a book. Bear explained that he wanted his book to be a linear story that starts and ends. No story arc, no climax, no character growing up or having to change. He compared his vision to a hip movie called *"Kids,"* which was released in 1995. "Just their daily lives in the underworld," Bear said.

I gave him my advice: Get a ream of paper, pull out 400 sheets, and write one page every day for a year. Then you have a book manuscript. "And you'll help me?" he said.

"I can't write it for you," I said, "but I'll help along the way, as you give me pages to read."

The whole thing made me dizzy. I just got off a prison bus, saw nearly sixty men on C3 whom I'd be with for the next who knows how long, and had made a friend who'd been upstate on and off for two decades. And he wanted me to help him write a book. I sat on my newly made bed and stared out the window at the serene May sky. Beneath that sky was the barbed wire that kept me here.

Our neighbor, behind the fencing, was Gowanda Correctional. Urkel said Gowanda prisoners stare out the long, glass-block windows (when they're open) and "wish they were here."

I told him, "The place looks like a building you'd find in Hell."

"It is," said Urkel. "When a C.O. gets punished for actin' like an asshole, beatin' people, or whatever shit, he gets sent here. You don want to be in G-wanda for nothin'."

In county jail, C.O.s were basically friendly, and you could talk to them. I knew many of them because I was a Lockport guy. Grew up there. Attended the same high school. A mean county C.O. was a rarity. In prison, it was the opposite, C.O.s were mean, vindictive, backstabbing, plotting, angry, thieving, hypocritical monsters. A friendly C.O. in state prison was thus a rarity.

"You ain't home anymore," Bear said. "You're in their house." I learned this quickly and, when I had a question about anything in this new place, I asked Bear or another inmate. You had to learn quickly because this was a totally different way of life. Rules applied, but not to C.O.s. Here, there was no logic, justice, responsibility, or anything that might be expected in the real world. In prison, there was chaos—you could count on that. In prison, there was no God to save you.

When a guy like me—good family, college education, accomplished—walks into prison, all the jail movie clichés run through your mind. I found that some were true. But it was the smallest things, like walking in line, that get in the way of sanity.

One inmate told me, "There are five pillars of corrections: punishment, retribution, rehabilitation, reintegration, and supervision." I understood but was skeptical. This sounded like something the Department of Corrections had written up in a plan to fund its prisons. And in reality, it was just words on paper.

I received my commissary order sheet to fill out. I needed Jolly Ranchers, peanut butter, coffee, sugar, and several other things. Then we handed our order forms in to the C.O. on duty and waited for our specific shopping day. On that glorious day (no mess hall food for a few days), my number was called, and I hurried over to commissary, which was in the school building, on a small loading dock. I got behind the long line and waited.

When it got to be 10:50 a.m., the clerk told us to go back to our dorms for

11 a.m. count. There was a collective sigh. Scanning the number of inmates at the dock, I figured there was no way each one of us could get through the commissary line. This was the kind of mind game the C.O.s played—give inmates a pointless task or impossible goal and see if they'll go along or just complain. If they complain, you can yell and write them up.

It was 2 p.m. before I was able to get back to commissary. I was surprised I made it back at all, and I was smart enough to not complain.

We were in prison, but we were still human, we still needed some quality of life to make prison livable—the opposite being a diet of bread and water, beatings and manipulation. Quality of life services included commissary, phone calls, and proper medical care. The prison was not being philanthropic—these services were farmed out to private companies, and in some cases, they were charged directly to us inmates. The result "spawned multi-million-dollar private industries," according to a March 2019 report from the Prison Policy Initiative. The report explained, "By privatizing services like phone calls, medical care, and commissary, prisons and jails are unloading the costs of incarceration onto incarcerated people and their families, trimming their budgets at an unconscionable social cost."

Waking up to a C.O. shouting "Count!" every morning at 6 a.m. makes you feel like you're in the military. The men in the dorm all stood next to their beds so the C.O. could count us, making sure no one had slipped away in the night. "Chow," or breakfast, was at 7 a.m., down at the mess hall. I was in Collins' general population, so I basically had no schedule for my first few weeks. I'd go back to bed after breakfast. After an hour or two, Heat woke me with a swishing sound. He was sanding his wooden creations, day after day, and getting sawdust on my bed.

During my first month at Collins, I learned that I needed to develop my tolerance of noises and voices, of people, of different cultures, of folks who had no tolerance, and of those who trespassed upon me, including those doing so with sawdust. Or cigarette smoke. I told myself, "Don't panic and don't rage out. Tolerate." Augusten Burroughs' *Dry* and *Magical Thinking* were a tonic of sorts to me, taking my mind home to the days of Four Loko and *Running with Scissors* reading sessions. If anyone had tolerated maniacs, it was Burroughs.

Once I woke up, I talked to Bear and read his morning pages. I made notes on them, realizing he was a good storyteller. Outside, when he bought crack, he had bought $400 to $1,000 worth—enough to entertain himself and his girlfriends. The book was about a network of drug addict thieves who crisscrossed the east, using a variety of drugs and committing crimes.

I was impressed. Every morning Bear gave me two or three pages to read, assess, and edit. He was off to a good start. For me, the novel was a trigger, making me want to get high.

The restroom, for sixty guys, had nine mirrors—seven of which were so scratched they no longer gave off a reflection. There were nine sinks and four toilets (one of which didn't work). There were two urinals. Everything was coated in cigarette ash, the air thick with smoke. I must have second-hand smoked two packs a day by the time I left Collins. The smell of smoke was everywhere, blending with sweat, fear, and fried food from the stove-top near the phone room.

The "wash hands" signs in restrooms impressed me, and not in a good way. By the time you reach your teens, you should know how to wash your hands. Collins gave us a handout: Wash with soap and warm water for twenty seconds, wash before preparing food, and wash after going to the restroom. Keep your hands clean to avoid getting sick. The second page of the handout was about foot care. The only thing I could think of was that the dorm housed grown-up crack babies (born in the '80s and '90s) raised in filthy, bug-filled apartments on the bad side of town who, learning what crack pipes were before learning about teddy bears, had never been taught how to wash.

Again, tolerance. But how could I tolerate this and say nothing? Saying something would have meant battling with someone raised in a home, or apartment, of anger, shouting (the primary method of their family's communication), arguing and doing anything to "win," even if it meant physical confrontation. We had many of these types in C3. They talked loudly and blasted hip-hop all day long, until they went to bed at night. In fact, they didn't talk. They broadcast. Whatever they were saying was so important, the whole floor, the entire prison, needed to hear it. Imagining what it must have been like to grow up in their houses, I shivered.

The officers called all meals "chow." We waited for the C.O.'s phone to ring. When he hung up, he'd yell, "On the chow." I inquired with several C.O.s, yet none could tell me what "on the" meant. Lunch came and went. Usually some type of slop ("chicken" and "beef" were both made of breast-enhancing soy) poured over rice or pasta. Bear said every prison in the New York State system served the same food at every meal.

As I was told by Bear, the chunks of slop in our meals were not any sort of meat at all. All the meals were tasteless, except for apple crisp.

"All the meat we get is soy," Bear explained. "Every prison in the state gets the same food we do, and all the meat has been replaced with soy. Our meals cost about $3 per person a day."

Patriot was nearby. "And soy makes your breasts grow. Estrogen. Don't worry, boys. I'm buying today."

"The women prisoners get regular meat," Bear said. "They sued because their tits were getting huge."

I couldn't help but look at my own chest.

"Eat up," Patriot said.

Either the cops, the kitchen inmates, or both were stealing food. The mess hall ran out of burritos on September 17, of wheat bread on the 28th, and chicken and fish patties on the 29th. The Collins solution? Feed inmates slices of American cheese. No bread, no lunchmeat, just three slices of cheese.

On September 18, C3 was called down to dinner so late that the kitchen staff had put the food away. So, we had to wait even longer to eat. So, who was really in charge of this system? Checking on things? Quality assurance? Nobody. An $80 billion system on autopilot.

Afternoons, I got to know my fellow inmates. There was always lots of chatting because "cube visiting" was allowed. Everyone's cubicle was the same: bed, locker, and desk. Near me was a thin man, a boy really, "Twiggy," with a ponytail that went down to his knees. He said he was part American Indian who had been wrongly convicted. Then he was silent, eyes closed, as if meditating.

Later, C.O. Hubbard said Twiggy was from a farm near Rochester and had been convicted of having sex with canines (beastiality). This was the same Twiggy who had Ayn Rand's *The Fountainhead* and *The Encyclopedia of Crime* on his little bookshelf. He stayed in his cubicle, alone, reading a Hindu book on peace.

In normal life, I would have not become friends with a sex offender. But the journalist in me, and our proximity to one another, invited a kind of sharing about our lives. The guy in question had the handle of Pastor Mark. We shared our life problems in long talks. His cubicle was near mine and we met (I did not yet know his crime) when he requested some sugar for his coffee. "I'll pay you back with my commissary next week," he said.

The question of "What's your story" was often first on the conversational list, unless the new person volunteered the information. The story isn't normally volunteered by sex offenders, who were notoriously difficult to interview. My story was easy: I was drinking too much after my divorce. I sold part of my painkiller prescription so I could buy more booze. I got caught.

Mark said he was a biohazard cleanup truck driver. He had a wife and daughter in Syracuse. A slight man with mustache, dark hair, and glasses, he looked and acted like the nerdy friend you had in high school, the one who went on to become an accountant or county clerk.

Pastor Mark was different from the others I'd meet. He offered his version of events during our first conversation. One evening, he said, after a few vodkas and a little coke, he was online "hanging around with the wrong crowd." He found a 14-year-old Lolita and engaged in a heated sex exchange with her. The teen turned out to be an undercover officer.

According to Pastor Mark, he had a solid home life and a great childhood. He turned out to be one of the magic five, along with Bear, who was going to help me through. For a nerd, he possessed a humorous charisma gleaned from clerking at his father's corner grocery store. "We were one of the most popular families in our town," said Mark. "Everyone loved my parents." They were generous to a fault, going out of business like so many others when the big box stores moved in and Main Street America died.

Asked why he got into Internet porn, Mark was the only inmate I spoke with who opened up. He claimed it was the stress of his job in biohazard cleanup. "There was a guy who lost his driver's license to DWI or something, so he shot himself right in front of the wife and kids. I was the one who had to get what was left of his mustache and teeth out of the ceiling of his dining room," he said. "We cleaned up murders, meth labs, and the scum of the earth."

Sitting in Mark's tiny cubicle at Collins and hearing his story, I noticed the religious paperbacks and leather Bibles lining his bookshelves. Prisoners in the dorm were not in old-fashioned, metal-barred 8x12 cells. Such cells were only for the seriously mentally ill (those who made snowmen out of feces) and particularly violent/suspicious characters.

Mark said his faith was tested and "increased" when he came to prison. Unlike most of the accused, Mark not only admitted his crime, but also asked his Supreme Court judge to sentence him to the maximum. His sentence for talking sex online to a "14-year-old" cop was five years. Everything he told me suggested that he really wanted to change, he told me that he wanted to become a pastor when he got out.

In Collins Correctional, Pastor Mark was enrolled in an educational sex offender therapy program designed to deal with issues "under the surface" like anger, fear, insecurity, past trauma—stuff that goes beyond sex addiction to get "to the root of the problem," according to Mark. He also saw the psychiatrist.

He said, "I knew when I did it, when I logged on, not only was the sex wrong but the ... context of it. She said she was underage and that made it naughty."

One day early in my time at Collins, we got a new guy in the dorm. He was a Rastafarian, with long dreadlocks. As soon as he set his bag down on the bed, he removed his state shirt. He was impressively built. The C.O. walked past him to the TV room for a floor check and the Rasta stared at him.

Then the Rasta hurried to one of the front cubes near the bubble and started pounding on a young, normally quiet black dude called Treat. My adrenalin started racing, and I could see the fight—they both went at it hard. Their arms were moving so fast, their bodies twisting and breaking into each other, it looked as if the Tasmanian Devil was spinning inside Treat's cube.

The noise was like someone pounding a sheet of tin. Over the sounds of other inmates yelling, I heard the C.O.'s radio. Soul and Cougar were over there and met up with two officers who'd come in. The mass of people pulled the Rasta from Treat; both were bloody and breathing fast.

They were both put in handcuffs and escorted from the dorm. Prison policy is that all parties involved in a fight go to The Box. It didn't matter who started it. From the amount of blood, it looked like both were going to the infirmary first. Though I hadn't even been involved, I couldn't stop shaking. I sat on my bed and tried to do deep breathing exercises to ward off an anxiety attack. The usual racing thoughts had begun.

In fact, when prisoners fought, it was normally in the bathroom, out of sight. The bathroom, with its dark symphony of flatulence, was the most popular place in Collins. You could smoke there, deal drugs, work out, get a haircut, fight, and defecate, all in the same place. And the officers turned a blind eye, letting the inmates sort things out.

I saw Bear a few hours after the Rasta-Treat fight. He knew Treat well and said the two were from the same neighborhood in Syracuse. Treat's brother had shot the Rasta's brother. The Rasta had been after Treat to even the score. From Treat's cuts, it looked like the Rasta had a shank, but, as Bear said, Treat hit his head on his desk when the Rasta shoved him.

"That's weird that the Rastafarian dude got moved into here, right near Treat," I said.

Bear looked me in the eyes and smiled. "It didn't just happen. Someone on staff doesn't like our boy. This was done on purpose."

Jack Henry Abbott, author of *In the Belly of the Beast,* wrote that he saw similar situations many times. Abbott: "It is routine to see guards make sure prisoners who have vowed to kill one another are forced into a cell together."

I received a letter that month from my Lockport friend Rachael. After her mother died of a heroin overdose (she and her sister were just, respectively, seventeen and sixteen at the time), Rachael had been in and out of trouble, even been to the county jail and knew the players. She wanted to sum things up for me when I started my Collins bid. She wrote, "Are there a lot of newbies there who now accept Jesus as their lord and savior? That God has a plan for them because their lives are now saved due to the fact that stupidity and ignorance led the way for them to be caught in their criminal acts? God, I hate those people. It seems like three out of four criminals are born again in jail, and God has personally touched them to send them down the right path, only for them to falter and throw it all away the moment they step out of jail. This is God's plan for his children."

My parents came through again. A package arrived from Palm Beach that included three shirts, shorts, and socks. The package room C.O. said I could not have either the shirts or the shorts because they were the wrong color—blue or with blue stripes. We weren't allowed to wear the same color as the guards. "Do you want to send them back or donate them?" said the C.O.

I had heard enough about the package room already to know that "sending back" meant my commissary account would be charged the postage. And "donating" meant some C.O. or his family would be getting free shirts and shorts. It was quite a racket—everything designed to hurt the inmate. I called my parents to be sure they never bought the wrong stuff again. I was cross, embarrassed, confused. I had to apologize to my parents that I was in such a shitty prison. I told my father, "With all the food and materials that they force people to donate, they must be running quite a store somewhere."

Luckily for me, my folks had also included books and magazines. Mom sent James Patterson and Michael Connelly (not my normal fare but good enough for prison) and Dad sent *Time*, *Smithsonian*, *National Geographic*, and Oscar Wilde's poems.

I kept in regular communication with them, through phone calls every other day. Though I was 50, my parents became my primary support. Just a few years prior, they wouldn't talk to me because, as my mother said, I'd call and "wouldn't make any sense."

My uncle was also a support. So was my friend, Rachael.

My daughter wasn't in touch because she was too young. And, because my wife had become my ex, I stopped communicating with her.

After socializing with all manner of men, from con artists to gun fanatics, it was time for chow. Specifically, dinner which was the first time I saw a regular occurrence—C.O.s, sergeants, and other staff stealing from the inmates' food supply. I saw three big Collins sergeants ease their way into the mess hall kitchen and come out with mouthfuls of buns and hot dogs, and additional ones in their fists and arms.

That is our food! I thought about it more and more, especially when the mess hall ran out of items like hot dogs, ice cream, and apple crisp. The highly paid staff could afford their own food. Two months later, I was incensed when I saw a C.O. walk out of the mess hall with a large container of ice cream. I thought this place was a racket and a half, and I began looking for the holes and flaws in every system Collins had. If the administration knew about officers stealing food, then they were just as much to blame, if not more. They tolerated the thieves.

Imprisonment was bad enough without a greedy officer taking your lunch while you ate raspberry Jell-O. After all, they made $40,000 to $80,000, plus overtime (which can be $44 an hour). As a reporter at the Lockport newspaper, I'd written about unions, including those at our local GM plant and in our schools. So, I wondered about AFSCME, which represented our C.O.s and 62,000 others in the country. The union literature said it existed to "fight for better pay and benefits, safe workplaces, and to uphold the standard of professionalism in our field."

It made me reflect on what I had witnessed so far. I did some research and found that each inmate was worth $60,000 per year to the state Department of Corrections. With 53,000 inmates, that meant a $3 billion annual budget. You'd think that, somewhere in there, enough ice cream could be afforded. Where was all that money going? Prison upkeep? How expensive was brown paint? Overtime? Theft? Costly mistakes and inmate lawsuits? *Maybe all that and more*, I thought.

The cost of $60,000 ($170,000 in New York City) to house one person for a year in a state prison compares most unfavorably to the cost of educating that same person in a community college for the same length of time (one year)—$5,000 to $10,000.

In the case of Houghton College's Hope House program in Buffalo, that $10,000 includes laptops, textbooks, bus passes and the services of a full-time social worker. This program is targeted to inmates transitioning to parole. The program's director, Rebekah Kimble, said this education can break the cycle of recidivism.

Kimble explained, "As for my feelings about education versus incarceration:

I see equitable access to education as a moral issue . . . many citizens returning (to society) never had access to quality elementary-, junior-high-, or high-school education, so they remain entrenched in a cycle of poverty that makes them more likely to engage in criminal activity. We have a responsibility to provide them with a better option than that. But there are people who don't see access to education as a moral issue, and to them, I present education as a cost-saving alternative to incarceration.

"Numerous studies show that returning citizens with a college degree are far less likely to recidivate than returning citizens without a college degree. So, spending $10,000 or $20,000 (paid through grants) to educate them for two years—and, by extension, reduce their chance of returning to prison—saves taxpayers thousands of dollars."

After dinner came free time, then recreation in the yard. When the C.O. called recreation, half the dorm gathered at the door, wearing shorts, t-shirts, and sneakers—unless they were poor. The poor inmates wore the standard green uniform with boots, even for basketball. The yard offered soccer, football, handball, softball, horseshoes, weights, and drug dealing. Gangs sat at the incredibly uncomfortable cement slab tables sprinkled around the yard. The Bloods from Los Angeles (Blood meant "Brotherly Love Overrides Oppression and Distraction;), Aryan Nations, Latin Kings of Puerto Rico, the Hispanic-American 38s, and East Coast Crip 69s—all were here. Rules dictated that only five inmates could be together at one time. More than that might invite a warning shot from the rifleman in the Tower.

As a WASP (mostly), I was not allowed at the tables, even though my friends like Cougar and Nobel were. Usually, a runner would approach a table, pick up whatever had been ordered by inmates, and then he'd meet the inmates or their representatives (dorm dealers) on the track for handoff.

Though you could buy drugs with commissary credit (food delivered to dealers on commissary day), the preferred payment method was money orders. The money could be ordered by an inmate's people (on the outside) and then picked up at an outlet by the dealer's people, on the outside. It was called a "Westie."

The Westie business was conducted via telephone, which was managed by Global Tel-Link. Inmates developed their own phone language with their people—coded messages to throw off law enforcement who listened in on calls.

Though I was from a small town, I'd met killers, robbers, and all their criminal friends. I'd traveled to the big American and European cities. But Collins was the first time I'd ever met gang members, or saw them admiring tattoos and throwing signs. Not only were gangs evidently present in every city ghetto in the country, but were especially in our prisons.

After recreation, at least on weekends, it was movie time. Most of the state-sponsored movies were rather obscure—weird art films or horror shows. Vin Diesel flicks were always on. Now and then there was a title that got people thinking and talking, like "12 Strong." Televised sporting events usually bumped movie night.

The person in charge of the TV remote was usually the biggest, blackest, toughest man in the dorm. That would be Nobel, but he often relinquished his duties to solve dorm issues and made his handoff to one of the other seven in the dorm pecking order. Cougar was number two. Until I got to know them, I thought they were the most dangerous men I had ever met. After I got to know them, I knew they were the most dangerous I'd ever met. Nobel was a trained boxer, and Cougar was a trained killer.

I met Cougar because he was right next to me in the dorm. He was quiet at first. Then he learned I was an author and started talking. With all those manu-scripts, he was well on his way to becoming an author. He was far from being a bragger, and rather secretive, but he did show me two bullet-wound scars on his right shoulder.

Cheap plastic shavers were given out at 9 in the evening. The restroom filled up and so did the showers. When you took a shower, you "needed" shower shoes (like flip-flops) because of mildew and because of the "activity" of lonely men. Men have certain needs, especially the young ones.

Now and then, as I wandered into the restroom, I'd see bath towels hanging from the top rail of the toilet stalls, blocking all eyes from seeing the active shitters. Not all the toilets held shitters. Some were, as Bear said, "cashing out," or "getting money," both of which meant masturbating. I found it revolting just thinking how I used the toilets versus how some others did. The place was coated in filth. There was just nowhere else to go.

A 300-pound muscle man named Gorilla made it impossible for me to block chicken-choking images from my mind. Gorilla "cashed out" nearly every day, carrying a jar of Vaseline, a towel, and two porn mags featuring "Big Black Butts" to the restroom. He always passed by my cube en route.

I had been on opiates for so long on the streets that, as I found out at the infirmary, my testosterone level was at 200. For a man like me in his late forties, the average is about 700. I didn't even think of sex anymore. As longtime heroin addicts will admit, you don't need sex. I hadn't been with a woman since my green-eyed friend with benefits, "Texas," in 2013. Though I found jail lonely, I had not adopted a grimy prison toilet as my new girlfriend.

One day after the morning routine, everything came to a boil in my head—the prison, my time, the dorm, the strangers, the nasty C.O.s, my parents miles away, my daughter and our estrangement. All of it raced through my head as I sat on my bunk. I was paralyzed with claustrophobia, fear, and anxiety, as if my Lithium, Haldol, and Wellbutrin were no longer working. I looked up to see the great wood sander, Heat, staring at me. And he read my mind. "This isn't going to last forever," Heat said. He was wearing a personal pitbull t-shirt that said, "It's Pit or it's Shit."

Then, as if summoned, Bear arrived with his morning pages. I dove into them as if running from the prison. My own mind was not my friend that day.

Morning medication time reminded me how New York State operates its prisons. It's probably similar at all prisons in America. The U.S. has the largest prison system in the world, and it's purposely built to keep running and to fail at the same time. Overcrowding causes long lines for nearly every activity, including the med line.

That day, I had gone to meds before my mini-breakdown. The C.O. ushered us out of the dorm, saying "Go get your Skittles." The attitude toward the mentally ill was somewhere between ambivalent and superior.

Breathing in the cigarette smoke of other med liners, I walked the grounds of C building and arrived a few minutes later at the big red-brick infirmary building. From the front door, a long line spilled out, going down the stairs and into the grass.

Two C.O.s were strategically placed outside to keep watch and coldly belittle us all. The officers didn't bother to stop the many men cutting the line, unable to wait their turn. In the normal din of conversations, I heard these comments:

- "We had a female C.O. in the other night and all the blacks were standing around the bubble, trying to impress her."

- "I was wild when I was young. The cell bars taught me to be slow to anger."
- "You a grown-ass man."
- "There's a MRSA case in C1. Wear socks everywhere."
- "That's not pacific [specific]."
- "How did Christopher Columbus discover America when it was already here?"
- "In the 'hood, if we go to another 'hood and kill people, we go to jail. Columbus killed the Indians. He didn't go to jail."
- "If you in business, that mean you an entreprenegro."
- "When I see something, I get excited about it. I just have to get loud."
- "When I smoke weed, I don wanna do nuttin."
- "He had an escape goat."
- "Avocado? Is that fish?"
- "Why don't they get back on the boats and go home? We're waiting. Do we have to drive the fucking boats?"
- "You know how we do."
- "Then you a low-risk type nigga."

In the med line, making it inside the building was merely the first step in the process. Next came passing the door marked "Staff Only." That meant only that you were no longer at the back of the line. Only when you could hear a sergeant bouncing a complaining inmate off the walls outside the doctor's office did you know you were getting closer.

"But I wasn't cheeking," the inmate yelled while being punched in the ribs. "I...didn't...cheek...med."

This was progress. Now you were close enough to smell the med nurse's perfume. Then you reached the C.O.'s desk. On it was a bumper sticker that read, "You can't cure idiocy. But you can numb it with a 2x4." That meant you were finally there.

"Name?"

"Brandon M. Stickney."

"DIN?"

"17B1378."

"I.D."

I showed my identification: Eyes: brown; Hair: brown; Birth date: 7/29/67;

Height 5'9"; Weight: 269. I missed being a kid, when I had blond hair and blue eyes.

This time the nurse was a guy, and one of the few good ones. When the nurse first met me, he said, "What are you doing here? You don't even smell like an inmate." Now, he handed me a cup containing 600 mg of Lithium and a 150 mg Wellbutrin. I took the meds, filled the Dixie Cup with water, and drank. The nurse watched me to be sure I wasn't cheeking. Certain meds that made it intact from the infirmary to the dorm could be sold for commissary, other meds, or drugs.

A fellow a few beds away from me received two 50 mg Wellbutrin daily. He'd get back to the dorm, pills in hand, and dry them out in the microwave. Then he'd deliver them to the buyer in exchange for rolled cigarettes. Inmates set up "contracts" like this for regular exchanges.

I received a letter at mail call from the administration—I had to attend Phase I. According to my little Collins Inmate Orientation Handbook, Phase I was "a program for all new offenders entering the ... state correctional system" to "prepare you for a smooth transition from living in society to being incarcerated." When was this ever smooth for anyone? It also said that this thirty-hour program "addresses topics to begin the process of preparing yourself for successful re-entry back to your family and community."

Phase I would be my first prison experience with wasted resources, and how the state's little booklets were loaded with half-truths.

I had to read and reread that Phase I description because it said they were preparing us for going to prison and for leaving prison all in the same class. Phase II said it was about making better choices in life, but added that it helped inmates with reintegration into society. The description of Phase III mentioned nearly the same purpose—getting us ready to leave prison.

The Phase I class was held in the gymnasium, a new building full of modern classrooms, refreshingly populated with more glass walls than wood and brick. There were five guys from the C3 dorm here, several others, and two inmate facilitators. There were test papers on all the desks, already completed by other students. There was also a TV with DVD player.

We did nothing.

No one seemed bothered by this but me. Freddie, a black dude with a gap between his front teeth and a huge afro (called a blow-out), was one IPA (or facilitator.) He chatted with his friends and ate a big pickle. Neal was the other facilitator. He was likely Latino, his skin covered in tattoos, real and jail-made. Neal (pronounced Nell) piped in every now and then. The talk was all nonsense: basketball, honor dorm thefts, Crips vs. Bloods, respect here at Collins, boxing, and the seriously challenged Package Room, which was always stealing from inmates.

The papers on the desks were only there to "look good" for when the C.O. passed by in the hallway. The classroom walls were glass. Freddie kept the conversation going with two inmates I had not met—they were all friends, serving a few bids together.

A small Latino in a Muslim kufi (hat) listened intently to the conversation. As Freddie or Neal, or one of the others, would end a sentence or thought, the little Latino would jump in with, "That's a fact." He said it so many times each class, my desk-neighbor and I began counting.

On Tuesday, I learned the little kufi man's nickname—Pudd. I couldn't believe it, but it suited him; he was an annoying little Pudd. I overheard Freddie call to him before class.

My neighbor at the desk was also Latino. He was a short man of about seventy. I wondered, *Why is this old man here when he should be home in Costa Rica with his family and grandchildren?* He was from my dorm, but when I asked him why he was in prison, he said, "It's a secret." I had been schooled by the other inmates. Anyone who won't tell you why they are down is a sex offender. I hoped not, but the more pressing matter was the "start" of "class." We had to count Pudd's facts.

In just the first five minutes of class, Pudd let one rip: "That's a fact," he said, responding to Freddie's still undiscovered urban philosophy. Pudd also said, "I ain't gonna lie" a lot. We let that go.

To count, me and the old man put "IIII"—four bars on paper for each of the four times Pudd said, "That's a fact." Then a fifth line would cross through the other four, for five times.

Freddie: "Ain't no one in that package room can be trusted."

Pudd: "That's a fact."

I'd zone out because the class was so boring. I'd look out the window at the June sky. I'd feel a nudge at my arm. It'd be the old man telling me to put down a new stick number—Pudd had done it again.

We counted twenty-four times. I figured we must have missed a few and vowed with the old man to do better on Wednesday.

After seeing the horrible job our "teachers" did in Phase I, I sent a note to the administration, asking to be an IPA. My request bounced around until it landed with Counselor Sword, who said I needed to look out for the next posting about IPA training. I could only imagine what kind of training the Phase I guys received. Months passed and I didn't see a posting, so I forgot about it.

An astounding number, 68%, of freed prisoners return to prison. Exit strategies may appear to be satisfactory on paper, as contrived by Albany pencil pushers. Officers who see the inmates every day have no stake in inmate success. Former inmate and writer Michael G. Santos said, "No one measures the so-called corrections profession by how many offenders it prepares to live as law-abiding, contributing citizens upon release." In fact, Santos notes that the prison system has "zero accountability" to the taxpayers who fund it. He quotes an unnamed prison education supervisor as saying, "We don't care anything about the preparations you're making for release or what you do when you get out. The only thing we care about is the security of the administration."

"Recidivism" was a word I saw on prison paperwork, and wall hangings, but no one really talked about it, at least not staff. Inmates talked of going back to the streets, dealing, stealing, wife-beatin', and gun runnin' as soon as they got out. And, of course, they'd get caught, again, and return to a cell in due time, which provided job security for correctional officers. I told my fellow prisoners that I wanted a Four Loko when I got out, and that grape drink would lead to drugs, which would put me right back here. That's what recidivism meant to me.

CELL #6

Unionized prison employees are awarded annual

pay raises and benefit increases, not necessarily

based on actual performance (safety, leadership,

advocacy). They are not publicly rewarded for

doing the right thing—neither are prisoners.

There is only one reward—more punishment.

Prison corrections officers act as weapon-carrying

police, though they have had no police training

(normally six months), and only two months of

C.O. training.

CHAPTER 6

LEFT FOR DEAD

"No matter how much I wanted all those things that I needed
money to buy, there was some devilish current pushing me off in
another direction—toward anarchy and poverty and craziness."
—Hunter S. Thompson, *The Rum Diaries*

Though I had a few good neighbors in the prison dorm, there were times when it all became too much for me. During the hot days of June, the building's bricks heated like an oven, so it was hot in the dorm well into the night. Four ceiling fans were not enough.

I took notes throughout my prison term. Angry one day: "My cube is missing a chair, a netbag for laundry, I have no ceiling fan anywhere near me. This is a well-traveled area and I have noisy neighbors: one is a desk-beating hip-hop wanna-be, and the other is a wood-working Geppetto. The puny punk kid near me closes the fucking window every time there's a nice breeze." Little things, except the noise, that built up to … At that point, I would have loved to be homeless again, rather than be here. At least I could walk away.

With Heat, or Geppetto, it was the little things that added up to this one big thing. Heat's morning noises, as I was trying to get just another half-hour of sleep, were, to use the old cliché, like nails on a chalk board. Tossing his vitamins onto the metal locker, stirring his coffee, and then slurping! Fumbling with his combination lock as if he didn't know the combination. The last time I'd lived this close to anyone was a few years ago, with my wife and child.

Heat's habits seemed designed to drive me mad. And why did he have that star tattoo on his neck? What did that mean? Heat claimed he was in prison because of his anger. No real tough guy would say that; people who always talk of winning fights are actually scared wimps. So, I'd get angry and almost say something to him, but I knew it would get me nowhere. You can't ever reason with a goon.

When I was blue, talking to a fellow inmate helped. Bear came to my rescue many times. Upon reflection, I felt I belonged in prison, not for my crime, but for all the other things I had done wrong in my forty-nine years of life. I was reminded of the disparaging things I'd said and the horrible things I'd done to people; all slammed right back in my face. Evidence of this presented itself often, especially when a C.O. called me "tubby," or something of mine was stolen. Anything I had done wrong in life? I was here for it. The Karma was here. The other shoe had dropped. The jig was up. There were times when I simply did not want to "be" anymore.

Then I'd overhear two of the big guys talking. "Black gangsters are not rich and successful because we are not organized." Suddenly, my mind was on a different tack, and I could go on after all. Go on by laughing.

June ended with a shred of good news. My parents had my college transcripts mailed to the Collins education department. That meant I didn't have to take GED classes, which I was sweating. Since 12th grade, I'd forgotten the finer points of mathematics. In fact, this would have been a nice point for my useless public defender, Katy Mock, to make before a jury. "There's no way Mr. Stickney could be a drug dealer. He can no longer add."

One day I, the optimist, the happy (as happy as one could be in prison) wanderer, got really angry. First, Qwikster came to me at 6:30 that morning to ask for coffee. I had just enough instant for myself, so when I said no, he gave me a nasty look.

Then Agony stopped by wanting "food, sweets, anything." Commissary was in three days. My last four cookies were mine. My Jolly Ranchers were gone. I had nothing for him. He boldly said, "Thanks for nothing."

I could have given them something, but I knew their histories—they never paid anyone back. If I gave to everyone who asked, my locker would be empty. I beg from time to time, but I pay back so I don't wear out my welcome.

During my homeless period just before prison, I lived with my friends Rachael and Sam (her longtime boyfriend and baby-daddy). When I first met Rachael, she was eighteen and was hanging out with my buddy Brett Garcia at Locust Street in Lockport. Before jail, I stayed at her trailer home. When we met, I always felt sick because of my divorce. She was the one voice of optimism and hilarity that I desperately needed.

Rachael wrote to me at Collins: "The best thing is having a routine to make the days go by. You can do this. This is only temporary. And we will all be here for you. Watch, listen, and learn their adaptations for one hell of a book. Please inform me of all the shady dealings at the prison."

Few real names were revealed in Collins Correctional. Every man went by a handle. You had to say "handle" because nicknames were for kids. They had prison handles. In addition to my associates Pastor, Cougar, Nobel, and Heat, there was a Polish pal of mine named Rico. Also Yum-Yum, Niko, Pops (who was not that old), Chino, Flacco, and rapo-hater Patriot. There was T-Bone and Fat Joe. And many others based on rapper handles and clandestine activity. It was very difficult to keep all these names straight. I just addressed most guys as "Dude" or "Man." Some names I could remember. Fat Joe really was fat, yet reported losing sixty pounds in prison.

Like others, Fat Joe took his handle from a hip-hopper. When I came into Collins, I became B-love. I weighed in at about 337 and wound up losing about seventy pounds in six months. When I was forced to give up alcohol, I ate. And ate. I needed to replace all of the sugar that I had been getting from alcohol, and so I turned to cookies.

Ears the Enforcer had a huge head (like the aliens in *War of the Worlds*), barely any hair, tiny ears, and a big attitude problem. The dorm's biggest gossip, he also dealt suboxone, a drug that, if mixed with water and sniffed, provided a heroin-type high.

Near Ears in the north side of the dorm were Oz, Oil, and a round midget named Pun. Pun was a loud black who claimed he was a pimp—as soon as he got home, he said he was "buyin' a new skin" (fur coat).

Brooklyn and Syracuse wanted us to know where they were from. There was Shy 150 and Shy 315. Knowing nothing of hip-hop other than disliking it, I later learned that many of the blacks and Latinos named themselves after rappers, which was unoriginal and predictable. I thought Homesick was a cool name, along with Caution, Dizzy, and Kilo. Rounding out the south end of the dorm were Agony, a child molester, Flip, Jinx, and Wiggles.

I got to know most everyone, interviewing some for the memoir I was planning about prison. You put a journalist in jail and what's he going to do?

I was new to this game and did not have a nickname. Cougar brought the subject up one day, saying he thought B-money or B-love would be appropriate.

"I like B-love better," I said because there was already a Money in the dorm.

"Okay, go with B-love."

"Thank you, Cougar. But why B-love?"

He looked at me quietly for a minute. Cougar was a low-talker and I often had to strain to hear him, even when he was right next to me.

Cougar, who had been writing in a notebook, sat all the way up and said, "Because no matter what, you can't stay mad at B-love."

Thus, my reputation as a nice guy. Prison didn't like nice guys. But I've never been a bully or a fighter. I might make fun of someone, but I'd never try to ruin them. As they said in prison, "People take my kindness for weakness." I didn't agree with that silly cliché, which told me no one was ever allowed to be nice to anyone. As the summer progressed, I found that no one took advantage of me, or tried. Looking back, I assume that was because of my friendship with Cougar. And Nobel.

As Cougar said, "You gotta walk right in here. Don' clown around and don' step out line, or a nigga or a C.O. will take your ass out. Don think dis here is a joke. Prison is like a snake. Feel me? Quiet for a while. Just when you think everythin' okay, it strike and bite deep."

Cougar and I talked nearly every night about publishing. He had several "How to Publish" books he wanted me to read to see if they were accurate. So I did, and we'd page through them together. Most of the dorm heard our conversations. I was pleased they were listening. If you were friends with Cougar, you had prison clout.

When I wasn't working with Cougar, I was busy with Bear, working on the novel he tentatively titled *Hustle*. I read his pages, made comments and corrections, and offered scene ideas and enhancements. Though I was in prison, I realized, I was right back in publishing, with two authors clamoring for my time.

At first, inmates didn't believe I was published. My folks sent me reviews of my two books, so the guys could see I was really in print. I had the *Publishers Weekly* review of *All-American Monster* and the *Daily Mail*'s feature about *The Amazing Seven Sutherland Sisters*. There were a few, like Ears, who wouldn't believe the reviews or the books were real, or that I was a real author. I ignored them. Bear and Cougar believed. They knew the truth, and that was enough.

Since Nobel knew so much about prison, I asked him for an interview. He agreed. Nobel sat next to my cube and Cougar was there too. I admit, I felt protected and, though I'm no hardened criminal (and embarrassed even to carry the title "felon"), I also felt like a badass. They were the two toughest and most dangerous guys in the dorm; Cougar was a former Blood, and Nobel was a trained boxer.

One of the things Cougar told me was "Don't take my kindness for weakness," Oh, that saying again. The actual quote, attributed to Al Capone, is: "Don't mistake my silence for ignorance, my calmness for acceptance, or my kindness for weakness.". Both a prison and an AA saying, it sounds like a mundane way to say, "Don't tread on me." It insinuates that you are powerful and will defend your territory. It also says anyone who is kind is also weak, so it's the perfect prison saying, especially in violent prisons where other inmates will walk up and take your food. Addicts are manipulative, so the quote has also worked its way into NA as well: "Don't ask me for anything other than advice," Also, "I'm a tough guy because I'm sober." Now, Cougar was being funny while issuing a warning. He didn't give anyone interviews, much less share his commissary food.

Nobel explained his time in Attica, where C.O.s punished inmates by turning off the power (all lights) and beat them in their cells. "You toe the line there, or you'll see," Nobel said.

Cougar said his time in Wyoming Correctional was similar. After a fight with an inmate, Cougar said the C.O.s told him they were going to run him to the Infirmary. Instead, he was brought to a hallway with no security cameras. There, he was given a handcuffed beating.

That wasn't his only run-in with the "po-po" at Wyoming. Cougar said he was with a sizeable "set" (gang) in the prison and he was helping with "work" (crack distribution). In his cell, Cougar broke up a cocaine rock with his fingers. A few days later, the prison gave him a random, routine drug test and he tested positive. Cougar couldn't believe it. He was a Muslim and hadn't used drugs in five years.

Apparently, handling the cocaine was the problem. It soaked into his hands—just enough to register. He got thirty days in The Box.

Nobel said Attica was filled with "ugly niggas" serving life sentences who didn't care about getting in trouble—they did whatever they wanted and the C.O.s looked away. "One man takes the young ones, promises he gonna train them to fight, bring 'em up right. They wind up trained, but then they gotta beat him. Either that or they get oiled up and he fuck 'em."

The Muslims are the only ones changing the prison system for the better, Nobel said. "I pray with the brothers to go the right way. Cutting versus fighting, you see. You fight like a man. People cutting people—it's only a coward to bring a knife to the game."

He continued, "Attica? Police beatings are the culture. But now they have cameras everywhere. They watched by Albany, and they takin' those night sticks away. Too many lawsuits." Nobel softly fist-bumped Cougar. "Lawsuit? Shit. They know they gonna get paid."

Cougar said our hometown area, Western New York, had built a reputation. "In past, people from Buffalo got beat up and beat down in those big New York prisons. Buffalo wasn't known for murder yet. Now there are more gangs of Buffalo inmates. Syracuse and Rochester slide up with us. Now we stick together."

Nobel told me a story about him and his girl. They started a credit card scam when he was in another facility. Nobel, as an intern in the Infirmary, processed simple paperwork. After a short while, he noticed the papers had Social Security numbers ... and if he took those numbers and names, he could "get money gangsta."

Nobel began giving his girl numbers and names over the phone. Though Nobel had been a low-level security risk for years, his calls weren't recorded back then. If so, he'd have been caught right away. More numbers were given to the girlfriend.

See, the woman's job was to put the information on credit card applications, and then sell the new cards to others. A card with a $5,000 limit would yield $1,500 for the Nobel team. Using the numbers, people were buying used cars, living room sets, and clothes while inmates' families received the bills. Investigators put things together after about nine months, but that was enough time for Nobel's girl to set up a big bank account in her daughter's name, so the police couldn't seize the cash.

Nobel already had a ten-year sentence. His conviction for credit card fraud added five more.

As I took notes, Nobel took my pencil away. It made me quite nervous, wondering what I'd done wrong. Cougar stared at Nobel. "Listen, man. You ain't gonna forget any of this. I been in fifteen prisons, starting when I was sixteen. I never fo'get a thing since then—jail brands you."

He got quiet. I said, "Sixteen? Weren't you scared?"

"I'd already been training since fourteen. Boxing, karate. Shit, I was scared for *them*."

Nobel was the center of the dorm's attention one afternoon. A Latino named Uzi discovered that his radio had been stolen before lunch. I knew who Uzi was, a rather rude chauvinist who claimed he assaulted a top Crips capo in Queens, though no one could prove it. Someone asked Napoleon, a C.O., to look up Uzi's crime. It turned out to be a conspiracy, so that could've meant anything from drug dealing to being a confidential informant (CI). CIs got arrested all the time, but their charges were greatly reduced or dropped because they were narcs, working for drug investigators.

Meter, Uzi's friend, was the "good looking one," a model-quality dandy who had no women to chase here in Collins. Recreation time came, and Meter found the suspect in the yard, and cut him across the cheek. He and the victim were escorted to The Box. Uzi had hired Meter, as we later learned. Whoever "borrowed" the radio returned it to Uzi's cube. The victim had been cut for no real reason.

All seven of the Muslim team, led by Nobel, waited at Uzi's cube for his return. When he got back, the Muslims surrounded him, and Nobel began his interrogation. The group was breaking the rules—no more than five inmates in one place—but the C.O. purposely ignored it. About five minutes of talk ensued in low voices; the dorm itself was silent. Then came the loudest crack I'd ever heard, even louder than the pine in my front yard snapping under the weight of an October ice storm. It sounded like a closed fist to the jaw. Everyone in the dorm watched as Uzi fell to the floor.

The Muslims picked him up, face red from the blow, and held him up. A C.O., not Napoleon, pushed through the crowd, put Uzi in handcuffs, and led him out to the Box.

Despite initial appearances, the inmates were in charge of this dorm. At least while I was there.

My uncle, Mason Arrigo, lived with his husband, Phil Barragan, in California. Because they were creating a graphic novel publishing company, they regularly attended Comic-Con and similar conventions around the country. Getting letters from them made me happy because they were a reminder of the world outside, which I'd be rejoining, by spring 2018, I hoped.

Mason was supportive of my literary endeavors with Bear and Cougar. Mason said, "We are very proud of you looking toward the future and using your writing skills to help other inmates. When you are released, look into teaching. There are programs to help parolees learn writing and skills to help them get ahead on the outside."

Our dorm had a treat the morning of July 4, 2017. I woke, as did many others, to a ruckus at 5:30. I had no idea what was going on near the C.O. bubble. The noise died down and Ishmael, Heat's friend and slave, saw my eyes open and whispered that one inmate had climbed under another inmate's bed to smell his feet. The C.O. saw him and the excuse for his behavior was that he had just returned from the restroom and gotten lost. The foot smeller was hauled off to The Box.

Ishmael waited on Heat as if Heat had once saved his life and Ishmael had to follow Heat forever-after. As I woke each morning, I'd see Ishmael making Heat's coffee. Ishmael cleaned Heat's cubicle floor and then waxed and buffed it.

I was appalled when I saw anyone using that hulking, clumsy buffing machine, whether they were shining a cube floor or the dorm's floor. I was imprisoned by the state; I was not going to clean floors for that machine. They could hire cleaners if they wanted it clean. Their own employees, the corrections officers, seemingly did nothing at all. It seemed their job was to stare at us and beat us when we were naughty.

Why would anyone work for "The Man"?

The Man was the enemy. I had developed a distrust of cops and government from a young age. Inmates weren't getting paid to buff those floors; they were sucking up to our captors. I wasn't going to do that, though. Once I explained this to Ishmael, I asked him why he cleaned floors. "I like a clean floor," he said. It was either kissing ass or obsessive-compulsive disorder, or both.

Ishmael was, to my way of thinking, quite rude. If he didn't think my bed was made well or if my floor was dirty, he'd point it out. Miffed, he'd say, "This makes all of us look bad." Of course, I was thinking, "Fuck you," but I'd just agree sarcastically. Ishmael had an anger problem. When in a bad mood, he'd fight anyone. And that was surprising because he was such a slight man. All the sit-ups and push-ups in the universe were not going to make him any bigger. If I needed a laugh, all I had to do was look over to Ishmael's cube: he was either doing his funny push-ups or waiting on Heat. Heat, I learned, bought Ishmael cigarettes and coffee in exchange for his labor. I never could tell (I was afraid to ask) his nationality. His skin was light green, so I figured Eastern Indian.

Unfortunately, Ishmael thought I liked him. He, too, brought me his writing to assess. Reading his work made me realize Ishmael was probably mentally ill. Undiagnosed, maybe. He didn't take meds. Time would prove that he needed them.

Ishmael got me thinking about the prison. It had been an insane asylum a century before. Thinking about how long the med lines were now and how weird my dorm was, I was shocked. The government had emptied the asylums in the 1980s, and now they were just putting us in jail. Prisons were the new insane asylums. As Piper Kerman wrote in *Orange is the New Black*, "Prison is ... where the U.S. government now puts not only the dangerous but also the inconvenient—people who are mentally ill, people who are addicts, people who are poor, uneducated, and unskilled."

Writer Elizabeth Koehler-Pentacoff recreated a classic scene of such institutional abuse in her memoir, *The Missing Kennedy*. "Patients were restrained in unclean, dismal, poorly lit cells with no fresh air or little hope for improvement. Many cycled downward," she wrote. "...Widespread overcrowding occurred with criminals, alcoholics, drug addicts, indigents, and mentally ill patients all housed together. Restraints such as handcuffs, locks, straps, and sheets were used regularly. Beatings and murders were not rare events." Now, Koehler-Pentacoff was describing a Depression-era insane asylum. Yet, shockingly, there is little difference between that and today's American prison.

Former C.O. Ted Conover once said that officers in the system don't care if we have psychosocial disorder, bipolar, depression, anxiety, or anything else. C.O.s just call us "bugs." Inmates said of someone having a psychotic episode that he is "bugging out." Officers are lightly trained in understanding mental illness even though "a large proportion" of their charges are sick or being treated. Instead, many officers assume the inmates are faking to get better treatment or wish to be housed away from the general population, gangs, or weapons.

I had a mental health counselor, so my needs were not completely ignored. But that was because my county jail had alerted the state prison system to my needs. I also raised my hand and said I needed the help. Others, however, needed help but claimed there was nothing wrong with them. They wouldn't get the help they needed, and the prison chaos would continue.

Entering the C3 dorm, I overheard, "She look official. She look like fire." It was from a guy at a bunk sitting next to another guy. They were sharing an issue of *Buttman*. I had recently walked the dorm, saying out loud, "Why does everybody have pictures of fat women on their walls?" And they did. The new poster style in prison, quite popular among everyone, except for the sex offender born-agains, were porn-star women with gigantic asses, and boobs to match. I also found out that this glossy magazine also had a phone app and a comic book division.

It was disturbing enough to see men sitting next to each other reading porn. But the cannonball asses were too much for me. These women had once been normal. Then they had fat injected into their butts until they were the size of weather balloons. This had become a ghetto fashion statement. Women other than porn queens were doing it to attract men; the kind of men they were attracting were my neighbors in Collins—men of questionable backgrounds and limited vocabularies usually quick to anger and violence. They were good at "getting money" for tattoos, SUV wheel rims, pit bulls, gold teeth, crack, bitches, and other status symbols of the street.

This was one of the times when my rural world experience clashed with the current culture. I was from Lockport, a small city of 30,000 on the Erie Canal. The population was primarily white, mostly Irish and Italians. Long ago, the Polish and Germans were our minorities. Now, they were Spanish and Jamaican migrant workers during the spring and summer months. The nation's politically-correct movement never touched my town. Townspeople lamented how "screwed up" television had become and wondered who the lunatic was who invented revisionist history, making Columbus a murderer and Malcolm a martyr.

As I walked the hallway of the dorm, I saw that, if anyone wanted to celebrate diversity, all they had to do was visit a prison. But no one celebrated prisons.

I focused on this from time to time. The dorm had WASPs like me from across the state, blacks and Muslims from Buffalo, Brooklyn, Rochester, Syracuse, and other points between, and several Native Americans. I saw no Asians or Eastern Indians. They were all in college or working, inmates said. And no one identified as Jewish in this dorm. Or transgender.

It was interesting how the dorm's two major religions differed: the Muslims used the dorm to worship, kneeling on rugs to pray toward Mecca, while the Christians prayed quietly at their beds or inside the little chapel near the Infirmary. Every now and then a C.O. would say, "No way. I'm not putting up with this shit," when the Muslims would gather with their rugs. They'd have to pray when he left.

At other times during the day, I saw some of the same religious folks gathered around cutouts from *Buttman* magazines. I think the limit was six page-sized "Buttwomen" on your cube wall at one time, but guys pushed that limit. The photos of these obese, oily women were like car accidents—you couldn't look away. Were they even human?

At the risk of sounding like a bigot (most of the women featured were black), I told Heat that in real life, the asses didn't look as they were photographed. "That's all nasty cellulite," I said, "These photos are airbrushed. Photoshopped. You name it."

Heat was as booty-brainwashed as the rest. "Look at that shit—chocolate goodness. She beautiful." Heat was one of the white fellas who "talked black" when talking to a black person. I heard it all the time, a man who sounded college-educated would suddenly develop an American big-city ghetto dialect when engaged in a discussion with someone who also spoke the language.

I had to write it down, in stealth, to study it and to try to figure out what they were talking about. I had no idea. I knew "that's a fact" thanks to Pudd at Phase I class. Then there was "Good lookin," which meant thank you. No one said "thank you" anymore, or "I'm sorry." "Thank you" was too white, and "I'm sorry" was admitting guilt or weakness.

I'm pretty sure I was the lone wolf who still said "thank you" and "I'm sorry." However, I did not poll all of Collins' 1,500 inmates to find any like-minded residents, so I may be wrong. I guess Bear said "thank you" to me. I'm not sure if he said it to anyone else.

There weren't many readers in the dorm (some were illiterate), unless you counted *Buttman* fans. Cougar normally read one of the many books on publishing. Bear and I grabbed books from the library.

I had never in my life lived with so many black people. I wanted to know more about them, but I couldn't just go to Cougar and say, "What's it like to be black?" Instead, I took out *Black Like Me* by John Howard Griffin, and *Black Boy*, as well as a biography of Richard Wright. I didn't expect to become an expert, just a little more aware. Interestingly, *The New Jim Crow: Mass Incarceration in the Age of Color Blindness* had so many readers in line, I never got a chance to see it.

I was profoundly moved reading *Night* by Elie Wiesel; some of his Auschwitz stories of captivity had parallels to what we were experiencing, psychologically. We had no power—we were controlled by (some) simpletons with agendas of pure hate.

Jack Kerouac wrote in *On the Road*: "The American police are involved in psychological warfare against those Americans who don't frighten them with imposing papers and threats. It's a Victorian police force ... (It) can make crimes up if the crimes don't exist to its satisfaction."

Dad told me in a phone call that he was planning a one-man show at a gallery near Palm Beach, and that he wanted a news release and press materials written to promote the exhibition. His new paintings explored the world of Hobo Hieroglyphics, code from the Great Depression that the homeless used, communicating with each other on their journeys across America. It was still in use today.

Dad had encountered the hobo code as a kid, riding his bike along the Erie Canal. He sent me examples of the code and a history from Google, as well as a few photocopied images from a book about Jean-Michel Basquiat, who incorporated hobo code into his popular 1980s works. Dad also sent images of his own first sketches and paintings from his "Hobo Hieroglyphics" series.

A second package arrived from my father that month with issues of *Artforum, Art in America,* and *Art News.* I used these magazines to write descriptively and boldly about Dad's art. I called to thank him for the package and told my mother I had been thinking about their offer to leave New York for Florida after prison. It sounded like a smart idea. Here, I was completely lost. A big life change was what I needed to get started again; prison was no help—it took from me and gave nothing in return. In addition, Mom needed me there because she was having a tough time with rheumatoid arthritis and forgetfulness. I finally had a new purpose in life.

I walked into the TV room one afternoon to find several irritated inmates. They were sitting, looking at each other. It was a bitch fest. The TV was off.

With brown eyes dead, and his face blank, Nobel looked at me and said, "Put this in your story. The cable is off because Collins don't want us watchin' the news. A C.O. been arrested for beatin' the shit outta his bitch." Though they were peace officers, sworn to uphold the law, as well as the prison's rules, officers were involved with the same problems as the inmates: child abuse, alcoholism, drug addiction, divorce, ill health, and suicide. A recent article on corrections.com revealed that C.O.s have the second highest mortality rate of any occupation. On average, they live only eighteen months after retirement.

So, Collins did not want its inmates seeing news reports of the incident, though, obviously, everyone knew about it. "Look, they're just like us."

The blackout lasted three days. Now, we were in the circulation area of *The Buffalo News,* I did not see a report of the incident there. Normally, the *News* carries all kinds of stories of police abuse, including routine murders by C.O.s at the notorious Erie County Holding Center. A lot of hangings and restraint stranglings. This was one of the places where my original distrust of corrections officers came from. Collins did nothing to change my mind.

The many workplace hazards that haunt officers are real, as if an unofficial battle is being waged by C.O.s and inmates against each other. An officer dies and there is retaliation upon prisoners. An inmate dies and it's payback time against officers.

HHS Public Access published a 2013 report on corrections officers injured or killed on the job. There were a reported 454,500 officers supervising two million inmates. C.O.s have one of the highest rates of non-fatal injuries at 125,200 in one year. The fatality rate was 2.7 per 100,000 officers, according to HHS Public Access. On average, eleven fatalities are reported annually.

There were some officers who were "nice" and, you could easily tell—they did not fit in with the good-old-boy network. As soon as Officer Hubbard arrived for his shift, voices in the hall rang out "Hub!" He was a tall, blond-haired Irishman who got to know nearly every inmate in our dorm.

Inmates could flood and frustrate an officer with requests: a sick-call form, a State Shop form, a cube move, permission to leave for AA, a better mattress, a bar of soap, a toothbrush, help with a lost laundry bag, and "Here's a great joke." Hubbard managed all requests with a smile or a kind word. I couldn't imagine him raising his baton to anyone. He didn't even wear one, while other C.O.s did. And I learned from Hubbard that C.O.s reveal little, if any, information about their personal lives. An officer might say he likes to go hunting or listen to talk radio, but they were mum on where they live and their families.

The justifiable fear was that an inmate, through his outside contacts, could target the C.O. Officers normally don't ask or go on the Internet to see what an inmate did wrong, thinking it might intensify their anger toward an inmate. I witnessed several instances of provocation by C.O.s telling other prisoners that one was a sex offender. That information could get a rise out of nearly any inmate.

We had three C.O.s per day, each working an eight-hour shift: 6 a.m. to 3 p.m., 3 p.m. to 11 p.m., and 11 p.m. to 6 a.m. Some carried handcuffs, though none had guns. Hubbard came in at 3 p.m. and got to hear all the stories about how abusive the other C.O.s had been to us. He heard positive stories as well, but a lot of the time it was, "Can you get me out of this?" Four or five guys at a time would be at the C.O. bubble even before Hubbard began his shift.

The "nice" C.O. is important. Despite the obvious hierarchy—C.O., sergeant, captain, lieutenant, warden, administration—prison is so chaotic and confusing, and the rules contradictory, that it seems as if no one is in charge.

The prison is a machine operating without oversight—the prisoner must go to the C.O. for guidance, yet some C.O.s, as I was learning, are hypocritical, bigoted, foolish, selfish, ignorant, and unforgiving. My characterization of the bad eggs was, "They provoke rather than protect." When affable Hub was on shift, inmates went to him for the sanity, expertise, and professionalism that some other C.O.s did not possess.

Every hour, a sergeant came into the dorm to check on the C.O. and see if he could catch any of the inmates breaking a rule. Sometimes the sergeant brought another officer with him and the three would chat for a bit at the bubble. Their conversations were sitcom-worthy, spirited because these men in blue had such strong opinions, like about yesteryear's American wrestling celebrities. One sergeant swore Randy Savage and Rowdy Roddy Piper were the toughest, while the C.O. said no one could beat Andre the Giant. The other C.O. said it was a shame when Jessie Ventura insulted the veterans and got punched.

Napoleon was an example of the ugly C.O. He was a short, thin man with a helmet of black hair, who smelled like Skin Bracer. He was of indeterminant race. He was all about order—even his tone of voice and word choice. Napoleon did not look you in the eye. Usually, his glance was downcast as if reading something. And he carried a night stick. That said a lot about him.

I could only surmise from college psychology that Napoleon grew up in an emotionless house where anything fun or celebratory went to die. His father probably told him "to be a man," never cry, never smile. A young man, Napoleon was thrilled to find a job where he could get paid to bully people and not get fired for hitting one, or many. The look on his dead-pan face led one to believe he suffered from anhedonia.

When called for chow, we were supposed to parade past the C.O. on duty and say our bed number so he could check it off on an attendance sheet and know who was there and who wasn't. Not everyone went to chow. The long-timers like Nobel and Cougar, and the wealthy, had food shipped in so they could cook in the dorm kitchen.

Preparing to head out for a meal, we gathered around Napoleon as he unlocked our door. Saying our numbers, we inmates exited and slipped by. I got to the second step when I heard, "Hold the fuck one minute!" Napoleon was having a fit, standing at the top of the stairs and waving his night stick, clipboard in his other hand. I knew he was talking to me. The whole line was held up. "Come here," said the C.O.

What a fucking asshole, I was thinking.

Why had I forgotten? Why did I wander through my days in a daze in prison? Why did I have trouble with the smallest tasks? Because of an affliction dubbed "Prison ADD" by writer Avi Steinberg. It's "the inability to ever be present because there's always something potentially heinous occurring nearby, something that is probably your responsibility."

I stood before Napoleon as he breathed hard and loudly, as if he'd just run a mile. "What the fuck is wrong with you?" Echoes of Elmira when they tried to get me to lead a marching line, and I led everyone down the wrong hallway. I was not supposed to answer the C.O.; that would have been asking for more trouble. I had to let him rant.

"What were you trying to do?" Napoleon acted as if this had been a planned escape. I zoned out as I often did. I didn't care what time or day it was, and I didn't care about petty rules. I hadn't even learned how to tell time until third grade. Not caring what time it is can get you in trouble a lot in life; even more so in prison. Napoleon knew he could yell only so long—he was, after all, holding up the whole dinner line. Circumstances were in my favor. "What's your fucking bed number?" I told him, and we all filed out of the building. He added, "Don't fuck around in my dorm."

The attitude of officers may not have been their fault. I saw plenty of senior officers in agitated states, but not toward other officers. Journalist and former C.O. Ted Conover wrote that some leaders only interacted by issuing orders. By failing to explain procedures, they "were eager to lay blame, and tried to humiliate us." Which is exactly the way some guards acted toward us.

Talking to Pastor Mark, I took issue with the false sense of entitlement state employees had.

"Entitlement?" Mark said. "With what?"

"C.O.s are always saying 'my gym,' 'my mess hall,' 'don't do that in my school building.' This is my complaint—these buildings are owned by the taxpayers, not the staff. The food we 'steal' from the mess hall is more ours than theirs because our families paid for it."

Mark pondered the question with me. "What about when they say, 'Don't forget to shower. The water is free'"?

"It's far from free," I said. "And when they fall asleep in the bubble, I feel like yelling, 'Don't sleep in my dorm.'"

Later that evening, Bear told me, Muslims gathered in the mess hall for some kind of ceremony. A fifty-six-year-old Brooklyn man had had a heart attack and none of the C.O.s or kitchen staff would touch him. Bear said prison staff are trained not to help people, so the state can avoid lawsuits from doing the wrong thing.

Two other Muslims dragged the man by the arms to the walkway outside. One sergeant ran to C building to get the AED machine to revive the man's heart. Once in the building, the sergeant learned the machine he wanted was broken. I thought a million questions and a lawsuit could come from just this one fact.

The sergeant then ran to D building, but by that time the victim had died. Three hours later, the ambulance arrived.

Bear said the guy had been serving a life sentence and had just completed year thirty-two.

"Where was the dude from?" I asked.

"Here," he said. "Our dorm."

I was shocked. I'd never met him.

"His name was Dr. Richard," Bear said. "It's weird. T-Bone just told me that Richard knew somehow. He'd been telling his brothers, 'I hope I don't die here.'"

Muslims were gathered at the windows, looking down at where the man's body had been placed. Death had come to our dorm. Few people talked about it or even noticed. The dorm was quiet; Napoleon had a free evening to read his newspaper.

To Bear, I went off. "This place kills people. No healthcare, no one to help you, no nothing. This is insane. That man lay on the sidewalk for three hours? Waiting for the ambulance?"

If officers were afraid of lawsuits, or if their union forbade saving inmate lives, why weren't inmates trained in CPR and first aid?

Bear said, "Nobody cares about you here. This is prison, man." He also tried to get me to understand the officers' thinking: "When a man hits the ground, the C.O.s assume that for the first ten minutes, he's faking to get out of prison and into a cushy hospital. They don't care if this is a critical time."

I thought about myself, of course. I was forty-nine, overweight, and had been abusing alcohol for nearly thirty years. Cocaine had been sprinkled in for more than fifteen of those years, and opiates populated ten. I thought eating healthy and working out were for geeks and wannabes.

A handful of Muslims quietly mourned the man's death. No one else in our population or in the prison seemed to care. This was a place where if one died, one truly died alone.

I'd read later that while the United States had a statistic for the number of inmates in our prisons nationally, it had no accurate way to measure the total annual number of inmate deaths. Journalist Beryl Lipton wrote: "Drugs, suicide, homicide, and more natural causes, like age or heart disease, are often to blame for the fatalities, but exactly how many pass away while in custody each year is not completely clear."

For various bureaucratic reasons, nationwide data is incorrect or nearly impossible to obtain. "Nearly three-quarters of inmates passed away before they had been convicted of a crime, added Lipton. "Forty percent of deaths happened within a week of arrest."

After my prison and jail experience, it's easy to wonder how many of those inmate deaths were of accused sex offenders. Word spread rapidly inside, and some prisoners, and officers, considered it a feather in their cap to injure or slay a "rapo."

Conveniently, the details of such deaths go unreported.

I shivered. This was no women's prison where they ask you, "How you doing?", where they celebrate birthdays and holidays with specially prepared sweets, gifts, and banquets.

I had no visitors. I was alone. My ex-wife wasn't coming. My parents, who were great supports, lived in Florida. My daughter was nineteen—I wouldn't want her to see me behind bars. My grandparents were elderly. My friends were either into drugs or had left my life because I was on drugs. "I figured that was coming," any of them would have said when they saw the April 1, 2015 headline in *The Buffalo News*, "Lockport Writer Indicted on Drug Charges."

Prison visits for my brethren turned out to be a horror anyway. Corrections officers put some visitors through strip searches, metal detectors, and a barrage of expletive-laced insults. According to inmates I interviewed off the record, some visitors were treated as badly as misbehaving inmates, even when children were present.

Inmates were denied visits for petty reasons like bad haircuts and defending their relatives in the face of C.O. abuse. Visitors were turned away for questionable reasons such as wearing steel-toed boots and arriving too early. Many visitors had driven hours to reach these rural prisons, only to go home angered or heartbroken. Grievances were filed, but what could be accomplished after the fact?

Officer behavior in these and other cases was reprehensible, and further evidence of a long-ignored system demanding change.

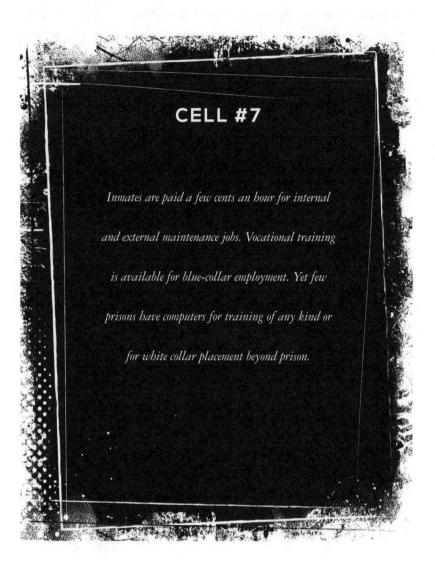

CELL #7

Inmates are paid a few cents an hour for internal

and external maintenance jobs. Vocational training

is available for blue-collar employment. Yet few

prisons have computers for training of any kind or

for white collar placement beyond prison.

CHAPTER 7

SUBOXONE DAYS

"...We exist ... in a prison environment which is,
by its very nature, suspicious of any and all groups
who do not conform to mainstream ideals of such a social system."
—Raven Wolf-Kindred, *Handbook of Asatrue*

The biggest "druggie" in the dorm was a tall gentleman nicknamed Iceman. He was called Iceman because he had eyes that looked like tomorrow. They were hypnotizing, like blue marbles. The dude was from white South Africa and had a pleasant English accent.

I scored from Iceman a few times, and I found that, in jail, he used alcohol, crack, GBH, pot, and suboxone. He made his own hooch from mess hall apples. The oxidation process made it stink, so no one went near him. Somehow, I made it without alcohol, or his hooch; maybe I was changing.

Iceman was a big, lifetime fan of '80s and '90s music. He had a ledger in which he listed the names of songs and artists. Sometimes he might record the name of the artist but not the song title. Other times he had the artist but not the song title. He employed me—my payment was commissary cookies—to tell him which titles were missing. It was a ball. We'd sit there reminiscing about tunes we loved and agonize over lyrics and song titles. Some were easy, like "Lowdown" by Boz Scaggs. Others were nearly impossible, like "All We Are" by Kim Mitchell (Canadian). We were having so much fun, other inmates like Pun, Nairobi, and Mark would stand by and listen in. Pun was extremely helpful with rap and hip hop, which I knew nothing about. Iceman did like a range of music.

"Can't Find My Way Home?"

"I know that. I love that song—used to make me cry when I was bombed. Let me think on that one. I gotta go through the mental filing cabinets."

"Let My Love Open the Door"?

"Easy. Pete Townshend."

"Okay. How about 'Every Day is a Winding Road'?"

"Again, easy. Sheryl Crow."

"'Motherless Children'?"

"Clapton."

"What about 'Helpless'?"

"Could be anybody."

"What year?"

"1980s. Alternative."

"So, it was on MTV. Hmm. Husker Du?"

On a sunny Sunday, September 10, we gathered in the TV room for the Buffalo Bills' matchup against the New York Jets. Cougar and Nobel were there along with Qwikster and several others. Seeing the Bills' uniforms up on the screen at Orchard Park gave me a small feeling of home.

The memories flooded in: My Grandpa Joe yelling at the O.J. Simpson Bills in the '70s, my mother crying in the mid-'80s as our team lost out in the playoffs—they were December tears because Grandpa Joe died at Christmas 1979—and numerous beer-soaked games with my friends. Today, I looked for John Lang in the crowd. He was the "Buffalo Bills Elvis" with muttonchops and a white "Go Bills" guitar. I had helped him write a memoir in 2013. Elvis could bust me out of here. My hero!

I wasn't supposed to be here. I had asked that narc if he was "working with the police" and he lied. Since when was it okay for the police to lie? That seemed like a recent thing to me.

As Bills quarterback Tyrod Taylor threw to Charles Clay for six points, the TV room erupted. The loudest was Cougar, who yelled, apparently at the Jets, "We ain't playin' witcha ho. We ain't playin'." This chant was quite funny, and Cougar tore up the room.

I was home with a bunch of strangers and my team. There *was* hope.

More people came in to watch the game. At any time, I could focus on the conversations sailing around the room. I was not disappointed.

- "I want a future, my nigga. I wanna own shit, my nigga."

- "He said he's not allowed to draw during Ramadan. It'll come to life."
- "I been on the terrorist watch-list since '94. I called a bomb threat into a school from the payphone there."
- "I'm feelin' some kinda way." (Jets fan)

That night, or early the next morning, I had a vivid dream of being on Washburn Street in Lockport. I was asking random strangers for change. Then I was at Jiffy Mart, the store where I usually bought Four Loko but, in my dream, I didn't have any money. I found $1.75 cents on the sidewalk, then another 40 cents on the store counter. Suddenly, that added up to $2.25. I only needed another quarter. I began asking store customers, and then the store clerk, for money. The clerk was some white guy who normally worked at Reid's Hot Dog Stand. The Eastern Indians who owned the store, who'd kicked me out for stealing Four Loko, weren't there. The Reid's guy gave me a cross look and tossed a quarter on the floor. Somehow, I had the money to buy three Four Lokos.

Then I was walking on Locust Street to my drug dealer's house. It was only 10 p.m. In real life, I'd never gone to Danny's house this late. Now, I figured I could get a few opiate pills. I found his apartment, went in, and saw his gal Maria. All of this was so real, so vivid, with everything in color, that I could smell spaghetti sauce warming on the stove.

I pulled a Four Loko from my bag and began drinking. I asked Maria if Danny only had suboxone. Then I was upstairs talking to the six-foot Danny himself, asking for a few Roxycodone, on a front. He said yes, and then I woke. Laying there, I heard the dorm's coughs, yawns, banging around, its awakening, I wished I was at my dealer's house, rather than here. For me, illicit drugs are subjects of nostalgia, like Jeep Cherokees, Grunge Rock, and Sunset Bay Beach.

Inmates tell newcomers to stay away from the three Gs: gangs, gays, and gambling. Messing with any of these can put you in a death situation. Or a cut-up one. I saw them around the Collins campus from time to time, the cut ones. These were the young guys usually—they had owed a gang money, had turned someone in, or knowingly (or unknowingly) enraged someone enough to cut them. A lot of the cuts came from drug deals gone wrong.

They had shank scars on their cheeks, a long-snakelike line running from mouth to neck. Some had three or more scars—they had really been attacked. They looked like aboriginal tribal markings, as if they'd been "scarred for life"; this must have been how the phrase originated.

Cutting. Busts. Theft. The underground thrived unabated in prison. The subculture was based on suboxone, K2, and psych meds. Suboxone was designed to help junkies quit. Abused, it caused a high. Most mixed it with water and sniffed. You could also tuck a tiny piece into your eyelid. K2 was synthetic marijuana—tiny pill balls rolled in a very thin cigarette and smoked. Psych meds cheeked from the Infirmary could be anything from Remeron to make you sleepy to Wellbutrin, known as jailhouse coke.

Other common street drugs were available at steeper prices. Subs (a.k.a. "chineta"), and K2 were the two most popular. Both were tiny, easily transportable, and required the minimal amount of work. Ladies could smuggle both drugs into the jail on visiting days—the drugs could be hidden anywhere, undetectable even during strip searches.

Suboxone (subs), or chineta, mistakenly thought of as "orange" in Spanish, used to come in pill form prescriptions. Its new incarnation came in wafers which patients melted under their tongues. The wafers were paper thin rectangles that came in two, eight, or twelve milligrams. Subs offered users heightened sensitivity, clarity, euphoria, excitement, hunger, and the need to chat with anyone around. Unlike heroin, suboxone couldn't kill you and would only get you to a high where you'd peak. Suboxone contains the active ingredient buprenorphine, a "semi-synthetic" opioid used to treat opiate addiction. It also is used for moderate to severe pain.

The female visitor passed the stash to her male prisoner through a kiss, or a handoff to hide on the recipient's body. Sometimes, it was stashed in the finger of a rubber glove and swallowed by the inmate. Because male prisoners got strip-searched, they had to be creative about hiding spaces. It's usually quite easy since the visiting room is like a big cafeteria, where inmate and visitors sit at the same square table. Conversations can be intimate. Many of the grumpy visiting room officers would rather be elsewhere and frequently "look the other way."

Once safely back at the dorm, the inmate dealer cut the strips into smaller, saleable pieces: $10, $20, $100, etc. Thus began the circus that was drug-dealing behind bars. It wasn't easy—commerce was much different from the street. There was no money in prison. It was so odd when a C.O. flashed a $20 for some reason. It looked like an ancient article. Here, commissary items and tobacco were our money equivalent.

Just about anything can be used as money in prison, as payment for doing someone's dishes to pummeling an enemy. Commissary is a small grocery store, mainly of junk food, though there also is meat, cheese, hygiene, and cleaning products for inmates to purchase. Ordering on someone's commissary sheet is a popular way for dealers to get paid.

A pouch of tobacco was about $5, cigarettes $10, and the rolling papers, lighters… Once you had a pack of cigarettes and were looking for chineta, you had to be careful. Though they often seemed like they were doing nothing, the C.O.s watched you. If you got a patdown on your way into the gym and the C.O. found a pack of Newports, he'd say, "You don't smoke. Why do you have these?" Carrying them for someone else was not a good excuse. Why didn't they carry them? And since you were white, why would you be carrying Newports? Some of the C.O.s were bigots who'd grown up in the same small town as the prison. Rural New York.

Usually the exchange was accomplished through teams. One inmate looked out for C.O.s, one passed the "cash," and another passed off the drugs. Thus, the necessary brotherhood of the gangs.

The most beautiful drug deal I ever saw took place on the Collins walkway, after dinner. During the walk (about fifty people were leaving the mess hall at once), the dealer caught up with the customer in full view of the other inmates and a team of C.O.s spread out on the walkway area and neighboring road.

Precision. Synchronicity. Impenetrability. The dealer and customer knew each other well because they had been working together since the beginning of their bids at Collins. I was walking behind them, knowing what was happening. They met amid a sparse gathering of inmates but, as they stepped together, inmates crowded around them like moths to a lamp.

As the crowd got thick, I could only see parts of their bodies amid a sea of green. And then in a flash of late afternoon sun and inmate cigarette smoke, the deal was done, both dealer and customer smiling, bodies slowly dispersing all around before reaching their individual dorm buildings.

It wasn't just visitors and inmates running the contraband game. Prison staff brought in more than inmates, according to a 2018 study by the Prison Policy

Initiative. The Initiative interviewed prison staffers, and learned that employees were dealing, from Alabama to Texas.

On the outside, I never really thought about money. My family had it, I had it, and then I went broke. When I finally stopped working in 2010, friends supported me. Prison woke me up to the value of things, even in those first few months. Suddenly, I had to be responsible again, especially if I wanted suboxone.

Someone commented in the press that Nixon/Reagan's War on Drugs was, actually, a war on black America. The war, however, celebrated diversity by putting all colors, races, and creeds behind bars. Our country had the highest number of incarcerated in the world. Prison for profit. It all made sense to my twisted mind. To be part of the resistance, I had to keep using. Citizens cannot be mandated to live sober lives—we have a right to the pursuit of happiness. High, I imagined I was making a stand. Or was I just afraid and trying to fit in? This was the easiest way to be a criminal among criminals, to make them trust me. Unless that was a lie and I was simply an addict, acting the part.

Dr. Gabor Mate published the seven signs America was losing its War on Drugs:

- Failure to reduce problematic drug use, including among young people
- Dramatic increases in crime related to prohibited drugs
- Skyrocketing public costs arising from both increased drug abuse and
- increased crime
- Erosion of public health
- Violations of due process and privacy
- Increased adverse effects on the poor and minorities
- Clogging of courts, compromised justice, and a loss of respect for the law

Even the name of this never-ending "War" on Drugs was inappropriate for this complex social problem. A solution, Mate said, should include "compassion, self-searching, insight, and factually researched scientific understanding,". He also said experts agreed that the war was "…an unfortunate confluence of ignorance, fear, prejudice, and profit."

An inmate had to secure invisible hiding spots, depending on the size of the buy. Early- morning drug and weapon raids occurred about every four months in the dorms. If his stash was found, an inmate would get a trip to The Box and maybe another charge. Hiding it was easier than you'd think since a piece of suboxone*** can be no bigger than the period at the end of this sentence. A powerful little drug.

K2 was also very small and concealable. Though it was compared to pot, it didn't look that way at all. It was sprinkled onto cigarette paper and rolled into a stick-like drinking tube. Users described a euphoric, paranoid pot-high, though the ingredients were just like the end result: always different. Unlike suboxone, K2 did not show up on most urine tests.

Collins, or any prison, could test for illicit suboxone use. The prison was frustrated into giving coma warnings about K2. When things go wrong with K2, users had an "eppy" or episode. Some were rushed to the Infirmary. Some just hid under a friend's bed until the eppy passed. Some went into comas and died. But that was rare—more of a scare tactic from the ubiquitous administration—a rumor designed to get users to stop.[3]

---

3 Like the addicts described in these pages, I wasn't sober on several full days at Collins and Marcy. I was using suboxone to de-stress, and to feel euphoric, in place where no happiness was to be found. While suboxone also provided clarity and energy, I remained clean after prison, when this book was written.

CELL #8

Prisons don't seem to follow rules, not even their own. Inmates are caught between a nightstick and a razor-wire fence. The American public is happy the bad guys (and gals) are locked up, but they fail to realize the inmate will become a citizen again and share the same environment, after being abused psychologically, and maybe physically, for years. Small crimes get big sentences and the incarceration system grows.

CHAPTER 8

CUTTING UP

"If every fool wore a crown, we'd all be kings."
—Welsh Proverb

Prisons in the United States began random drug testing in the early 1990s. However, inmates could legally question and protest the testing process. C.O.s who administered the tests were not medically trained personnel and often made mistakes. They forgot or improperly completed urine sample labels, or forgot to refrigerate the samples after testing.

In each prison's mini-court, an inmate testing drug-positive could receive an extra thirty days on his sentence or time in The Box. Other punishments included loss of good time, phone time, cubicle confinement, and commissary. But if an inmate can show that a C.O. erred on the test, all can be forgiven, or forgotten. At Collins, eleven toxicology tests had to be discarded in July 2018 because they went unrefrigerated for the weekend.

That there are drugs in prison is no surprise. Yet suboxone and K2 are so specialized—both are nearly impossible to find by officers because doses, though highly effective to users, can be so small. A high percentage of inmates were convicted of in-prison drug crimes, earning additional state time—and the party goes on.

Getting to know Easton was another of the three Gs that I broke. He was albino-white with a wisp of thinning hair. He eased into C3 and stayed on his bed after unpacking. Easton's bed was next to Mork's, a former kitchen worker who'd been fired. The hallway was on Easton's other side, and I introduced myself when walking past.

I did not know it the first time we spoke. I thought maybe, maybe not. That night I scored from asshole Ears and let the chineta melt under my right eye. It hurt like hell, but Jo Jo said that meant it was "a good hit." Feeling good, I thought I'd make a new friend with Easton, I could sense he needed one.

Easton was reading one of Mork's *Entertainment Weekly* magazines. I walked into his cube and said "Hi."

He lowered the magazine, looked over at me, and said, "Your eye is really red."

"Oh, allergies," I said.

"In one eye?"

"Sty?"

"You're asking me?" he said.

"Don't answer a question with a question," I said, covering my eye with my hand.

Easton laughed. "You're visiting?"

"I wondered if you were cool," I said.

"About most things," he said.

"Why are you here?"

"The police found meth, a king's ransom, and coke in my apartment. An old friend, who I guess is no longer a friend, tattled because I broke up with him."

"What a bastard," I said.

"And I was sleeping with someone else. Well, several people."

"You get around."

"Oh, I was just angry. Trying to make a point. He's the one who went too far."

"Jealousy."

"Exactly."

I was feeling very talkative and quite high. My guard was down. I offered Easton a small piece of the chineta and he said okay. He showed enthusiasm, but hid it behind cool. We'd just met after all.

Easton had first been imprisoned in Sing Sing on twenty-one drug offenses, many of them felonies. Easton said he had a beautiful apartment in Manhattan that served as "Grand Central party station" for two years. His friends were artists and models, transgender and transvestite, who filled their bodies with meth before going out on the town.

"It seemed like I had hundreds of friends," Easton explained, "and then the po-po busted in on me and my new man in bed. We had left drugs and needles and pipes lying about everywhere." A swirl of the hand.

On two possession charges, he was sentenced to three years prison, two parole. Only one person (not his boyfriend) showed up at the sentencing. At first, Easton took the recommended "Shock program," a physically and mentally punishing military-style jail stay. It was a six-month program, rather than the three-year prison stay. After one failed week in Shock, Easton dropped out and was shipped to Collins. His chronic depression made him ineligible for Shock.

"I got money stashed away that is kind of secret," Easton said. "So, I'll have an apartment for at least ten months when I get out."

I asked about his tenure in Sing Sing, the very definition of a notorious prison. He mentioned predictable C.O. and inmate abuses, concentrating instead on how prison is "a formidable society in America," since there are so many prisoners, and so many long sentences.

"Prison is the 'me too' club," Easton said. "A returning, repeat offender sees an inmate he once knew before and he says, 'I ain't seen you in a minute.' After their bro-hug, it's time to compare notes.

"One says, 'What you doin' here, son?' Answer, 'Oh I beat my bitch good, and I stole some shit. You know … robbery in the first.'

"'No shit. Me too.' Then a party ensues. High-fives. It's like they're celebrating more incarceration."

Easton was right. I'd seen this very behavior in county jail, in Elmira, and in Collins. It happened just about every time a new inmate came into the dorm.

Easton borrowed my copies of *Artforum* and *Art News* "for something high-brow to read in this sea of Mongols. I'd rather it was moguls."

Afternoons, before dinner, we played a game of Scrabble using the dorm's battered set. Despite being a writer, I lost to Easton every time. He lisped once, "You must leave your brilliance on the page."

Things got creepy toward Thanksgiving. I found that, like most prisoners, I marked time's passage on a calendar in my cube. I didn't care about politics, sports, or anything in the news (who was I to report for?) except rock star deaths.

Scott Weiland of Stone Temple Pilots died of an accidental overdose on December 3, 2015, when I was in County. Chris Cornell of Soundgarden hung himself May 17, 2017, and Tom Petty died of an overdose October 2, 2017, when I was in prison. Then there were David Cassidy and Charles Manson dying two days before Thanksgiving 2017.

In 2017, during the ongoing epidemic, there were 49,068 opiate deaths in America. This number makes it look like opiate dealers should be jailed for life, which some politicians have mentioned.

But those deaths aren't all 17-year-old high school kids who took pills from Mom's dresser drawer. The deaths include purposeful overdoses (suicide), street-level junkies, middle- and upper-class addicts, cancer patients who overdosed, ER mistakes, and those forced into use, for whatever reason.

According to the National Safety Council's 2017 analysis of accidental death, the leading cause of deaths that year was by opioid overdose. For years, the top spot had been held by car accidents. Americans had a one in 96 chance of dying from an opioid overdose, up from car crash's one in 103. Illicit fentanyl was blamed for the drug statistic.

The list of the dead from all drugs was 72,306, according to the National Institute on Drug Abuse. Other drug-related statistics include heroin deaths at 15,958; cocaine deaths at 14,556; cocaine mixed with opiates at 4,184 deaths; and benzodiazepines at 10,684 deaths.

These numbers can be questioned. How many were really suicides? How many involved the mixing of heroin, cocaine, and "benzos"?

While the numbers are startling, the fascinating fact is that the National Institute on Drug Abuse reports accurate numbers, or claims to, while our system of incarceration cannot report an accurate number of annual deaths in our correctional systems.

My death by fentanyl overdose would be reported, while my prison death from having my head dented by a C.O.'s baton would not. For example, the Erie County Holding Center is known for officers who act as judge/jury/executioner. ECHC has one of the highest rates of "suicides" in the nation, or at least deaths classified as suicides, according to Chris Stevenson of the Black Agenda Report.

The temperature was much cooler, the rains more frequent. It had been a cool, rainy summer. I told other inmates I put a curse on the summer so my judge, Richard Kloch, would have as crappy a summer as me. And it worked.

Since October, I had been watching the hills near Collins during sunset for the changing of the trees. Not because I loved fall—to me, it meant winter was coming. Not all Buffalonians like winter. To me, it was like living half our lives—up to eight months—indoors because of freezing temperatures and impassable roads.

Now I "yearned." It seemed I never understood the word's meaning until, from a prison perspective, I looked out the window at the woods' yellows, reds, and browns as art. An indescribable work by an unknown artist, signifying the phenomenon of change as a part of life.

And signifying nothing.

As dusk arrived, I recalled studying in the Lockport Library with Anne, riding around at night with Joan, and sneaking into a bar with Misty. Old girlfriends. Why was it fall when I always fell in love? Fear of being alone in winter? The romance of a new high school year? My first experience with the manic depression that would turn me into a drunk? A writer, but still a drunk. As I watched another fall die, I thought: "Alcoholics know something about living that others don't." It was our secret, and the dearest tragedy.

In my wired mind, everyone was a drinker, and they were soon going to invite me over. I drank with them, for them, and sometimes against them. Every patron at the liquor store was my friend. We would soon drink at their house, where I could tell them about myself. My friends were starting to vanish, so I'd make new ones. I'd introduce myself to strangers and they'd scowl; I was just too much for some folks.

One summer day, I was walking down Church Street and a voice from a porch called out my name. I walked up to him and we shook hands. I had no idea who he was; still don't. He invited me to his fenced-in backyard for cocktails with his wife. What were we talking about? Hours later, I left. In a couple months, needing a free drink, I walked down Church and could not remember the guy's name or his house number. None of them had a beer garden in the back yard. Did I imagine it?

I must have sensed a dark energy in the air. I should have taken the vision as a prophecy. Within days, I received a letter from my daughter, who was in college. The letter made me swoon (in a manly way) because it was our first communication in a year and a half. Inside was good news—A's at college—and bad news, her grandfather, my ex's father, David, had died in October in a Lockport hospital. My daughter gave me no cause of death.

For me, David had been a god of sorts, paving my way in life. He was in his seventies and had had trouble breathing. He was admitted to Lockport's hospital and died shortly thereafter. I was not moved to tears because Lithium dulls emotion and because my ex's side of the family shut me out completely when I moved out of Morrow Avenue. It seemed like I lost 100 friends overnight. On Papa's passing, I mostly felt bad for my daughter and her heartache—she was lucky to have such a close and affluent family.

I had written to my daughter ever since entering the county jail, and continued by doing so in prison, sending her long letters with humorous drawings of us, though I did not hear back from her. I didn't think she was angry with me; I just thought she was young, spending time with her friends, and her film and writing projects. Her generation communicated by Facebook and Twitter, which I did not have behind bars.

In her letter, my daughter talked about college, her boyfriend, her volunteering projects, and the new films she was making, including a country song video for a close friend trying to break into the business. My daughter also included six examples of her compelling animal photography. Whenever I felt no sense of security, or my mind was racing, I knew from her that a world of the arts still existed on the outside—a Walden for creatives to go to.

Rev. Thunder, Pastor Mark, and Easton began planning our Thanksgiving dinner. This was rare. There were ten of us pooling commissary funds for a communal meal. Rev. Thunder was excited—he knew how to cook. We had to sign up for time because others wanted to use the oven on Thanksgiving Eve.

I was short on cash because of chineta purchases. Keith was spending all his money on it, giving me pieces whenever I wanted. Suboxone and Lithium helped beat the depression back. I found I wasn't the only one feeling it. A guy named Devil, in a cube up by the C.O. desk, apparently failed a piss test for drugs and went to The Box. Now his cube was empty.

A few days later, he was dead. Pastor Mark came up to me and asked if I knew. "Yeah," I said. "He got busted and went to The Box." Mark slowly shook his head. "Yes, and he killed himself in there—hung himself with the bed sheet. Left a note. Said he owed the Bloods too much money and … Well, he did it to himself before they did."

I felt horrified, anxious, and then numb. Had I talked to the dude? What of his parents, wife, kids, if there were any? I didn't even remember his face. Just like the Muslim whose heart gave out, he was suddenly gone. Another death from our dorm. And as happened in the case of the Muslim, everything in the dorm continued as if nothing happened. No one mourned visibly or acted any different. I know Rev. Thunder and Pastor Mark prayed together, "for this man's sad soul to have quick delivery to heaven." I attended the prayer group—it was five sex offenders and me. Cougar looked at me and shook his head.

Prison suicides were very much on my mind; we were still in Western New York, host to the notorious Erie County Holding Center. The center often had suicides, but covered them up, C.O.s handing up reports that there had been a "disturbance" in cell #17 rather than a successful suicide. The center was state-cited for that practice. Along with Alden, ECHC was "the worst in the state," said a *Buffalo News* report by Matthew Spina on May 29, 2018.

The recent suicide from our dorm was one of thousands of deaths in the state's prisons. The total number of inmate deaths was 3,479 (in 2013). Six percent of those prisoners took their own lives.

Being so close to death let my mind wander to the real dangers here. Inmates were being killed all the time by officers at the Erie County Holding Center, which was just fifty miles away. I was new to prison life, aware that life here wasn't guaranteed. We faced two main threats—morally bankrupt C.O.s and other inmates.

Writer and inmate Jack Henry Abbott said in 1991: "…More prisoners are murdered today in American prisons than any other place on earth. About ten percent of America's prisoners are seriously injured or murdered annually. Every single prisoner every day must exist with the imminent threat of assault at the very least—and from any corner."

Collins' officers had indirectly murdered the Muslim man by not working quickly enough (or at all) to save him. He was a lost statistic for a part of the government that purposely does not maintain accurate records.

As time stumbled by inside Collins, I learned how prison drugs tore men's skin from around their souls. It was similar to life on the outside, only more quickly controlled by The Prince of Darkness. Inmates sought happiness and escape from prison absurdity—nothing of intelligence or love happened in lockup. Peace was non-existent. An inmate with only one day left in his sentence felt no joy—only fear and paranoia—because anything ugly can happen at any time in prison, from an assault to a new charge, adding time to the sentence.

Getting high for the first time in prison gave me a separate peace, just like it did for the average inmate. So, the drugs were sought a second time and the bill to the dealers went up. Drugs then became a regular thing. The inmate might run short on cash, but that was okay. The dealer said he could wait. The bill got paid off and the inmate's credit was extended. The inmate spent all his commissary and began asking for more money and Western Unions. The inmate's people grew tired of the begging and either refused temporarily to send more money, or stopped altogether. The dealer continued selling drugs on credit. Then there was no way out—the inmate owed hundreds and had a heck of a habit.

Ways out:
- Get transferred to another prison
- Steal from other inmates
- Tell officers your life is in danger & transfer to P.C. (Protective Custody)
- Break a rule and go to The Box
- Get beaten up, shanked, or killed

Keith got in very deep. He told me he owed Ears about $200 he couldn't pay. That's like $2,000 or more on the outside. Ears got his suboxone from a gang. They'd be the enforcers should Keith fail to pay. Cuttings were common at Collins, though not as frequent as in maximum security. Ears was demanding and receiving anything he could get from Keith. Keith was visibly nervous, shaking even. Yet he'd still score more chineta from other dealers. I knew because he'd give me some. In return, I'd give him a bit of my commissary.

Then, two inmates I didn't know were drug tested, failed, and were sent to The Box. They both owed Keith money that he'd been counting on to pay his bill.

Once you're gone, there's no coming back to the same dorm. Keith was headed toward a nervous breakdown. One morning, Keith was absent from breakfast. He showed up about an hour later in the dorm and told me he'd been given a urine screen. He packed up his stuff and around 11 a.m., our C.O., Hubbard, escorted Keith to the door. He was gone.

Cougar, Bear, Urkel, and I stood there, dumbfounded. Well, at least I was dumbfounded. A conversation ensued about "Keith's clever escape," as Bear called it. During chow, he must have gone to the infirmary and told them he was having mental problems or that someone was out to get him. Bear explained, "All you gotta do is say you're afraid for your life and you go to P.C." He couldn't have failed a drug test, or he would have been escorted out in handcuffs like the others. Officers made it look as if you've been arrested.

Keith lost his debt without getting hurt. Ears was pissed. The Bloods were really pissed. I owed Keith $15. I got off the hook too.

April 23, 2017 was my last day of freedom. I was homeless, staying at Rachael and Sam's house in the town of Lockport. Awaiting sentencing, I was trying to put my life back together after being in an out-of-county jail for drug court. When you go to jail, the authorities don't care if you have rent to pay, appointments to make, or any other responsibilities. That's why many inmates are homeless upon release. In Lockport, if you are poor, there's no one to help you find a home.

One month earlier, my grandmother was dying. During a late February pre-sentencing hearing, I asked Supreme Court Judge Richard Kloch if I could get out of jail, before sentencing, to see my grandmother and attend her imminent wake.

Unbeknownst to me, the judge had researched my background. Kloch asked the district attorney if letting me out was prudent. The DA said, "Mental illness combined with addiction? I'd say no. Not a good idea."

Kloch said, "We don't normally see this type of person in my courtroom. Did you know he has two books published? Well reviewed books. He has worked successfully in business and is a professional."

It was almost as if I hadn't been charged with a felony.

The judge, suddenly my best bud (so unexpected), decided to let me out, which never happens. My useless public defender had told me not to talk to the judge, but I did anyway. And it worked. He said I needed to meet with my proba-tion officer and "come back to me in a month."

I couldn't believe it. I was thrilled. I was walking, but where? I had no home, nowhere to stay in Lockport. Quickly, I thought I'd stay with my longtime friend, Danny. He had a house near the Erie Canal. Failing that, maybe Lockport Cares, the homeless shelter. Plan C was my pastor's house. My mind was racing between excitement and paranoia. I actually had $20 due to me from jail commissary; the deputy on duty gave me a check.

I had a long haul ahead of me, up the tall, twisting snake of Niagara Street Extension, thinking only that once I reached Danny's house, I'd be able to score some opiates. I heard a car approaching. I turned and saw a brunette in a Jeep. She actually stopped and rolled her window down, saying that she knew women shouldn't pick up men, but I didn't look weird. I did a small jump for joy and she laughed. We chatted about hydrocodone during the whole ride. My paranoia surfaced again, telling me she might be a narc, trying to score from me. I'd be right back in jail, whether Grandma was dying or not (she really was).

The girl said she was going out to a bar that night—I should meet her. She was girl-next-door attractive—silk blouse, jeans, tall black boots. She didn't need a coat—it was sixty degrees on this particular Friday, February 27. I had her drop me off a block from Danny's house, in case she was a narc. I shouldn't have been so paranoid—I might have gotten laid.

I had been in the county jail since late October, waiting for sentencing. I knocked at Danny's door and was welcomed by Maria, his longtime girlfriend, and mother of two of his children. The kids started yelling, happy to see me after so long. This was my new family. I'd known Danny for ten years. My real family had abandoned me because of my addict lifestyle. Danny's was the family that did not judge.

That night, I had half an Opana—just half so I didn't overdose after being clean in jail for these past four months. I drank a Four Loko too. I'd never stayed at Danny's house before, but when I asked, he said I could stay downstairs in the abandoned apartment. I had a lamp line running from Danny's upstairs to the living room window to downstairs. Danny had run out of room—he was a bit of a hoarder. And when the family downstairs moved out, he rented that too from the landlord. There was a TV and a couch downstairs. That was it.

I stayed there for the month. Then Danny closed his little store and needed to move everything into that old apartment. I was using and drinking every day, getting money from Danny for odd jobs. After that, Rachael and Sam took me in. My alcohol tolerance had really changed during those months in jail. Any time I tried Four Loko while on suboxone, I vomited. Before drug court and jail, I could drink several Four Loko and be on suboxone in a single night. For the uninitiated, Four Loko was a grape drink I liked that came in a malt can, with twelve percent alcohol. One Four Loko equaled four and a half normal alcoholic drinks.

There wasn't much to do at Rachael's, though we used to do all kinds of things together. Now, instead of a neighborhood where we knew everyone, they lived in a trailer park. Total isolation. So, we talked about old times, updated our Facebook pages, and watched old episodes of "Mad Men" and "Californication."

Trying to keep my mind off my court case, I drank as much as I could and watched TV. I took notes on everything that happened to me. Then came that day in April when Rachael dropped me at county court. Judge Kloch had trusted me for two months, but I never took a urine test at Northpoint Outpatient, as I was supposed to. A Chinese Dragon Lady, Liz, ran the outpatient program. I met with her a few times, saying no to every test I was told to take. So, Liz turned me in to Officer Fender, who went and ruined everything.

The "Brandon the Felon is Free" deal I made with Kloch was that I'd get regular urine screens from Northpoint. The suboxone I took told me to blow it off. The judge was disappointed in my bad behavior, and showed that disappointment—a sentence of two years in state prison. I wouldn't see freedom again for a year and four months (at minimum).

My yellow journal had a photo of The Who in concert at the bottom right, while top left was a bum napping on a park bench. My signed "BMS" notebook was called "Diary of Madness." My last journal entry said I felt like I was "moving forward with my life." I figured Kloch would just sentence me to county jail. The journal said I was changing Northpoint counselors—Liz was out and Chuck was in. But they were lying to me. Liz had already made that call to probation and I was fucked. The rest of my journal was blank.

Collins wanted to know what shape I was in. Dr. Chris completed a full physical and deemed me nearly disqualified for any inmate work, except for pushing a broom. Back and knee problems had persisted since the car accident. The following boxes were checked on my inmate medical form: no strenuous exercise or competitive sports, no lifting greater than twenty pounds, no pushing, pulling, bending, twisting, or prolonged standing, and no working around or controlling machinery. This document guaranteed that I never have to take a top bunk.

At the Collins dorm, I learned from Bear and Heat that there were nine sex offenders among us. Sex offenders, or rapos, are the lowest on the inmate chain. Heat and Patriot, a Gulf War vet, were the most open in their hatred of these men, but it remained verbal only.

We were in a dangerous category—general population. I asked Cougar why there weren't more fights and harassment, especially with the sex offenders.

"If you got a good crib, a dorm that's in control, you don't want to mess up that gig," Cougar said. He, Nobel, and the other inmates "in charge" kept the peace. The rapos were protected … almost.

The state made each new inmate view a 2015 PREA anti-prison rape video starring real inmates (and victims) from Fishkill Correctional. PREA was the Prison Rape Elimination Act of 2003. Posters with stills from the video, with taglines "Report It" and "Stay Safe," hung in the mess hall, infirmary, and other prison buildings. While 200,000 sexual assaults still occur annually, the penalties typically imposed today represent a heavy deterrent—not as depicted in "Oz" and "Shawshank Redemption."

Unfortunately, according to the Committee Against Torture, prisons without PREA still have significant rape issues.

Moreover, the DOCCS inmate orientation handbook had three pages, at the document's beginning, on how there was zero tolerance for sexual abuse among inmates and staff. The very next page covered suicide and communication.

Zoom was his prison handle. Had been down 20 years (several in Woobourne in the Catskills) for a crime he said he did not commit. Like Mark, Zoom was a man of faith. Zoom liked to say, "Every time I turn around, God is showing me things:

humility, people, situations. But there is so much more that God is trying to get me to understand."

Zoom nearly always was smiling. "When I speak," he said, "I'm not only hearing my own voice. I'm hearing the angels speak." When we first met, Zoom had twenty-four months to go before his release. He spoke of the day his wife (how does a wife hold on for 20 years, especially to a convicted sex offender?) will pick him up at the prison gates. They'll go home and have a long-overdue dinner." Said Zoom, "We'll get reacquainted."

Zoom walked to the campus chapel at about eighty mph, thus the handle. He was impossible to keep up with. Yet he stood by his friends with his counseling, philosophies, experiences, generosity (a bottomless pocket of peppermint candies), and an expectation that you would treat his friendship responsibly.

"My incarceration," said Zoom, "is the result of an old whore of a money-grubbing ex-girlfriend who, with her friend, accused me of rape. The judge was a woman who would not listen to me—her mind was made up that I was going to be the example."

Zoom adds, "So, I do what I did in the Army. Deal with it. It's almost over." He grabbed his well-read Bible from the top of a James Patterson stack, and we were off. In the chapel, I was struck by all the poster-style images of Jesus and average Joes at worship, as if the prison population is somehow represented by artists' ideas of blue-collar America. "Fight the War," one poster says over a praying man, "On Your Knees." Of course, the anonymous poem "Footprints" was represented, as were images of a Latino Jesus and a wall-length map of "His Journey."

We were in a church of sorts, but not for religious purposes—not on this day. Pastor Mark was here, along with Zoom, four other inmates, and a civilian facilitator. A non-participant corrections officer sat nearby. This was a meeting of Cephas, an in-prison support group focused on post-prison planning and life. Not all prisoners, especially sex offenders, had family or friends to go home to, much less an actual home or place to live. Led by a civilian from the community, the group helped with advice, listening, and links to post-incarceration services.

Life outside prison for sex offenders was chaos, according to those I interviewed. There were many strict rules to follow, including not living near a school or playground. The other inmates joked, yelling to rapos: "Put down the rattle and step away from the stroller!" Some sex offenders were held longer than their sentences because they could not find lodging that parole would approve. Breaking even the most mundane rule landed them back in prison. One (or possibly more than one) made it out of prison for only a single day before an infraction brought them back.

I didn't find Cephas very helpful, though it was nice to meet Jane, the civilian who ran the meeting. She reminded me that I did not have that long before I'd be free. The sex offenders in the dorm had to live here much longer and survive. I was a drug offender, so no one was hunting me down.

Despite his eccentricity, Zoom worked in the law library. He was there for me, again, when I needed his help. In my frustration, I had started a story that I thought of on the walkway. The administration mandated that all prisoners were to be treated the same, as if we were. In a perfect world, if nonviolent prisoners were granted as little as an hour per day of individual attention, the outcome of incarceration might be different. Studies have proven that individual psychiatric attention is superior to group rehabilitation, because everyone is different. And they have different needs.

The way most staff, in my experience, treated the inmates (horribly) got to me. I took it personally. Creating a satire, I imagined a Collins with a 600-headed monster made up of 600 linked prisoners. I left it to the reading audience to imagine how they were united. They were connected during court as the judge lumped them all together with one grand sentence and tossed them in the slammer.

The monster went on a Daniel Boone-type journey, wandering the prison, department to department, getting different and strange answers as to why he was bad. I wrote all of this in a yellow legal notebook, unsure what it would become. I envisioned a satire for adults in the form of a kids' book. I let Zoom read it and he agreed to type the manuscript for me at the law library.

The story involved people from each prison department, battling to see who was most bureaucratic. Corrections officers beat the monster, stole food, and were oblivious to the inmates' drug dealing. God watched the monster's journey and ordered America to build more prisons and "keep them filled."

In the end, the monster was saved by an angel, who explained that the monster was not bad—it had just done bad things. Goodness was inherent in the monster, prison was a single stop on the road, and the future would provide opportunities for the monster to live well and serve others. The monster floated over the fencing and was finally free.

The end was kind of smarmy. I wanted a happy ending to wrap up my indictment of a prison operation that simply enraged me.

Once the story was typed, I shared it with Pastor Mark and Cougar (who offered laughs and positive reviews). Zoom asked me what I was going to do with it. I said, "Look to the alternative media."

CELL #9

Until all prisons are managed like proper educational institutions, giving inmates more to do (yard time doesn't count), the internal atmosphere will be as absurdly criminal as the lives prisoners had before being locked up.

Prisons perpetuate crime and foster recidivism.

Recidivism is a pristine business model to keep our jails up and running, and our prison staff employed.

Roughly 68% of paroled inmates return to prison, while .role models for younger inmates are non-existent.

CHAPTER 9

AA (ANXIETY ATTACKS)

"In my younger and more vulnerable years, my father gave me some
advice that I've been turning over in my mind ever since.
'Whenever you feel like criticizing anyone,' he told me, 'just remember that all
the people in this world haven't had the advantages that you've had.'"
— F. Scott Fitzgerald, *The Great Gatsby*

Agony (he gave himself this handle) was a young man with a creatively sculpted beard, like Elliott Gould circa "MASH." Vocal inmates did not like Agony, saying he was convicted of child molestation (kissing an eight-year-old below the navel).

Agony said he could play guitar with Five Finger Death Punch, Anthrax, or even Megadeath. He said he'd ridden professional motorcross, and "can beat the shit out of the biggest knuckle-dragger" in the dorm. (In fact, Nobel or Cougar could finish Agony with one look.) And Agony's pathological lying went on. He said that he was a trained sniper.

Driven by his faith, Pastor Mark met nightly with Agony in the cubicle next to mine. Mark said he wanted to help Agony dispense with some of his lies and "try to make him see some reality." Mark was perceptive—Agony might not even know why he was in prison. Considering the medical and mental health care I had so far received, I agreed.

At times, Agony raised his voice in frustration. "I don't believe in no God." And it was obvious, through overhearing Mark's conversation with him that Agony wasn't really listening. Or seeing reality. Mark, however, remained patient, like the pastor he wanted to be, meeting with the young man every day. Was Mark altruistic in his intentions? Was Agony, the sex offender, worth the effort?

Agony's delusions were medicated, but maybe not enough. Collins was supposedly one of the New York prisons that catered to the mentally handicapped. The ill. Those who were "out there." Some were in the darkest of places, Delusionville, even though many years had passed since their crimes. I did not interview or seek out these people—some were in solitary for good reason.

In this Twilight Zone were the sex offenders, many of whom admitted their guilt, but others who said the victim or child was sending strong signals that they wanted the sex, no matter the intensity of abuse. They believed the child or victim had seduced them. Though still a journalist, I saw no reason to show these people to the world.

While many sex offenders tried to hide their identities from the prison population (even though threats of harm had been reduced by PREA), Elmira Reception "outed" them with mandatory haircuts, with bald patches, skull skin cuts, and eyebrow shaving. Imagine, crazy hair or a missing eyebrow informing the world of sex offender status.

Some "rapos" were much less fortunate when entering Reception. A man who, with his wife, sexually abused their four under ten children, was given a "wash down" upon entering his cell on day one. A C.O. took a fire hose and sprayed the man right into his locker and the wall. The man was simply left there to dry and nurse his own wounds. A day or so later, the same C.O. lit a roll of toilet paper on fire and threw it on the man's bed.

I finally found out about the tiny, beer can-shaped Spanish man in my Phase I orientation class. According to a C.O., he had been convicted of abusing a small boy he had been babysitting. And I also found out, through Pastor Mark of all people, that Collins was sixty-percent sex offenders. Thus, the lack of "rapo" talk and abuse, as at Elmira and some of the more dangerous maximum securities like Wyoming, Sing Sing, or Fishkill. Cougar's assertion that we wanted to keep things quiet was partially correct.

The abuse may go on unabated in the tougher jails. Said Tucker, a sex offender in my dorm, "A C.O. asked me, after he had punched me unprovoked, if I was going to fill out a grievance (form).

"If you want to," said the C.O., "first I'll handcuff you, and then I'll hold a plastic bag over your head until I'm certain you're not breathing.'"

It was only a threat. Unforgettable, certainly.

Patriot used to "run his mouth" in the mess hall, surrounded by dorm-mates and others, including many sex offenders.

"I hate rapos," said Patriot. "I'd like to kill them, fuck their eye sockets, and shit in their mouths." Rapo comments were also common in the Infirmary's medication line, and along the pastoral walkways dividing buildings and grounds. "I hate spics and spooks too, and that's all we got."

Patriot, holding a clipping from the *New York Post,* was thrilled to announce that Rep. Rick West of Oklahoma wanted rapists to undergo "chemical castration," drugs used to nearly eliminate male libido. He hoped New York would pass such a bill. Yet catcalling was as close to danger as most sex offenders came in Collins. The violence and fights were usually among the gangs in the yard.

Asked why sex offenders seemed to have it easier these days in New York state prisons, a C.O. told me, "There's more of them now. And more laws protecting them." Laws like longer sentences. Reports indicated that child abuse increases in a down economy, and, today, the Internet provided a whole new world for offenders like Mark to get into trouble without actually touching anyone.

Surprisingly, all the sex offenders I met in Collins were socially outgoing. Some avoided more public places like the TV room or the gym, but they wanted to make friends, especially with each other. I'd walk up to a group Mark was standing with and realize I was the only one who was not a sex offender. I'd look around the room, self-conscious that I had been seen with "them." Inmates said, "If you are with them, you are one of them."

You didn't really make traditional friends in a short-term prison bid. I associated with some sex offenders and learned a great deal. Even if they were treated almost normally in general population, they still wore the sex-offender scarlet letter, even in chapel. The C.O.s were rather chatty about the sex offenders, as when a new one would enter the dorm. Otherwise, a crazy haircut, or radically oversized clothes (another Elmira trick) would give them away.

During the notorious hazing at Elmira (which included psychological abuse at the hands of club-wielding officers), the state supply center purposely handed out oddball clothing sizes to the sex offenders. An inmate who traditionally wore a large-size shirt and had a 30-inch waist would receive a 4XL shirt and pants with a 60-inch waist. The man would have to wear these garments because they were standard prison uniform; appeals to the state shop or to the C.O.s for properly sized clothes were met with either silence or laughter.

And how about size twelve boots for size seven feet? Punishment for not wearing the mandated uniforms included a stiff Tier-Two ticket, which went on your permanent prison record, which might result in more prison time. Or the offender just might get one of the tough punishments a C.O. could think up, like 100 pushups, a jab or two with the nightstick, loss of recreation time, or cubicle confinement.

The scariest, and deadliest, fates that haunted the Collins campus inmates seemed to revolve around young New York City gang members (some looking no older than ten), who peppered the facility and the dorms. The walkways and the recreation yard were hazardous if you were a gang member, if you owed money, if you were part of a vendetta, or a handful of other reasons. Also, if you were a drug user, it was easy to get into debt for the two popular jailhouse drugs of this period.

As part of ongoing fights, gang members shanked, or cut, people's faces (along the jaw line) with the regularity of mosquitoes biting picnickers. Our trips to the infirmary for nightly medication were often delayed by the latest gang member who got half his face slashed or cut off. The infirmary was small and could take only so many patients at once. Teens and 20-somethings with big cheek scars stood out on the campus.

Ted Shady was the only sex offender I saw doing drugs, but there were others. To purchase suboxone, Ted told the dorm's drug dealer he'd trade him packs of Newport cigarettes from the commissary. He dissolved the pieces in water and sniffed them, or he'd place them under his eyelids to dissolve. The high produced an energy-inducing euphoria. You could tell who was high on chinita because they would be excitedly talking to each other, running around the dorm chatting to anyone who would listen, or enthusiastically cleaning their own cubicles.

Ted Shady and I wound up at his cubicle, sharing drug stories, and I popped the question: Why are you here? He clammed up, which drug takers never do. I was pretty sure I was with one of *them*. The sex offenders.

Ted Shady gave a long sigh. He slowly explained that he had a picture of his girlfriend's two-year-old daughter naked, "playing at the beach," and he "accidentally" posted it on his Facebook page. Somehow, it got forwarded to the addresses of all his friends, associates, and co-workers. A co-worker took offense and called child protective services. The girlfriend broke up with him and added her name to a list of complainants, which grew rapidly. Now he was in Collins.

My bullshit detector was showing red. So, despite the chemical encouragement, I never got the real story out of Ted Shady. I imagined volumes of child porn hidden away someplace.

Punishment. It's known that some drug offenders in New York State get more time in prison than sex criminals. Something the legislators might want to take a look at, right?

A convicted crack dealer I met grabbed me by the shirt when he became aware that I was interviewing sex offenders. "The DA recommended eighteen years for me," he seethed. "A rapist in court at the same time as me ... He sodomized a little boy and raped a little girl—the same DA recommended six months in jail with ten years of probation. Don't fucking tell me about sex offenders and justice because there ain't any!"

The sex offenders at Collins usually avoided the benefits of today's New York State prison—flat-screen cable TV, weekend blockbuster movies, refrigerators, and commissary, cooking utilities, stocked bookshelves, gym, yard, workout facilities, libraries, and more. The first sign of trouble, dorms became overrun by C.O.s there to break up any fights. Raids for drugs and weapons were routine.

After learning I was a journalist and author, each sex offender I met, except Agony and Mark, said they wanted me to help them write their story. Each wanted to "tell the world what really happened" and "set the record straight."

About ten different people used these exact same words. Pressed for details and to set a date and time to begin formal interviews, the subjects always balked, citing any number of mundane reasons why, after all, they could not talk.

I met Livingstone at Collins. His cubicle was located near mine. His story: He worked for a company that catered to the elderly. One of his clients, a woman of 67, fell out of her wheelchair one day and accused Livingstone of groping her.

The prosecutor supported the woman's complaint with unique details: Her attacker kissed her, pulled her from her wheelchair, and began removing her clothes.

Livingstone said stories about him and the woman (who he said had Alzheimer's) had appeared in news accounts, branding him a rapist prior to trial. According to Livingstone, the media was in cahoots with the prosecutor and judge, "who are all related," as was the female victim. "They all stand to make millions suing my employer" because of the conviction.

He said, "It's a set up; even the old gal's in on it."

How a woman with Alzheimer's could be part of such a conspiracy, I did not ask. Pressed to set a date to begin our interviews for his "tell-all book," Livingstone always had something more important to do. The world had to wait, seemingly forever.

I went back to AA, which was held in a classroom near the library. I brought a pocketful of Jolly Ranchers to stay awake.

Leon was the first to testify after readings from the Big Book. "Well, my ex-wife…"

I should have known it was coming. This was only my third AA meeting at Collins and the "meeting killer" had already reared its head. When AA attendees, specifically men, opened up by talking about the "ex," it was time to go. These were guys who simply couldn't leave it alone. They ruined meetings because AA discussions were supposed to be about alcohol and alcohol-related problems.

When you put "ex" before wife or girlfriend, it was over. She was an ex. It's over, man.

If she asked you to give up drinking, she's already planned the rest of her life, without you. You may give up drinking for her, but that won't work. You were going to be out of the apartment or house as soon as she could convince you it was all for the best. She was a desert oasis, looking like a lifesaver, but not there at all. She asked you to move out, just for six months, then a year, then it was a trial separation. The verdict was already in on that trial—you were guilty. She was innocent. It was all your fault.

Once Leon started, I heard a collective sigh. The whole room was amped up to talk about their former lovers, girlfriends, and spouses.

Because I liked to drink, I'd been attending AA since 1996. It drove me crazy when attendees said AA, or their Higher Power, saved their lives. *No, it didn't,* I thought. *You saved your life.* It also made me crazy when judges included AA as part of an offender's sentence. What happened to separation of church and state?

Here in prison, I was looking forward to a discussion about alcohol. It took me seventeen years to get over my ex. What these men needed to do was stop:

- Thinking of her every day
- Being angry or homicidal toward her boyfriends
- Drinking/taking drugs despite her
- Wishing her pain and misfortune
- Worrying about the impact of her actions on your offspring (another form of jealousy)

My list does not account for the unforgiveable and intolerable situations of child abuse or financial entanglements. If she asked you to stop drinking, you had to prepare for war.

"I'm Brandon. I'm an alcoholic." I didn't want to give up on something that brought me thirteen years of joy and two years of joy mixed with misery. For me, alone in those apartments, the end was drug-soaked, and blah, blah, blah. Losing your love always ends the same—desperation.

Five inmates told their stories of woe. Then no one else had anything to say. I wondered if there were more divorced women in America than married ones.

I don't remember my exact words, but I introduced myself as "a proud alcoholic," and then addressed the room: "Brighter days are ahead. Once you let go." There was no response. After a ten-second pause, our group leader excused us for the night.

Outside, walking to the dorms, I asked "no nickname" Paul, in prison on a third DWI, if what I had said was appropriate. He didn't answer.

"It felt preachy," I said.

"What?" Paul said. "Oh, I wasn't listening."

Bear progressed well with his novel. I was happy to help him as I had helped many authors publish over the years, from Marsha Kight's *Forever Changed* to John Lang's memoir of rugby, football, and being the "Buffalo Bills' Elvis" superfan.

Bear's story centered on a group of twenty-somethings crossing the country, shoplifting to buy coke and meth. It was kind of a poor man's *Less Than Zero*. The characters in *Less Than Zero* shopped at Prada; the characters in *Hustle* stole from Prada. Nearly three months into my Collins time, Bear was still handing me two or three new pages each day to review.

I slept a lot during this time, depressed and simply trying to pass time in a dream-world that was better than my reality. It took a month and a half for me to get used to being in prison, and I was in the process of giving up. I had no power, except when I was writing or editing. That's what I told myself, trying to make some sense of something that made no sense.

Other inmates kept busy with loud conversations, cooking, cleaning, working out in the restroom (using the top toilet stall bar for pull ups) and yard, dealing and using drugs, talking on the phone, working the many jobs for The Man (mowing lawns, painting the campus, etc.).

In the restroom mirrors, one could see guys doing workouts without weights. Guns, the Cosmonaut, Abs, Catfish, and Ashes engaged in vanity and pride before the mirrors. The mirrors that worked, anyway. They were usually at home in the yard with the big weights, five times a week. They curled the biceps, pulled the triceps, worked the pecs, and crunched the abdominals.

At the dorm, these bodybuilders posed before the two silver-framed mirrors, hurling the lingo: "You do bis and tris today?" Golden bulges in the mirror, a hand framing a square face. Superhuman. Guns with arms that looked like tree branches, tattooed arm "sleeves," and an ego the size of Cuba. The Cosmonaut, tall, ski-jump nose, a mountain man. Abs, the guy everyone liked was built like a statue, with arms ready to fly.

Catfish: "Yo', ma nigga," and the rest of his statement in Spanish. He danced back and forth in front of the mirrors, rapping in a foreign tongue and jabbing like a B-movie boxer. Ashes, here eight years, was the quiet one, his own veins popping from his softball-size biceps.

Flexing and reflecting. Then they lit cigarettes and lounged against the toilet stalls.

Bear had to leave for a few days for a court date in Rochester. Though Rochester was only ninety minutes away from Ellicottville, he faced something like a three or four-hour bus ride, in shackles, just to get there. He'd stay overnight in the county jail and then go to court the next day. Then another overnight after court and the long ride home.

I worked more with Cougar while Bear was gone. Cougar let me read one of his notebooks, which contained number five in his 'hood book series. It was a lively story and a voyeuristic look at a life I hadn't really known existed. Nowhere near my Lockport, it was centered on Pearl Street in Buffalo, with rival gangs battling for drug turf.

I'd answer hundreds of Cougar's questions about publishing. And there was the night that we realized we both had lived in Charlotte, North Carolina, twenty years apart. The Cougar and I had a lot in common.

Despite the Lithium and other psych meds, prison had overwhelmed me. All I wanted to do was sleep. And I wanted to be back home in Lockport, drinking and scoring pills from Danny****. At times, it seemed I had been ripped away from that life by God, but it was only the justice system. Collins had copies of Bibles with book covers that said, "Not Arrested. Rescued." Well, I didn't feel rescued. Most of the time I didn't know what I felt other than disgusted and lost. And worried people were out to get me.[4]

Mark had given me a "rescued" Bible, but Patriot tore pages from it to make rolled cigarettes. He used the ultra-thin pages from the "maps" section, so I was still saved.

I was lying face up on my bed. Cougar was across from me. It was before lunch.

"I want to die when I'm high," I said. My urge to get high was increasing since I had been cut off. Also, I hated it when AA folks would talk about an "old timer" of theirs who died. "At least he was sober," they said. I wouldn't want to die sober.

Cougar heard me and said, "You don't want to die at all. You want to get back in the game." He said I should stay away from drugs and reminded me to stay away from the Three G's (gangs, gays, and gambling).

Something about him made me open up about my depression, as if I was Huck and he was a badass Jim who could help me. I said to him, "We are prisoners on the outside too. We got taxes, relationships, money, work, bills, food, clothing, religion, community, kids, and ex-wives. Oh, and then death."

This time he just shook his head.

I felt I had to break Cougar's rules. I wanted to get high—the only thing that makes prison tolerable. In county, I bought a pill for three soups, and all it did was keep me awake all night. So, hell, if prison was such serious, gangster shit, then I wanted to get serious too. O.G. Or something like that.

4 I found out later that Danny died in early 2018 of complications from a stroke.

More suboxone, it turned out, was right under my nose. I just had to work up the courage to ask for it. It helped that I'd met a new inmate. We got along well. I didn't care when I found out he was gay. My uncle on my mom's side is gay. So there went two of Cougar's rules.

I got angry with Cougar anyway. He wouldn't let me borrow any sugar. That was a big, hairy deal in prison. Also, it seemed like every time I wanted to take another depression nap, Cougar would grab neighbor Urkel and play a loud game of cards on the wall between their cubes, shuffling over and over and slamming winning cards down. I was steaming.

So, I got up from my bed, slipped on my sneakers, and went looking for Ears. A guy had told me he dealt suboxone. It's amazing how quickly you can go from hating someone to liking them when they have drugs to sell.

When I got to his cube, Ears was talking to Patriot about the latter's need to wear a "pad" in his underwear because he often shit himself. Ears held up his hand to me and said, "Later."

I walked back to my cube, where Heat and Bear were grilling the kid, Agony, about touching a little boy's ass.

"You think that was alright?" Heat said. "Putting a Matchbox car in his butt?"

"I was high on heroin," Agony said.

"So that makes it alright? Millions of people have been high on heroin. That didn't make them stick their fingers up little kids' asses," said Heat. "Bear, can you help me out here?"

"Have you touched other kids?" Bear inquired. "Other than this one?"

"No," Agony said.

"I bet you have, man," Bear said, laughing angrily. "I bet you have."

Agony said, "I don't use drugs or alcohol anymore."

Heat said, "Why would that stop you?"

Across from my cube, Urkel was listening to hip-hop tapes on his "Walkman" radio and singing all the lyrics he heard. Yesterday, he tried to tell me he was in jail for nineteen years for a stabbing. I did not believe him.

I touched Urkel's arm to get his attention. He looked at me and removed the headphones.

"Do you know where I can get any, um…" Why was I nervous?

"Any what?"

"You know, chineta."

He put the headphones back on. But then he said, "Ask Jo Jo."

Out of the whole dorm, Jo Jo was the more obvious one. He was white and looked like a smooth character who might have worked at a bank or investment firm. He always sat in his cube with his neighbor, Bean, next to him. Urkel told me they were drug buddies, but I didn't know they sold drugs, or if Jo Jo did.

Disliking Ears, I felt better about dealing with Jo Jo, as long as he was cool. In fact, once I got to his cube, that's what I asked him. "Are you cool?"

"Of course. You're Brandon, right?"

"Yes, and I'm not a rapo."

He looked at me funny. "I kind of figured that. What did you do?"

"I got two years for selling suboxone to a C.I."

"Oh, yeah? Do you buy bricks?" He meant cigarettes. One $10 pack equaled one piece of chineta. If I bought bricks, that meant, because he'd never seen me smoking, I was potentially a good customer.

"Yeah, in exchange," I said. "I'm looking."

Jo Jo nodded. "I'm going out to the yard tonight. I'll let you know."

I thanked him, waved to Bean, who nodded, and went on my way.

That night, I skipped rec in the yard. Jo Jo was nowhere to be found, so I figured he was outside, as he said he would be. I wandered into the TV room and caught an episode of "House, M.D." Dr. House was making a bet with his friend Dr. Wilson about how long they could have live chickens in the hospital before security noticed. It was my favorite series. But the patient in this episode tried to kill herself.

I felt myself starting to seize up with an anxiety attack. I had watched "House" when I had my own apartment. Every time the good doctor popped a Vicodin, I'd match him with a pill of my own, washing it down with Four Loko. I felt scared and bewildered. That art gallery-sized apartment, my independent life in my hometown, my friends, my possessions, my pills and booze, my euphoria—it was all gone. I was now babysat by creeps in uniform. Douglas Dodd, author of *Generation Oxy*, shared my experience of going from cloudy drug happiness to a crash landing. Dodd wrote: "Although prescription painkillers took me to all-time highs, they led to a downward spiral that brought my life to a deeper, darker place than I could have imagined." Completely isolated from the world, I was surrounded by strangers, many of whom had abused children. Some had killed people.

"You okay?" an inmate asked. He was one of the few I'd not yet met. There were only three of us in the TV room. Nearly everyone else, including the big-mouths, were out at rec.

I was holding my head as if it was going to roll off my neck. "I think so. I just thought of a bad memory."

The inmate said, "Don't do that. You not gonna be here forever, O.G."

I thanked him and wondered if my meds were off. The sleeping depression, the anxiety attacks, feeling at any moment as if the other shoe was going to drop and I'd be hauled off to The Box.

I stood and went to the window. Outside, a soccer game was being played, and I was transported back to those innocent times on the field in Charlotte. It was 1978. I was eleven. At the window, I did breathing exercises. But prison wouldn't go away.

Back at my cube, I saw Cougar, now back from rec. That meant Jo Jo was also back. I think two hours passed before Jo Jo decided to come my way. I tried to keep busy reading *The Goldfinch* by Donna Tartt, a real solid find from the prison library. It was a guaranteed intellectual escape from my surroundings.

Then came Tartt's line about people like us: "What if the heart, for its own unfathomable reasons, leads one willfully and on a cloud of unspeakable radiance away from health, domesticity, civic responsibility, and strong social connections and all the blandly-held common virtues straight toward a beautiful flare of ruin, self-immolation, disaster?"

The library, in the school building, held universal wisdom—musings that helped me understand where I was, why I was there, and, sometimes how to get to that clean, happy, inspiring place called the future. But there was an ogre in polyester at the door—the librarian. There were also three inmate assistants for the six or seven prisoners who'd go to the library at break time.

The Collins library, located on B side, was the size of a family camping tent, but packed in was a wide selection of new and popular titles, classics, Spanish language books, modern American literature, coffee table books, biographies, politics, and more. There were also current magazines and newspapers. Wanting to read a book on the Attica riots, I filled out the form and handed it to this gubba librarian, who refused to speak to anyone, at least every time I was there. Even the prison assistants avoided her.

I said, "Excuse me" and handed her my form. She took a fast look and said, her neck waddle shaking, "No way. I can't order this."

"Why?" I said.

"It's about a prison riot," she said, returning to her desk work.

"It's a history book, not a how-to," I explained, politely and calmly. "I am doing a project."

"I told you, I'm not fucking ordering it."

She sounded … identical to a C.O. *Was the Podunk town of Collins cloning these obtuse robots?*

In the end, I never got the Attica tome. And that was that.

I heard Jo Jo approach, "Hold out your hand, low," he said softly. I complied. His movement was so fast, I nearly missed it, but there in my palm was a square of orange suboxone. "You owe me a brick," he said, easing away. I wasn't worried about the money—friends were supporting me for commissary. But I was worried and paranoid about getting busted.

Urkel, who saw the exchange, actually winked at me. What was he, twenty? I figured he was a crack-baby, now all grown-up. Bear said the adult crack-babies were here to torture us. Crack-babies became prominent in the 1980s when smokable cocaine was all the rage in the cities, and addicted soon-to-be mothers showed up in emergency rooms. I recall the child abuse stories then—babies left in a car seat, car radio blasting bass-based hip-hop, while the parent lingered at the gas station, making the buy. It added up: the screaming at home then, the noise in the dorm now.

I looked around to see if anyone else was watching me. Pastor Mark walked out of his cube on his way to see Zoom. No one was eyeing me. I sat on my bed with the piece and my fingernail clippers. I cut the piece in two, one for now and one for tomorrow. I hadn't had a sub since being at Rachael's before court.

I took my water bottle and poured a drop onto my plastic spoon and dropped in the sub. Then I put the spoon deep into my locker so the sub could dissolve. For a second, I thought of selling the other half (exactly what put me in prison), and decided it'd be better to wake and bake first thing tomorrow.

I let five minutes pass, pretending to read Donna Tartt. Making one last check that no one was watching me, I caught the C.O.'s glance. But Napoleon, having scanned the dorm himself, had gone back to reading his *Buffalo News*.

The book *Recovery by Choice* explains that "sometimes a near-relapse situation arises because the person never understood or has forgotten why they stopped drinking/using to begin with, or because the situation has changed so that those reasons no longer pertain."

Thinking about how ugly my life had become, I decided that using a drug was my way to get back at The Man, the system, the cops, the C.O.s, and even my ex-wife.

You all locked me up, but you can't stop me from using. And it made me feel great.

The sub dissolved, I took the spoon and bent my knees, so I was completely behind my walls. I sniffed the water drop in and felt part of it hit my stomach. Addicts have preferred systems of intoxicant delivery, and the nostril had been mine, ever since my cocaine days. I used to use both nostrils. Randy, a friend from Lockport, told me it all went to the brain (and lungs and stomach) anyway, so choose a nostril. I chose the right, and it had been that way ever since.

My wife once told me Billy Joel sniffed a hole in his nose from cocaine use, though that may have been an urban legend. Still, I'd been waiting for my hole to open up. I gave up cocaine because of anxiety and switched to opiate and other pills. I had sniffed Opanas, Roxycodone, Hydrocodone, Oxycodone, Adderrall, Wellbutrin, Xanax, and Ativan, and I couldn't remember the others. Oh, suboxone too. In a span of about twelve years. Alcohol was a standard all through those years.

I hid the spoon in my locker, and then hid the other piece in the front pocket of a pair of my underpants. Growing paranoid, I looked to Cougar's cube and saw he was somewhere else.

It took about ten minutes. I was high, feeling the euphoria, thinking it was finally time, after three months, to clean my cubicle. Massive energy boost. I grabbed the broom and mop from the slop sink room and went to work. Pastor Mark stopped by. Leaning on my wall, he told me about his religious test case—Agony.

"He says after he serves his seven years, he's going to join the church," said Pastor Mark.

"I don't like Agony," I said. "He has psychosocial disorder, or something that makes his personality a kind of poison. I'm sick of him."

I looked at Pastor Mark and smiled—I was really feeling the drug now.

"What's gotten into you, B-love? Actually cleaning? Will you do my cube next?"

I said yes. Everything was beautiful, being in prison didn't matter, and I loved everyone. There was clarity, my noise didn't matter, my bid wasn't that long. I was funny, fun, and full of literary ideas that I scribbled into my notebook. I gave an encouraging speech to Bear (he knew what was up), who said thank you. I wanted him to keep up his passion about the project.

After about two hours, I got a terrible stomachache. I knew the sub had gotten me when I sniffed too hard. When my mouth got that pre-vomit spit going, I knew I was going to throw up my coffee and a honey bun. Scooting to the restroom, I had to ask Drea, a smoker, to clear out of a stall. "I feel sick," I said. Drea moved fast and I made it to that toilet just in time. Most of my dinner came up. So did the coffee and the honey bun. But I felt so much better, lighter and happy—and ready to rest. At 8:30, I fell asleep in my cube and stayed that way until our 10 p.m. count. My sleep felt like I was riding a carpet of peace, love, and safety. Where no one could hurt me.

Not that night.

With a big smile on my face, I was up at 5:30 a.m. I had more chineta to start this wonderful day. Snores hummed all around me in the half light. The best thing about drugs was that they insulated you from the world around you. While all the stupidity, fear, and madness swirled about you, you were in your own world and others could visit, but only if you let them in.

The drug was in that pair of underpants. I slid the piece out and repeated the same process with the spoon. The C.O. was someone I didn't recognize. And he was asleep, under his jacket. The dorm was cool in the early morning hours, because these morons kept their windows open. Of course, thin man Urkel's was closed!

I got smart and sniffed gently at the sub water, so it wouldn't go straight through my nose and down my throat. I felt it stay, right in my nose. Just a tiny drop of sub water. I pressed my nostril down to get the sub to soak in and congratulated myself for having addiction down to a science.

The C.O. called count at 6 a.m. and I was wearing my greens and boots, ready for chow. I read a little of *The Goldfinch*, smiling the whole time. I briefly got paranoid, figuring some fellow inmates would see my dilated eyes and know. So, I decided to wear my reading glasses, unpolished, to throw everyone off.

Normally the walk to chow—down three flights of stairs, and up the walkway to the mess hall—was a bitch. When there was no wind, I was surrounded by clouds of cigarette smoke, and cigarette exhalations. These guys were chain smokers.

Today, I didn't really care, just strolling along, nice and hungry. Breakfast was cracked wheat cereal, coffeecake, and apple juice. I was ravenous. I didn't even feel sick when watching guys pour their milk over their coffeecake. We were all equals. No one was below me. This prison thing wasn't so bad after all. And I could see clearly why the law wanted me locked up. I was a naughty boy.

Two days later, our C.O. regular disappeared. In his place was another guy I didn't know. It was about 8:30 when we learned morning rec had been canceled. That sucked because I wanted all the nut jobs gone while I read and edited Bear's new pages.

But everything seemed off. There was no movement outside. The normal noise of the prison day had been replaced by eerie silence. I was reminded of a passage in John Howard Griffin's *Black Like Me* that I thought applied to the various races of his dorm-mates. But it was really about his moment. "Tension hung in the air, a continual threat, even though you couldn't put your finger on it."

Ears (the know-it-all) interrupted everything with his weirdo wigger talk. "Yo, my nigga. Rec was canceled because nigga's getting raided—"

"Get to your fucking cubes!" interrupted a screaming C.O. who came stomping into our area. Ten other officers rushed in, looking and sounding as if they'd just completed a 5k.

"Get to your cubes now!" shouted another. "Stand in front with your hands behind your backs. Watch them!" he said to the other C.O.s. "If they reach in their pockets or put anything in their mouths, take their heads off!"

The noisy sergeant, Jebstick, did his best to order us around and intimidate us. I admit I was fearful at first, this being my first drug raid ever. But some of the characters in here had been through multiple raids in their own homes, with Grandma and everyone. On their faces were ironic grins.

"No talking!"

We were ordered to strip down to our underwear and put our clothes on our beds, without going into our cubes. So, shirts and pants began flying. My Lithium was working, so though my legs were shaking from adrenalin, I was in control. Thank goodness this raid hadn't happened two days earlier.

Jebstick continued to yell. "Stay out of your cubes. Face the wall. Don't look at me."

I wondered how long this was all going to take. Pastor Mark looked terrified. Urkel seemed to be somewhere in outer space. Bear just shook his head, whispering, "Routine shit." Cougar waved his finger at me as if I'd been bad and had caused this. He grinned, then put on a serious face, as if he was changing masks. I wasn't sure why. And Heat was sweating. He had tattoo contraband in his cube and who knows what else.

I found out later this raid was really a weapon search. Sometime right after breakfast, a Latino named Monk (not to be confused with Easton's neighbor, Mork) had been frisked, a shank was found, and Monk was now in The Box. The COs figured we had more shanks to hide.

Systematically, the goon squad rifled through our belongings, taking over two hours to find nothing. The one inmate I knew who was holding swallowed his balloon of suboxone just in time.

We all had to take our cube chairs to the TV room. Having arranged them in three rows, we all sat there—claustrophobia setting in—wearing only our underwear. We waited while individual inmates were picked out and given extra scrutiny—via questions, and even some anal probes in the laundry room. These goons were thorough.

Then, one by one, we walked through a metal detector. I guess if a blade could be hidden under the skin, this device would find it. Inmates are known for boofing shanks, so there was that possibility too. The line would have gone faster, but the C.O.s wanted to yell at and belittle everyone first.

Maintenance workers had been summoned to open wall heaters and cubicle walls, but only three guys showed up, so that plan was scrapped. I laughed. The

Man couldn't keep his shit together.

"We'll be here all day," one C.O. said. "We asked for eight guys."

Once the raid was over and the Gestapo split, it took hours to put our stuff back together. The C.O.s had flipped tables, messed up the kitchen, and left everything for us to clean up. Cougar's books, notebooks, and letters were strewn about. I helped him once I was done with my cube.

Everything I owned was taken from me before entering prison. The administration handed out rations of toothbrushes, toothpaste, soap and toilet paper. And trauma and grief—those were free, and you got your fill of it every day.

I had no cup. Lithium made me very thirsty, all day long. A cup was necessary. I drank out of an old, cleaned-out peanut butter jar. My garbage can was an empty cashew container. I didn't have a pillow, or a laundry netbag. I had to use my cloth pillowcase as a netbag.

I am a writer and an only child, so I am used to being alone. That was a problem for me when I got divorced and went to inpatient treatment programs, where I was surrounded by thirty to sixty other people, and staff, for twenty-eight days. The counselors and therapists said I was "too alone." In addiction, they claimed, I had to be around other people to heal and "start living a new life without intoxicants." Now it never mattered to me whether I was alone or with others. Getting high was just plain fun. And my Higher Power loved it too.

Throwing responsibility out the window was my thing. During my marriage, my wife told other people, "Brandon thinks he can do whatever he wants."

The inpatient programs weren't that bad because I knew I would be going back home. I enjoyed Christmas at Mount St. Mary's Hospital because we all drew our "best Christmas tree." It was nice being surrounded by thirty addicts for the holiday. We made the best of it with brownies and Kool-Aid.

To suddenly live with sixty other guys, in a dirty PRISON, where no one was going home very soon, bent my brain into horrible shapes. I couldn't think. There was nowhere to be alone.

Because of the constant restroom smoking, the whole place smelled like an ashtray. And sweat. I became disoriented. The guy next to me did not know what "obnoxious" meant. Everyone seemed selfish. The same reaction to situations was nearly universal among my brethren: "That's crazy" and "This shit crazy." I had to sit on my bed whenever I got dizzy like this, so no one would know. My dream last night set in a summer park, then a mental institution. Kurt Cobain and I were sitting together on a park bench, watching a wide river flow. The top of Cobain's head was missing. Panic attack. Death was only a nightstick away.

Walking helped me breathe. I went to the restroom. Astonishingly, no one was there. I went into a stall to urinate because I didn't want to see anyone; the smell of smoke made it seem as if others were there. Flushing, I opened the door and went to the sink to wash. Suddenly, behind me, a C.O. I didn't recognize accused me of smoking in the restroom.

I listened and let him finish. Then I said, "I've never smoked a cigarette in my life."

Neck veins bulging, the officer shouted, "You're a fucking liar! I ever catch you smoking in here again, there'll be a kind of trouble you've never seen in your life!" Then he exited.

Smoking in the restroom was tolerated by some officers, outlawed by others. Sometimes, when an inmate was caught sneaking a puff, the officers would punish the whole dorm by confiscating our microwave, toaster, hotpot, and stove top. Ours was a master-servant relationship.

I saw my mental health counselor, Mr. P., once a month. In his spacy, quiet, air-conditioned office, I felt almost alone. He spoke softly—he reminded me of a high school English teacher. Adverb. Gerund. Metaphor.

I told Mr. P. about my anxiety and why I suffered from it almost daily. He listened, took notes, set his pen down, and joined his hands together as if ready to pray.

"How do you feel about yourself?" he said.

I had to think about that. "I don't like myself," I said. "I don't like anyone here. Not that I am supposed to, you know. I feel claustrophobic, angry, and poisoned by the atmosphere. I want to rebel against my captors. I'm surrounded by sex offenders, but they are the only friendly people. I feel all of this at once."

Mr. P. said, "You express yourself well. I hear claustrophobic a lot. Do you meditate? Take time out and just breathe? Try to clear your mind?"

I thought of the Muslims kneeling and praying on those magic mini-carpets of theirs. I laughed out loud, at myself.

"Well, you're laughing." Mr. P. said. "That's healthy."

Getting back to the dorm, I saw that Bear had returned from his out-of-prison trip. He was rather happy, noting that some smaller charges in his drug case had been dropped. And he had been cleared to leave for his treatment class for early release.

Somehow, despite at least three searches on the outside, he made it back into the dorm with several hundred dollars' worth of wafer-thin chineta. I told him he'd missed our drug raid. "I'm just lucky," he said. Then Bear searched the fold in his pant leg and produced a $10 piece for me. "A little more payment for *Hustle*," he said.

Some weeks back, the administration had granted a waiver so I didn't have to take GED classes. If I had to take the GED, I'd have aced the English portion but likely failed the math. Then I would have had to take math classes. Being poor at math proved I was not a real drug dealer. To me anyway.

However, I did have to sign up for and designate a vocation. I met with the Vocation Committee at the school building. The committee consisted of three folks—two women and a man. I had been on a bench in the hallway with other inmates, awaiting my turn to see them. The process involved a twenty-minute wait for a three-minute meeting. The guy was balding but deeply tanned. His head looked like a golden saucer. The women were opposites: one had blond hair, bad skin, and a 1970s paisley dress. The curly-haired brunette had large lips and tiny ears, rhinestone shirt and flowered jeans (was this 1971?).

I had a copy of my medical report, detailing my arthritic back and knees from the 2012 car accident. It said I could not work, basically, and couldn't lift over twenty pounds.

"What are you interested in, Stickley?" said the bald man.

"I don't think I can work a job here," I said. I did not want to work for The Man.

The brunette said, "Well, this is more like school."

"We won't work you too hard," said the bald dude.

I handed them the doctor's report. The brunette eyed it quickly and handed it back to me.

"Let's see," said the man. "Let's put him in plumbing."

They nodded, and I said, "I'm more of a white-collar worker."

That's when I realized Collins had no white-collar jobs for inmates. They had plumbing, painting, groundskeeping, mess hall, etc. All the jobs supported the prison's upkeep—as if we were being forced to dig our own graves. C.O.s or staff never lifted a finger. The prisoners did it all.

"Mr. Stickley," the man said.

"Stickney," I corrected. I could *not* become a plumber. Cleaning toilets?

"Mr. Stinkflea," said the bald guy, "here is your registration. Plumbing starts on Monday. Thank you." And he pointed to the door.

I was fucked.

I was in plumbing class with fourteen other inmates at different levels on the learning hierarchy. The table before us was covered with the stuff you see in everyone's basement, except here it was all taken apart. It all looked like junk to me.

I couldn't believe I had to be here three hours, five days a week. I told myself to stop whining. The plumbing class, run by a rugged dude named Mr. Noodle, was held in the school building's first floor. There was a guard on duty, making sure none of us felons wandered off with any dangerous plumbing tools. I could make $100 by pocketing a screw driver. Bear would have it sold faster than you could say "contraband."

On the table were copper, galvanized steel, PVC, and PEX pipes. There were also cap, coupling, adaptor, union, and elbow fittings. I did not know this equipment—Mr. Noodle was naming them, and saying we had to memorize them, along with all the tools in the "shed" at the end of the room. I took notes for the test, later.

The walls of the room were lined with "jobs": a shower, a toilet, sinks, basins, pumps, and other mock stuff from household and building locales.

I would have been much more comfortable working in the library. I wanted to learn, of course, but not about this. The whole thing was a conflict—plumbers were men's men with workers' hands. As far as I was concerned, Noodle was speaking a foreign language, and I was only just starting to figure out ghetto speak. (I could write the ghetto speak dictionary and become the Collins professor of jive.)

Plumbing classes were supposed to last six months, after which the student would receive a title, like plumber or plumber's assistant. It included creating graphic designs—without a computer—of plumbing installations that the student had to successfully install.

A tall, wiry guy who'd been in the class a while told me: "It's a myth that it's only six months long. You only graduate when you've passed all your tests."

I had been counting on getting out after six months. Students were all at different levels: some were beginners like me, others had been there for three months, and still others were working on their own plumbing designs.

I felt as if I was in an ugly kind of alone. I was not on the same level as any of these future plumbers of America. I told a guy across the table I didn't watch WWE, and he looked at me like I was the dummy.

He was just one of the kooks in plumbing. A stinking plump dude who sat next to me told a slopehead buddy that "microwaves cause cancer." The guy had a thousand theories, each more profound and life-changing than the next. "All medicine is poisonous," he added. "It kills your liver."

Our teacher might as well have been named Mr. Moody. Some days he spoke with us, and other days he was silent. Two days in a row, he made us watch fire safety videos from 1978. In the videos, the actors' outfits were just as snazzy as the guy who testified about getting burned. "I did not know I was about to be engulfed in a ball of fire," he said.

Other than that, it was stare-out-the-window time.

A visitor broke the boredom. On Noodle's desk was one computer, dating back to when Apple itself launched. Two days after I started plumbing class, a C.O. and two inmates informed Noodle they had to remove the computer for "security reasons." The same wiry man said, "They've taken all the computers at Collins and locked them in a basement. They caught an inmate trying to get porn."

The plumbing computer was the last one to go, putting the entire campus back to the 1970s. It was a theme here, and I hummed a bit of "Stayin' Alive."

CELL #10

It is true that we focus myopically on the existing

system—and perhaps this is the problem that leads

to the assumption that imprisonment is the only

alternative to death—it is very hard to imagine a

structurally similar system capable of handling such

a vast population of lawbreakers.

CHAPTER 10

INTERVIEW WITH AN OFFENDER

"All men are liable to error; and most men are, in many points,
by passion or interest, under temptation to it."—John Locke

P ressure, fear, and anxiety continued to chip away at me. Was my medication really working? I started going off, about smokers, ghetto speak,
and the mess hall. Everyone complained about the mess hall food, with
good reason. Soy and no meat? That was just the beginning.

The mess hall wall had a poster-sized sign that listed twenty "don'ts", including talking loudly, fighting, and wearing hats. Kufis were okay. The sign said we
had twenty minutes for chow. Actually, by the time they called our dorm for chow,
we got out of the building, walked to the mess hall, stood in line, and sat down to
eat, most of that promised twenty minutes had been eaten up. I recall taking just a
few initial bites and the sergeant saying, "Okay, let's wrap it up."

The abuse by the C.O.s was particularly bad at chow. The heat I took for
forgetting my spoon at Elmira was nothing. C.O.s routinely frisked and roughed
up inmates in search of food they tried to "steal" from the mess hall. Well, they
were taking the food because dinner was at 5 p.m. and there was no more food until
7 a.m., unless the inmates had commissary or a package from home. The inmates
also took food because they didn't have time to eat it during chow. I didn't think it
was stealing—it was our food, paid for by the taxpayers. It was the C.O.s and other
officers who were the thieves. But inmates got stripped, slapped, wacked with a
club, and given tickets.

C.O.s would try to intimidate inmates by standing next to us and staring at
us as we ate. Glaring, actually. As if the inmates had done something wrong. Meals
were ruined by this psychological abuse; they were already ruined by food quality
issues.

Most meals were "meat" sauce poured over rice or pasta. Sometimes there was
grilled cheese or the rare real chicken meal. All meals were bland, tasteless, and

needed salt. We had some derivative of apples fourteen times in two weeks: an apple, apple sauce, apple crisp, apple jelly, and apple juice. The baloney was green. Complaints were lodged. The kitchen manager with the drunk's nose told us it was because of oxidation. Big word. Air did it? How come none of the other baloney I ever saw in my life was like this? It all added up to "inadequate nutrition," according to "Survivors Speak," a prison abuses report by the American Friends Service Committee.

The apple crisp was delicious, probably the best thing the mess hall served. Seeing the C.O.s walk out of the mess hall with take-home containers of apple crisp was sickening, though. A female C.O. told me on a Wednesday afternoon that she loved apple crisp, especially since the kitchen served it to her on Mondays. Sarcastically, I said, "That's sweet, Officer." She didn't pick up on it, which was good since I could've gotten the night stick, a ticket, or both for being disrespectful. Male C.O.s pounded your head in if you were disrespectful to any female.

At meals, we often ran out of apple crisp, chocolate cake, vanilla pudding, and, of course, ice cream. I'm surprised the C.O.s weren't fatter.

We also received beans at nearly every lunch or dinner. The worst case was chili which, obviously, came with a side of three-bean salad!

The two worst meals were on Fridays: Wheatena for breakfast and veggie pasta with vegetable sauce at dinner. *Yuck*. Wheatena is basically fiber-wheat birdseed with a watery brown gravy. You could add a hundred sugar packets and it still would have no flavor.

The grape juice came in plastic containers with silt at the bottom. The bread was so thin it was transparent. All the other bread items, like hot dog rolls, were stale. And the mushy oranges had white fuzz on them.

After a few months passed, talk increased of getting out. The prison offered a couple of addiction treatment programs that, if passed, would reduce an inmate's sentence by about four months. Prisons play with time when it comes to when a prisoner may be freed.

I had a merit date of May 14, 2018, which meant I needed to do everything the prison asked me to do and not get in trouble. Then there was the conditional release date of August 28, 2018, which was if I didn't do anything wrong but didn't complete any classes. Finally, there was the end release date of December 14, 2018, which was the longest they could hold me on my two-year sentence. I had already completed four and a half months in county jail, which counted toward those two years.

Bear was waiting for his treatment program to start. He'd leave Collins and go to another prison somewhere in the system—Collins did not offer addiction counseling. Because our prisons were filled with drug offense convicts, you'd expect every jail and prison to have a comprehensive, on-site treatment program.

Bear urged me to sign up for a program like his. It wasn't hard to make the decision, yet I'd soon learn that Albany's written descriptions of prisons and their programs leave out the reality of day-to-day life at its facilities, as in the case of my old friend Stan, who received a felony DWI when his car crashed in Lockport and his seatbelt-less passenger was killed.

Stan went to the state's friendliest prison, Groveland. I was told over and over that Groveland's prisoners had the most freedom: the yard and libraries were open all day, the C.O.s were civil, and it didn't even seem like jail. That didn't stop an inmate from trying to cut Stan with a shank—another inmate intervened and stopped the attack.

My complaining about Collins was valid, though I did not yet know how bad things could really get. I asked Bear why he was always so happy and motivated after twenty-three years in prison. He said he was used to it, he knew he'd soon be free again, and his incarceration was simply the result of his love for drugs. His enthusiasm for the book he called *Hustle* was what kept me going during my prison misery.

Inmates crawled out of the woodwork with horror stories. I noticed that Cory (no handle) was missing teeth on the right side of his head the time he asked me if I wanted to buy some K2 from him. I said no, but we talked for a while because he was from Western New York.

Cory said he was at another prison dorm before Collins. The C.O. who came on duty at 11 p.m. was drunk, Cory explained, and fell asleep at his desk, or "bubble" as it was called. He was holding up his head until his arm slipped over. The C.O. then accidentally hit and injured his eye on the corner of the desk.

But instead of telling the truth to the sergeant, the C.O. claimed that one of the inmates had hit him in the head with a padlock placed inside an athletic sock—a so-called "slock" was a common weapon among prisoners. The C.O. wasn't sure whose it was.

"After that, the C.O.s came in, handcuffed a bunch of us, and beat the shit out of us," Cory said. "I lost four teeth." What kind of a coward handcuffs a guy and then beats him up? Cory claimed the inmates banded together on a $35 million lawsuit against the prison. Journalist and former C.O. Ted Conover explained: "... That there is a current of brutality in corrections work is hard to deny. Anyone who follows the news knows you don't have to look far to see correction officers at their worst."

That's the truth. Then there's the "truth" that comes from street cops and corrections officers who commit crimes against victims and inmates and then hide behind "the blue wall of silence." Truths are inverted and twisted to exonerate officers, not victims.

Essayist Ron Daniels wrote in *Police Brutality*: "... Because of the 'we against them' fraternity mentality ... it has always been difficult to prove police brutality cases. Police officers often refuse to come forward and expose brutal and corrupt fellow officers. Police departments seldom vigorously investigate allegations of police misconduct." The corrections departments I saw had some good, trustworthy officers, but there also seemed to be a lot of bad eggs, almost proud to be corrupt, and happy to make their malicious presence known.

The court, unsurprisingly, is often on the side of the cops. "Few police officers ever face trial for shooting deaths, let alone are convicted," said reporter Madison Park for CNN in an October 2, 2018 report. Some corrections officers cover up their own crimes against inmates. Trials are held annually to find out a reason, and a responsible party.

The noise got to be too much in the dorm, in the mess hall, on the walkway. Certain groups of inmates would get excited about something and they'd all have to pipe in at once—no one listening, everyone shouting. I was the small-town boy witnessing a big-city ghetto thing that I didn't understand and didn't want to. I just wanted them to shut up. Just as James Baldwin had written in the 1960s, the laughing he heard outside was not from joy. It was angry, mocking laughter.

I found the inmates from the five boroughs to be the hardest to tolerate—they all seemed to have that New York thing, where you always have a rude comment or complaint about something. They were critical of everyone, constantly smelled odors they didn't like, and argued in front of the TV, especially during basketball season. As a rural child, I found these noise boxes to be a daily hassle. My ears were bent by the audio assault. Writer and former inmate Jimmy Lerner said, "A New Yorker will tell you exactly what he thinks—to your face. None of this 'Have a nice day' bullshit and then stab you in the back."

My prejudices seemed to come out in the mess hall. Because I hail from Lockport, I believed that a majority of Americans are bigots. They didn't admit it and they kept quiet about it. I am sure that there were people in certain cultures who disliked me because I am white. It's funny. On the news, political pundits call each other racist. As if it's a capital crime. There is no law against being a bigot. You don't have to like other races if you don't want to. But that doesn't mean you're going to hurt someone you don't like.

The prison cultures, the voices, the dances, all rubbed me the wrong way in the mess hall. There they were so disrespectful—it was obvious they never had the gift of a role model or mentor, and whose fault is that? I'm a "Heinz 57," said a white man with many European nationalities in his genes (me). And there's folks of my own color who had stepped over the line long ago.

Jack Henry Abbott put you right there in the mess hall with him in his memoir, *In the Belly of the Beast*. Abbott said, "How would you like to be forced all the days of your life to sit beside a stinking, stupid wino every morning at breakfast? Or some loud fool in his infinite ignorance to be at any moment able to say (slur), 'Gimme a cigarette, man!' And I just look into his sleazy eyes and want to kill his ass there in front of God and everyone."

As payment for editing the first draft of his manuscript, Bear gave me a bunch of things: food, chineta, and, on the best day, a set of earplugs! Evenings and mornings were a breeze; I went to sleep and stayed asleep. Most of the time, the voices around me mattered not. I finally learned to tune them right out.

The noise boxes included Gotti, Pee Wee, Young Life, Bo, Heat, Cowboy, Patriot, and Nairobi. The final inmate on that list was in a category all his own. But at the top of the list came "The Cyclops," a man of forty with one bulging eye and the other cloudy, bathed in a pool of goop, lower than the bulging eye. The damaged eye revolved around his head, below cheek level, a kind of broken satellite. He was a tall, imposing man, yet held his arms and legs like the Scarecrow, as if they had been pinned.

When The Cyclops woke at his cube each morning, the mouth got going. He rose for the restroom, brushed his teeth, got new clothes, and slipped on his boots. The activities were interspersed with vocalizations and moans:

- Oh, Body
- Shiiiit, Body
- Pshooooooooooooo
- My pain, Lawd
- Holy Jesus, Joseph, and Mary

These proclamations would stop when one of his neighboring Muslims would speak to him, or when he started in on his coffee.

Now Nairobi was also in a noise box category all his own. He was the darkest black I've ever seen, tall with short nappy hair. Walking around, sweaty and shirtless, he squared off like a kickboxer or cage-fighter.

On this day, he was standing in the middle of the dorm yelling about pickup basketball games. He spoke as if they were March Madness rivalries. Unchewed popcorn spewed from his mouth. "You trippin' nigga," he said. "You foulin', we foulin', we playin' our team."

Behind me, Urkel's voice rose, interrupting Nairobi. "I got a squirter," Urkel said to Bear. "She blew me, and her pants got all wet. Soaked the front seat of the car.".

I had earplugs and wanted to wear them all the time. But they were contraband, so I had to hide them, especially during count. Most times, I wished I were deaf. I told Pastor Mark that I was going to take a pen and poke my eardrums out. A radio would help. Commissary sold radios for $30 each, and some inmates had them, but the price seemed steep to me, and inmates said the reception was poor because we were in the hills. At times, that was the worst part of prison (in addition to psychological abuse)—the constant audio assault. Human noise. At least no one engaged in ghetto speak in their sleep.

We walked to the Phase I classroom and saw a TV playing a DVD. I was excited. Maybe we were going to see a movie or educational show—anything was better than another six hours of ghetto speak by our IPAs and their "That's a fact"-uttering minion.

The stage was set. The faux test papers lined the tables. We were all in our seats. Our leaders, Freddie and Neal, checked the DVD player and put on an educational show. Freddie then turned the volume all the way down so they could talk. I wished I'd brought my earplugs.

The beer can-shaped Latino man tried nodding off on his arm, but Freddie woke him, saying the C.O. could walk by at any minute.

I thought, *What if I get to Phase II and am responsible for everything I was supposed to learn in here?* I couldn't turn Freddie and Neal in to the administration because that would be narcing, which is forbidden in any prison. That's what the guys with the scars on their faces had done—narced. And they remembered it forever.

Former inmate Michael G. Santos spoke of narcs in his book, *Inside: Life Behind Bars in America*. Santos wrote: "…Some men find it to their advantage to whisper into a staff member's ear or pass a note. In exchange, the informant may receive exoneration from a disciplinary infraction, a transfer to a preferred prison, a cigarette, or an extra scoop of cereal. Staff members do what they can to protect and coddle their informants…" But they can't be everywhere. Sometimes that narc is going to wind up getting cut.

Marathon chattering—the Phase I brothers sure could keep it going on food, Islam, boxing, women, fights, shootings, Farrakhan, thefts, thug life… Pudd was at it with his, "That's a fact."

A C.O. came by near the end of class and woke up a pudgy kid in the back. We were let out shortly after that, only to find that same C.O. sleeping at his desk.

That night at dinner, Pudd decided he'd get in my face. Maybe he knew that the Beer Can man and I were making fun of his "That's a fact" stuff. I'm not sure, but there I was, waiting in the dinner line for my slice of meatloaf when Pudd said, "There you are." I nodded to him. Then he started talking baby-talk to me and mentioning little kids, as if he was trying to indicate to the dinner crowd that I was a pedophile. As he tried to fight his way through the line to get near me, Pudd was wearing his kufi. I immediately knew how to handle him.

Back at the dorm, I called for Cougar and explained the situation. Cougar nodded and called Nobel over.

"He's beefin'," said Cougar.

Nobel said, "What is it, B-love?"

"This guy," I said. "I call him Pudd. He looks vaguely Latino and Eastern Indian, wears a kufi, is in my morning Phase I class. He disrespected me."

Nobel knew him almost immediately. "What do you want to happen?" My mind wandered as to what I could order up for this little jerk. The code says that if I attacked Pudd, I'd bring the wrath of the Muslims down upon me.

But my relationship with Cougar put me in good stead with Nobel. Nobel had already agreed to do an interview with me about his years in prison.

Nobel said, "Let me take care of it." And I knew he would.

My mind turned to getting out of here. Bear was nearly done with his book, he said. *Hustle* did indeed move at lightning speed, a sexy how-to for crackhead shoplifters. There was scene after scene of burglaries, robberies, and cocaine parties, as well as the hilarity that ensued. I urged him to give the plot an arc where the two main characters—based on Bear and his girlfriend—could turn away from this life and redeem themselves. Bear said no, the plot had to move as a linear tale with no redemption.

Bear stressed he wanted his book to follow the format of *Kids*, the controversial 1995 movie by Larry Clark about skateboarding stoner youths in New York City. So, while Bear wanted no solutions, I urged him to offer his characters "an out." I suggested that he have Shauna, the lead female, stop her car at a country church. After a bad weekend of meth use, she would wander into the church—the way Hemingway's characters visited churches in *The Sun Also Rises*—to stare at the crucifixion. Bear used the idea but had her do a primal scream, instead of a prayer, which got her kicked out of the church.

I tried to talk with Bear about the publishing process after revisions. He had a good novella on his hands. Bear needed an agent and a publisher. Cougar had a copy of the *Literary Marketplace*, but Bear shied from using it. At that point, I concluded he might only have one intended reader for the manuscript: his girlfriend.

Our conversations were often about the time I had left in prison. I just did not understand merit time, release dates, "good" time, accrued time—In fact, anything to do with calculating when the fuck I was going home. Not that I had a home to go to—I had bounced from county jail to halfway houses to hospitals to homeless shelters. That was drug court's way of making me quit, and I refused to quit.

Once I left prison, I figured I'd wind up back in a homeless shelter, facing two years of parole. Parole liked to catch parolees using drugs, so their parole terms would be deemed "violated" and the offender sent back to prison. As I looked ahead, I just wanted to get out to drink and inject—what happened after that, well, who cared? A normal, responsible person would not understand this. Bear did, and that's why he'd been in prison for two decades. The drugs are indeed more important than anything. Bear was good at explaining how the state didn't just give everyone a leave date. There were three leave dates with variables—ways to get out early for achievement in school, vocation, and good time. On the other hand, bad inmates could earn more prison time.

There was only one solution, and I knew it. Back with the parents in Palm Beach.

Bear told me to sign up for a class called NYASTP, a six-month program on addiction that would earn me three months off my prison time. NYASTP stood for the New York Abstinence Support Treatment Program. It was "administered" by the state's Department of Corrections and Community Supervision (DOCCS). No one really runs, manages, or supervises anything at prisons. They're created to run themselves with minimal work on the part of humans. And they don't do what they say they do. Nothing is corrected. But the fact that prisons exist make old people and Republicans feel safe at night. These institutions also create a whole bunch of jobs for folks who wouldn't get hired or employed anywhere else.

Because I was no expert on "recovery," I asked Bear what this program could really accomplish for me. He shared the prisoners' skepticism about anything to do with DOCCs. Though I had a successful journalistic and business career, I had struggled with mental illness and addiction for thirty years. How could I pass NYASTP? I was angry at prison, the system, and myself, and I wanted to keep using drugs. "Just take NYASTP and, if you succeed, you get out of prison early," said Bear. "It's worth a try." Bear slapped himself in the forehead and added, "And what if you learn something?"

Right around then, I received another letter from my Uncle Mason, my mother's brother. Mason was well-aware of my addictions, though we had not spoken in a few years. I wasn't mad at him. I really wasn't mad at anyone except my ex-wife—we were supposed to be together in sickness and in health. I got sick and was kicked out.

I was thrilled to receive his letter. Mason wrote: "…I'm happy you are safe and clear. I know prison is a terrible place to be, but it gives you the time you need to learn about yourself and stay clean."

After countless inpatient rehab programs and many trips to the psychiatric hospital, I had learned the only thing that could make me stop, was me. I was not powerless against alcohol, if I personally committed to go without. But I did not have that commitment all the time.

That night, Jo Jo asked if I was in for a twenty. I said sure and he promised that after recreation, I'd be all set. I gave him some commissary food as payment. He showed up after rec to report that his contact almost got caught and had to swallow the balloon. So, to get our stuff, we had to wait a few days until the moron shit it out. I'd never pay Jo Jo again. I had been counting on him, and now I knew he was lying—one does not ask for payment in advance unless they are going to screw you. Against my better judgment, I got a $10 piece from Ears. Which just shows that no matter how much you hate someone, you can never tell them. You might need them to score for you.

Fall came to the Collins campus. From my dorm window, I saw, off in the distance, a dense forest that led to the hills of the Southern Tier. The colors of fall reminded me of freedom, of women I had dated, of rainy nights I had walked the streets of Lockport with my friend Bill Hannigan. We'd pass a small bottle of whiskey back and forth and visit girls in the wealthy section of town. My college years seemed so carefree—a time when nothing mattered. It was when I could do whatever I wanted and not worry about trouble.

When I was in junior high school, I first noticed the smell of cigarette smoke on my shirt. I'm not sure why I didn't notice before; maybe junior high was when I learned to first use my voice in protest and to stand my ground, at least with my parents. Going somewhere in the car, I'd ask Mom or Dad, or whichever smoking parent was driving, to crack their window just an inch. They'd complain that it was winter and tell me to put my passenger side window down. "Then all the smoke will go right in my face," I'd say. So, they'd huff and puff and put their own window down a bit.

I learned in state prison that, in most cases, nonsmokers cannot become friends with smokers. To a nonsmoker, smokers are elusive, clan-like, dependent. Before prison, I observed co-workers and friends smoking in the last places smokers were allowed to go in America: porches, parks, back parking lots, designated smoking rooms, and shadowy alleyways, near dumpsters and stray cats.

Like an addict, the prison smoker is always on the quest for more. Take the case of our dorm's Leroy, a Vietnam vet, who had lost all his teeth. He was a kook who always looked as if he was sucking his lips in. Leroy's cube was in the dorm's center aisle. When it was empty, that meant Leroy was in the restroom smoking a rolled cigarette, the cheapest way for smokers to get their fix. Commissary sold bags of tobacco and rolling papers.

When Leroy was in his cube, that meant he would soon walk to the restroom. When he was out of his own tobacco, he bummed rollies from others. "Can I get a bust down?" meant "May I have the last few puffs of your cigarette?" If you were bored, you could watch Leroy walk to the restroom, find no smokers there, and walk back to his cube. Then he'd leave his cube and go again to the restroom. He'd sometimes complete the process three times in five minutes, unless he found a smoker from whom to beg.

He was a true nicotine addict. The prison—and thus New York State—encouraged the addiction by selling cigarettes at the commissary. The state profited from the sales. And, of course, there was no smoking cessation program at Collins. The majority of prisoners at Collins were sex offenders, then drug addicts or convicted drug dealers. This mirrors the national statistic: Sixty-five percent of our 2.3

million inmates are addicts as well.

At times, there were at least ten smokers in a restroom that had only three toilets and two urinals. A cloud was always hovering and swirling. A smoker like Ears or Urkel gave me a dirty look whenever I told them I needed to use the stall—I was interrupting their Newport or rollie. I felt some days as if I had second hand-smoked the equivalent of two packs of cigarettes. I inhaled smoke on the walkway, outside the dorm, on the way to get meds, in the restroom, and even in my own cube. Heat, when giving a fellow inmate a tattoo, never failed to light up. I complained loudly when I could not get a toilet stall, but to Heat and his buddy of the day, I said nothing. It wasn't worth it to antagonize a smoker or a cube neighbor because things would just get worse.

My two closest inmate friends were Bear and Pastor Mark. I confided in both of them that I was writing an essay on how smokers cannot befriend nonsmokers.

I told Bear, "It's not Max Perkins, but I'll at least prove these prisons shouldn't be profiting from or selling cigarettes."

"This prison is profiting from us in many ways." Bear said, "Cigarettes are one way, and imprisoning addicts is another way. Prison is a business, and America leads the world in providing space for and profiting from us."

Pastor Mark said, "Who is Max Perkins?"

"This guy who edited Hemingway, Fitzgerald, and others," I explained. "Perkins was very opinionated and got in a lot of trouble for his views. Like H.L. Mencken."

"Well, you'll have that down," said Bear. "You get cigarettes banned from prisons, you'll get killed."

"That's why they have cigarettes," said Pastor Mark. "To keep these maniacs calm. Could you imagine what would happen if they didn't?"

Bear said, "Stickney'd be dead. They'd smoke him."

The majority of my dorm-mates were smokers. Leroy found a lot of bust downs. He paid his benefactors back once every two months when he received a package from his wife in Freeport. He received tobacco, rollies, chocolate, chips, coffee, and other sought-after items. It was sad really —he would be mobbed by "friends" who took whatever they could, like seagulls going at a bag of Doritos. They were practically robbing him. I thought he was lying when he said, "I don't give a fuck. When I get it, I give it away."

I wondered how these chain smokers could survive. Leroy's case made me study all of them. If they were going to choke me, at least I was going to get something out of it. Upon waking to count at 6 a.m., I fought the urge to go back to sleep, but instead I watched them. Some were already awake, hitting the restroom for that first one of the day.

Chow was called, and we filed out of the building. Some smokers already had unlit smokes between their lips, ready to fire the lighter upon reaching the exit downstairs. They smoked on the way to the mess hall. Not allowed to linger and finish the cigarettes at the mess hall entrance, the smokers put the burning end, or "cherry," out in their hands or on the pavement.

Once breakfast was completed, it was time for another on the way back to the dorm. Those who went to get medication had another on the way there and one on the way back. The others went to the restroom upon returning from chow. They stacked the smokes. Those who went to morning GED class or to work at Buildings & Grounds lit up there and back. Buildings & Grounds workers smoked during their entire shift.

Sometimes, when an inmate would be caught in a minor rule infraction, the C.O. would order him to pick up cigarette butts near the flower gardens or in front of the dorm building. The inmate would smoke during that assignment.

That was ten or more cigarettes before noon.

The there-and-back routine was repeated at lunch. The restroom was filled after lunch. At 2 p.m., work and classes were called, and more cigarettes were smoked. Dinner was the same. Smokers were always in need of lighters when theirs died. The borrowing of lighters could throw a smoker's whole schedule off. Nothing was more important. An inmate seeking a cigarette would take a ticket for being late to class. On the walkway, I often heard some version of, "This lighter was new two days ago. Now it's shot." They had no idea how many cigs they were smoking. It was their new way of breathing.

The smokers I observed were creative, sneaking lights from the oven, and from electrical outlets, and, when out of papers, using toilet paper roll covers and Bible pages for rollies.

The rest of every night, the restroom pumped smoke out into the TV room. At bedtime and in the middle of the night, I could smell smokers going at it in neighboring cubes. So, in fact, I was second hand-smoking two packs a day.

Disgusted, I told Bear, "Smoking kills, but not fast enough."

Outside prison, in real life, my relationships with smokers had been challenging.

As the Tex Williams song said, everything gets dropped or interrupted so they "can smoke that cigarette." The term "nonsmoker" connotes something negative about the individual, as if he or she is missing something. Smokers and nonsmokers travel in different circles, especially in prison. Caught on the walkway without a cigarette, a smoker would walk away from a conversation, mid-sentence, with me, to run up to a passing smoker to bum one or to get a bust down.

I wondered why I was dropped so suddenly. When the wind was to my face on the walkway, I was happy to be rid of a smoker. Just as in the car when I was thirteen, exhaled smoke and cherry smoke blew right into my nostrils. Marking their territory, smokers left their stink on me everywhere.

"Just try it—you get high the first time." That was Ears' advice to me one afternoon in the restroom. I stared at his Newport and actually considered it. Because, as an addict, I wanted to get high. I was desperate to get high to beat The Man at his own game. This was before I found my chineta connection. "Maybe later," I told Ears. Because he was a bully, he just wanted to make me sick or give me a new habit I couldn't afford. In the long run, I'd become Leroy.

Heat finally left. He did one last tattoo in his cube—a New York Jets logo for a dude I never met—smoked a Newport, and began packing. Heat was the first inmate I would see leave the dorm on good terms, on his end date, and not going to The Box or to another prison.

I asked him if he was happy. He said, "I'm going to get laid in twenty-four hours. I'm already hard as a rock." Of course, I had expected something disgusting to come from him. And I was jealous. I wanted to go home and was counting the months on my fingers: May 2018 was nearly a year away, and I had to hold out. It might be next August or even December if I could stay out of trouble and pass whatever classes I took. NYASTP, which Bear had mentioned, would get me out early, but I had to go to another prison. NYASTP wasn't offered at Collins, and I couldn't find out where I'd be going. Ideally, it would be a proper treatment and recovery facility with individual counseling and staff support.

Absurdity slapped me in the face in the form of DOCC's bureaucracy. My first application to NYASTP was denied; now I understood why Moe always bopped Curly and Larry in the head—frustration that they could be so stupid. DOCCs denied me NYASTP because I had "a criminal record." The boneheads even listed my crimes on the letter: DWI (in 1996!), two shoplifting charges (for Four Loko), and the reason I was incarcerated—criminal sale of a controlled substance. My record put me in prison—everyone who took NYASTP had a criminal record. I wanted to scream.

Journalists learn fast. Bureaucrats want you to play their game, fill out their forms, and wait in their long lines to get what you want. They want you to "think" as they do. On Cougar's advice, I wrote an appeal, saying I was in AA at Collins and needed NYASTP to learn how to live sober successfully, to make my life matter. In a month, my appeal won me a spot in NYASTP.

Heat gave me his colored pencils. I had not learned to like Heat, but I accepted the pencils anyway. His leftover commissary went to Bear and Cougar. His illegal tattoo kit went to Pun. Heat took all his woodworking equipment home, including 400 popsicle sticks.

It seemed like his preliminary goodbyes went on forever. Fist bumps. A few hugs. I think he said goodbye to each man in the dorm, fifty-nine or so, including me. I was witness to a language transformation I had heard somewhere in the past. When Heat said goodbye to white and Latino people, he spoke "normally." When he wished the blacks well, he slowed his words, dropped S's from words, and basically talked "ghetto black."

I was educated in the 1970-80s in nearly all-white schools in Lockport. College was a culture shock for me. However, I'm not a bigot. There is the Queen's English. There is ghetto talk. People have told me it doesn't exist. It does (reverse prejudice), and I witnessed it with Heat. He was "code switching." It was quite fascinating to hear, really. Despite his "real" tattoos, gun charges, and pit bulls, Heat was a big fat phony.

Heat finally cleared out his two years' worth of junk. Bags packed, he walked out of the building into a blue van that I guess was taking him to a bus stop. His cube sat empty for a day. Then Albany told a New York judge, "We've got to keep those jails full!" A new guy arrived.

That was the day the doorknob fell off. It was on our exit door to the dorm, which wouldn't open without the knob. Maintenance was paged, and the metal door was propped open with a mop handle by the C.O. Hours later, three guys from maintenance fooled around with it, putting a whole new knob unit in and giving the C.O. new keys. A day later, both of the new knobs fell off. Again, they were repaired. An officer accused all sixty of us of tampering with the door. We all laughed at that and the matter was dropped. It fell off once more, a month later. It was quietly repaired and stayed intact afterward.

Pun sat near me, Patriot, and Bear at dinner. We were treated to chicken patties, home fries with chicken gravy, and rice pudding. I complained about the door knob fiasco.

"New York State's finest," Pun said, taking a long, uncomfortable pause before saying, "at work." Many addicts were known to pause right in the middle of a sentence, as if they'd gone blank to distraction.

Then Patriot pointed at his dinner tray and said, "There's not enough food here for a seven-year-old. I heard *you* say that."

"This meal cost the state one dollar, maybe less," Bear said.

Patriot ate all our rice pudding because we hated it. The rice was barely chewable. Then Patriot shoved his chicken patty down the front of his shirt. "For snack tonight," he said.

I began weeks of notes to J. Luce, the Collins vocational supervisor, explaining that my medical paperwork advised against handling such jobs as plumbing, and the only station I might be able to work was culinary. I wrote that I needed a job "that would complement my mental health success."

I didn't want to "take up a spot in plumbing that another inmate could appreciate." I picked up this point from a plumbing inmate whom I told I didn't want to be there anymore. He said, "Then sign out, nigga, and give u spot to somebody want it." Sage advice.

J. Luce responded that he addressed my medical concerns with the plumbing instructor. Luce also said, "Plumbing can be beneficial to your programming needs." He was correct here, but I didn't find that out until later. I left plumbing after three months, after talking with Bear, who again advised I enroll in NYASTP. It turned out that, if I'd completed six months of plumbing, I could have achieved my merit date and left prison in May.

Luce said, "I advise you to continue your positive participation throughout the entire class module, working to fulfill your merit time eligibility requirements and learn as much as you can to help you with gainful employment ... and be an asset to your family's home needs." Here, he was partially right, but Luce should have made it blunt: "Nigga, you jam on plumbin' an gradiate, you be outa here earlier!"

As I tried to find a leaky pipe, I could only focus on wading through pools of shit. And how could a journalist/writer of twenty years' experience suddenly become a plumber?

On Bear's advice, I concentrated solely on NYASTP and finally got in. Due to the duration of the NYASTP program, my late start, and an error on the counselor's part, I was in prison three months longer than I had to be. But I knew none of this then.

On October 1, I wrote my first grievance, at Zoom's urging. The C.O. working the afternoon shift told us at shift start that he would write up someone, any-one, with a "random ticket" if the noise level increased while he was there. That included inmates watching sports on TV.

This random ticket thing ate me up. It was like a police officer in traffic who sees an accident, has no idea who caused it, and issues a ticket to the victim stand-ing closest to him. What if three dudes were getting loud, as they like to do, and I got the ticket? That's blaming the victim. And was this random ticket matter a rule in Collins' *Policies & Procedures*? Zoom, our law librarian, said it wasn't. As a rule, C.O.s simply made up new rules on the fly.

Now, white noise can reach a peak. Other C.O.s, like Hubbard, simply ask us to "turn it down."

This C.O., after his announcement, took the chair out of the bubble and went to the hallway connecting ours to the dorm next door. He sat down to chat with the other side's C.O. Zoom said, "That's abandoning his post. That's leaving the dorm unattended."

After Zoom went back to his cube, I took my write-up and hid it in a book. I realized Zoom was manipulating me. Where was Zoom's write-up? I didn't need reprisals from filing a complaint, and I wasn't going to be in this prison long enough to change the way its officers behaved.

I owed money to a new dude named Funk. Funk was a white Muslim who made getting suboxone too easy. My bill with him was about $70. That meant I had used seven times in two weeks. A regular junky in prison time. My commissary would pay $40, but then I'd have no food. I could get crafty and tell Funk I made his food order (he gave me a list), but the commissary was out of some things. I'd have about $10 for myself.

I was embarrassed and wanted more. Once again, I had become the guy I had been before jail. Someone who owed drug dealers money, and in such a short time. The hedonist in me had not changed at all, just changed locations and dealers. Guilt.

Cougar found out about my debt. Prisoners are shameless gossips. So, staring at me from his cube, he just started in. "It's gonna happen and you not even gonna know it. That how fast these boy work. When you walk, you watch out."

He meant I was going to be cut. Over the debt.

Beginning to panic, I stared back at him, blankly. I wanted him to know I was giving Cougar da Admiral respect and that I was listening. At that moment, I knew what I should have known all along. Nobel and Cougar were silent business partners. That was how Cougar learned of my outstanding bill. Someone else owed him money too and was blaming me. I actually owed Cougar, and, from my experience, no one wanted to owe Cougar anything.

I'd estimated weeks earlier that Cougar had between $10,000 and $50,000 in a bank account his "bitch" managed for him. I knew the amount because of comments he made to me about the possibility of self-publishing all of his 'hood books at once.

His deep tone was one of disgust. People in this prison got cut over an owed dollar of commissary.

Cougar talked "at" me for about twenty minutes. I said nothing, not wanting to get in deeper, or to make him angrier. Even though I was on Lithium, I had that old feeling of impending doom in my stomach. Fear.

"And that's a fact," Cougar said. He walked up to my cube, gave me a three-second glare, and walked off to the TV room. My mind was racing, but I thought I had a pass no one else had. I was a writer, and he had hired me to help with his books, as well as publishing research. I had been to The Show. And he was still looking for a backstage pass.

I remained hyper-aware, and paid Funk as much as I could. And I stopped using. I was terrified that I'd earn a long cheek scar from a gang. Cougar might have even prevented what he might've originally instigated. Nobel remained just as friendly as he always was to me—I could only wonder what he was thinking.

I dreaded being in prison in December. The snow was coming—the lake effect. We got a dusting in November, and often had to walk to meds in the rain, and the dorm was cold. The brick buildings heated up in the summer and remained cold during the winter. The yard was closed until sometime in March.

For me, that was fun, to watch the smokers try to light their cigarettes in the rain, against punishing Northeast winds.

The morning of December 3, Napoleon told me to pack up my "shit," I was going to NYASTP. I said goodbye to Cougar, Nobel, Pastor Mark, Zoom, Easton, and several others. My drug bill was fully paid. No more gangs, gays, or gambling.

Pastor Mark gave me a picture done in colored pencil. It was of a tree with a honey bees' nest. Next to the nest was a bespectacled, flying bee, wearing a graduation cap with tassel, named "Professor B-Love." I was moved because, to me, it meant I could rise again from these depths, that I could accomplish anything.

I was cautiously happy to be moving forward, to be making a change. A few inmates gave me their home addresses and said "stay in touch." Easton and I promised each other that when we got out, we were both going to Florida. The first thing we'd do would be visit the Salvador Dali museum in St. Petersburg, and then retire in the sun. To me, that day seemed an eternity away.

But it was only eight months.

MARCY
CORRECTIONAL
FACILITY

MEDIUM SECURITY

CELL #11

Is it a fantasy or a future reality that we will move beyond

the current paradigm of barbarism? Writer Scott Gutches

said we could realize such a vision. "Progress toward a

punishment devoid of cruelty and unusualness. Perhaps in

a hundred years it will be impossible to distinguish between

a life before and a life after prison walls." Punishment and

discipline anger and confuse the inmate, destroying his sense

of future, of purpose in the outside world

CHAPTER 11

A "HANDS-ON" FACILITY

"Do you want them to come out (of prison) angrier,
meaner and more dangerous?"
—Path of Freedom, GO Project Films

My Lockport friend, Rachael, obtained my new prison address. She wrote and asked, "Are you making new friends?"

I was.

She added, "Keep your head up and your ass low."

I passed judgment on Marcy's people as soon as I left Collins. Collins' crowd was tough, hard-nosed, protective, and serious. They were guys' guys, basically—what you saw was what you got. Buffalo-area people.

Then there were my initial impressions of NYASTP's F1 dorm: immature, touchy-feely, gossipy old maids, selfish, narcs, and harsh judges. No one wanted to get in trouble, so there'd be no fights...maybe.

After spending time with friends Cougar, Bear, Pastor Mark, and Zoom at Collins, I changed for the good. But that was all but erased when I met the critics in Marcy. As I'd learn, there were some good, bad, and worse people here. Plus, the bureaucrats.

Soprano weighed 292 pounds, according to his Marcy prison I.D. But his brown skin glowed with health and he looked like a famous fat guy. The look on his round face was of supreme confidence—at any moment, he seemed about to break into a smile or carefree laughter. A circulating inmate rumor confirmed that he had been a contestant on "American Idol" in 2012. I didn't believe him until he gave me a detailed explanation. It was the year that rocker Philip Phillips took the win. "We practiced for six hours right outside the studio," Soprano said.

"I was exhausted by the time I got to see J. Lo."

He claimed that jailors who'd seen him on the show were shocked when he walked into their prisons. Soprano was down for two years on a drug charge, just like me.

His cube was behind mine in the F1 dorm. My cube was next to a window on one side. It looked out at the expansive recreation yard, and in the distance was the Central New York Psychiatric Center. It was an imposing, oddly shaped structure—five floors and a great many windows. It was the state prison system's insane asylum, housing serial killers, men who ate their own shit, and inmates who tried to rip their eyelids off. It was part of DOCCS' mental health network, serving 8,500 of this state's 52,000 inmates.

The center had 220 beds and housed dangerous sex offenders as well as those who fell under Section 402 of the state corrections law and were hospitalized involuntarily, including kids as young as seventeen. There were no C.O.s there, or unlocked doors, or four-man rooms.

My dorm was like all the others at Marcy: cinderblock walls painted brown and off-white, dented metal cubicle dividers, football-style numbers painted on each cube (1 to 60), metal lockers, metal-framed beds, plastic air pillows, sheets, and small blankets.

Gandhi was on the other, windowless side of my cube. Named thusly for his belief in nonviolent protest, Gandhi was six-two with black hair and blue eyes. He claimed he was Mexican on his mother's side, British on his father's. Gandhi had been a highway drifter on the Eastern Seaboard ... and an addict. The man had been to thirty-five states, but not out west. He was addicted to Robo-Tripping—drinking excessive amounts of cough medicine to get high.

When Gandhi first entered our dorm, he was put on one of the bunks at the end of my cube. New inmates had to take bunk beds. I had gotten lucky with cube six—no bunk. To get to the top of a bunk bed, new inmates had to step on the bottom bunk, climb onto a locker (that has wheels), and jump to the top. They'd have to be in good physical condition to do it. According to the Infirmary, if you weighed 300 pounds or more, you got a bottom bunk.

When Gandhi and I first met, he asked me my astrological sign. I told him "Leo" and he opened his locker and pulled out *The Only Astrology Book You'll Ever Need* by Joanna Martine Woolfolk. Having quickly turned to "Leo," he began reading aloud. Our bromance started that day—if there's one thing Leos love, it's to hear positive things about themselves. Gandhi would be the fourth of my five.

Woolfolk wrote that the Leo is "enthusiastic, powerful, expansive and creative, generous and extravagant, dogmatic and fixed in opinion." Prison tried to eliminate some of these qualities in me, though I certainly stayed "fixed in opinion," even when my opinions were dangerous to hold in prison. I kept my enthusiasm for creative writing—that was my only power.

The astrological author also mentioned that Leos most likable trait is "exuberance". And apparently we were "prone to being victims of slander."

That part was true.

The prison language barrier was worse when it came to Hispanics. I had nothing against Latinos; in all likelihood, I was likely part Hispanic. And several Latinos like Rafael and Nacho were very friendly to me. A few others used their Spanish against me, starting on day one. I had bussed it from Collins to Marcy, a long trip that included shackles but not showers.

I was so exhausted when I got to cube 6 and unpacked that I socialized a little and called it a night, falling asleep before "lights out." That was a big mistake. I did not know I was being watched and evaluated by Chevy, Shorty (the midget), and Pato. This was the first time they had seen me, and they assumed that after my long, horrific trip, I'd want to jump right into the shower.

The gossip was hot that night while I slept, and was red hot the next morning when, all over the dorm, people were telling me to shower. Someone even wrote a note to Hudson: "Stickney has not showered since Tuesday." That was a total of two days, but the way the note was written made it seem as I hadn't showered since 1985. Hudson called me out to the entryway to the dorm, where we were alone, and gave me a lecture on the importance of cleanliness. By that time, I had already taken a shower, though the Latinos had done their damage. I was branded as dirty. It lasted for two months until I got so mad, I stood up to them.

The showers had a doorway to the toilet room. As I disrobed, the hooting and hollering began, in Spanish. It was the same three—Chevy, Shorty and Pato. I knew what they were doing, saying I was dirty and fat, and others should stay out of the shower "when Stickney's there." Also, "it's about time"—fifth-grade bully crap.

I looked right at Pato and said, "Are they talking about me?"

The other two were laughing, staring at me, poking at each other.

Pato paused, then said, "Yes, they are."

"Tell them this: Only Latino whores hide behind Spanish when criticizing someone. If they are men, they speak English and say it to my face." I thought I was dead—inmate fights happened in the showers, out of sight of the C.O.

Pato translated. It took him a long time in Spanish to say what I had said in English. Chevy and Shorty weren't as fluent as Pato.

I became so enraged, I sounded like I wanted them to stab me. My hands were shaking, the adrenaline pumping. Suddenly quiet, Chevy and Shorty flushed their cigarette butts. Then they walked out of the restroom. Not bothering to ask what they were really saying to me, I told Pato thank you. He nodded to me and left.

I waited a paranoid week for retribution. None came.

One day early in my Marcy stay, I was feeling down. My counselor kept playing with my leave date, and the other inmates were getting to me. Gandhi saw all of this and said, "One day all of this will end. And you will be free."

He gave me a gift. It was a single sheet of notebook paper with various brands of cough medicines. "You can get high from these," Gandhi said. "And it doesn't show up on a drug test."

Robitussin, Coricidin, and Cough & Cold HBP were on the list. Any cough medicine that had "DM" on the box, for active ingredient Dextromethorphan. Plus, and that included a lot of pill brands. He said I could drink an eight-ounce cough medicine or take sixteen pills and I'd be "high as all get-out." Gandhi broke our eye-contact and gazed out the window as if remembering a particularly great personal episode.

When I asked, he declined to tell me why he was in prison. But, after listening to several of his lectures about homeless living and cough medicine, I figured he was a booster. Too many times caught at Rite Aid or CVS with a backpack-full of Robitussin bottles.

After life among the sex offenders at Collins, I felt I knew enough about those men to exclude Gandhi from their ranks. He didn't seem like he was hiding something; it was more the way I felt, like we were above all this.

The astrological book helped him make friends. The predictions were like facts, and this dorm's inhabitants wondered constantly about the future. The past haunted us, and we could not change it. The present was routine, yet anything could happen—a fight, a stabbing, a death—at any moment. The future was unwritten, yet we were trying to lay our hands on the tablet as soon as we could. Astrology was a glimpse into the why of yesterday and the possibility of tomorrow.

I came to rely on Gandhi to help me straighten my thoughts. Usually, in prison, such things do not usually happen. Gandhi got mixed up with the blackjack players and gamblers, spending most of his time in the TV room with the cards. He told me Leos get jealous when their friends pay attention to other people, and I guess he was right. I was a little peeved he was entertaining the gamblers and not me. Of course, I let it go.

He suffered for it. On Friday and Saturday nights, inmates were allowed to stay up until 2 a.m. in the TV room playing cards, dominoes, Scrabble, and chess, and watching the flatscreen. I was tired of prison by 10 p.m. and wanted my sleep. The dorm was silent by 11 on those nights. Gandhi, however, was a night owl, and he wound up sleeping heavily during the day, missing meals.

Soprano was also helpful to me. This former "American Idol" contestant might have worn a 4XL shirt, but he radiated confidence and positivity. At times, he was obnoxious with his prison radio, which constantly played soul music and hip-hop, the latter of which was expected in this environment. Hip-hop is the new social programming, creating followers who do anything a hip-hopper will do: money-getting, guns, champagne, and "bitches." That's what life is. Right?

He claimed that the white BMW in the photo taped to his wall was sitting at home in Mom's garage waiting for him. Soprano had photos of three black women on his wall—all current girlfriends, he claimed. His big-man size must have been hiding a powerful weapon besides his voice.

I asked him how to manage criticisms about my weight, which always sent my self-esteem oozing onto the floor.

Soprano took his do-rag off and said I was going about things all wrong. "You're a grown-ass man," he said, rubbing his stomach. "Here and now in America, we are *in*. The ladies seek us out. I know. You gotta start looking at this shit and saying, 'I don't give a fuck.' The shit people say mean nothing to you once you got some attitude."

An inmate named Balam sat down with me one time in the TV room. He was appointed to provide F1 orientation. He went over "job functions"—chiefly cleanup assignments from the counselors. I was in charge of wiping down the four phones and booths. I was very distracted by Balam because he looked like he was dying, his black skin gone gray, his eyes watery and sad.

Balam also explained "cube standards, dorm rules, program standards, and schedules." Basically, he talked about the numerous times and days the counselors made us clean the dorm. He told me about laundry (the dorm had three washers and three dryers), "treatment assignments, and mandatory recreation." All my life thus far, I'd never heard of "mandatory exercise."

He also spoke of sick call and commissary, quiet time, hygiene standards, the C.O. warning logbook, and the mess hall schedule. Also, every time we left the dorm, we had to sign out, and upon returning, sign back in.

I was grateful Balam lived through his mini-orientation for me.

A day or so after my arrival, I asked one of the counselors what NYASTP was all about. I asked if there was a brochure to read, so I'd know what to expect. We were in a prison, not a treatment center, or a proper hospital. I got nothing but confusing information from the counselor. An Aryan named Bo searched through his paperwork and gave me his copy of the DOCCS' "continuum of treatment services" (whatever that was) program overview, which discussed the history of NYASTP and outlined the "intensive" program. NYASTP started in 1991, and in 1992 reported its highest number of participants at 26,155.

NYASTP goals were as follows:

- Focus facility resources on the needs of offenders with a history of alcohol and substance abuse.
- Better prepare participants for return to their families and communities upon release.
- Reduce drug and alcohol relapse rates and recidivism rates for program participants.
- Ensure appropriate aftercare services in the community.

-   Increase coordination among pertinent state and local agencies, service providers, and community organizations.

The goal that glared back at me was reducing drug and alcohol relapse rates. Drugs have long been available in prisons and jails. This fact has not changed. How was NYASTP supposed to reduce relapse in Marcy if the prison, like others, was soaking with K2 and suboxone? NYASTP counselors preached no convincing rhetoric here. I saw inmates dealing and using nearly every day during my eight months at Marcy. In fact, a couple inmates who came to NYASTP from other prisons brought drugs into Marcy with them. A man I met at gym boasted of making hooch (prison alcohol) in C2 dorm.

NYASTP began experiencing a decline in court-mandated and volunteer enrollment because of the Drug Law Reform Act of 2009, when municipal drug courts started popping up, diverting offenders from state prison. I failed drug court because I continued to use drugs— suboxone and Four Loko.

There were days I had tried to stop, and days when I did stop. But there always seemed to be a compelling reason to use, from thinking I wouldn't get caught, to giving The Man the finger. The reality was different and a lot more complicated. I was addicted, divorced, homeless, unemployed, and suicidal. Like a parachute over a fallen soldier, drug use covered up all those dreadful realities for four hours at a time.

Allison Moore, a former Maui police officer and meth addict, couldn't handle reality either. In the book *Shards*, she wrote, "… When I started to come down, I couldn't face being plunged into the icy cold water of my real life. I did another line, bigger than the first. It made me feel calm, confident, excited about my future. Meth was the answer to all my problems."

Drug court diversion caused many NYASTP programs in our state prisons to close. By 2011, there were only 289 participants, which is quite ironic. Lockport drug court failed offenders each week, as did every other city court in New York state. The eight work release facilities in New York state decreased to two after drug court's expansion. This meant that for quite a number of offenders who completed their time in county jail, plus those who refused the NYASTP option, there was more time to serve in state prison. (Work release followed NYASTP completion for some inmates.)

The report was missing statistics on the number of former inmates who remained drug free. In fact, other than the hollow program goals listed, there were no measurable outcomes to show how NYASTP failed or succeeded. The declining number of participants may have said more about the program than the state report itself.

On a related note, a counselor shared the return-to-prison-after-parole (recidivism) statistic—40% through 2010, and 68% through 2018. Parolees were sent back for parole violations such as failing drug tests or failing to meet with the parole officer. Hadn't they already served their time? Parole turned the system into double jeopardy for inmates who had drug problems and issues keeping appointments.

I thought that the 40% return rate was outrageous and represented a huge failure for the employees of prisons/DOCCS, not the former inmates. Not to mention the jump in recent years.

Marcy Deputy Supt. Laird Strassmeier claimed that the solution to recidivism was poor treatment of inmates. "The power here is tilted toward us on purpose. We train for that. It's supposed to be miserable for you, so you won't come back," said Strassmeier. I thought. *How could that work when inmates have always been treated like dogs, and worse? If his way was working, why were the prisons growing?*

I wished someone had given me a NYASTP brochure, but brochures like that didn't exist. The report I read made me confused and depressed. What had I gotten myself into?

Everyone had a favorite C.O. in F1 dorm: Valefor, an average-sized bald guy with a grin that suggested an infatuation with irony. A Howard Stern and hard rock fan, he had none of the ugly qualities of the other C.O.s, or if he did, he just hid them well. He was approachable, friendly, self-deprecating, hilarious, and genuine. He had four kids and his own home zoo: three German shepherds, a tabby cat, and a hamster. The only correctional officer who'd become one of the five people who helped me, Valefor said that with the pets running around, he often felt like he was on a reality show.

Unlike the other C.O.s, he never yelled at our dorm. Valefor was respectful toward us—we would never challenge his authority. And we would have acted the same way toward any other officer who acted as if he respected us. At least three of our C.O.s slept through parts of their shift with us. Others spent most of their time on the phone. F1 was low maintenance, unless inmates were provoked.

Some Spanish dude who knew only a few words of English was my Marcy dorm neighbor at one point. He was slated to go to another jail or home in a few days. I asked Valefor if Gandhi could move into the cube next to me. I laughingly told him I wanted a "half-white, half -Mexican" neighbor for a change. Valefor nodded and said he'd take care of it.

You know how I found out whether Gandhi was cool or not? I asked him, with a hypothetical question, "You're at a party and you throw up. Do you go home? Or stay to get more wasted?"

"I stay and tip a little more cough med," he said.

That was the correct answer. True bohemians, after some rum, heroin, or a few pills, puke and keep going. In a prison dorm, you did not want an officer to see you vomit. That generated immediate reportable suspicion... and drug testing.

So that was how Gandhi wound up next to me. And I never let him forget it; without me (and Valefor), he could have wound up next to a real asshole. And there were several real assholes in F1.

I've thought of God as an irresponsible creator, bringing humans to life but giving them so many flaws. Creating a beautiful planet Earth and filling it with so many stupid, destructive people who torture other life forms, including themselves. In prison, you get what you can, and I had to thank God for Gandhi, the man who'd help me see beyond the chaos into that new world awaiting me.

Gandhi (like God) had a twisted sense of humor. Gandhi looked at me dead-pan one morning, whispering, "I found a black pubic hair on my underwear. Do you think they're secretly raping us at night?"

Bunking next to Gandhi in the dorm was Ace Lanza, a white supremacist. A slight man, no more than 130 pounds. Brush cut, tattoos, prison clothes.

Lanza and I became friends when he heard I wrote a book on American terrorist Timothy McVeigh. Ace claimed he was first cousins with Adam Lanza, the shooter in the Sandy Hook Massacre. It wasn't just that they were related, he said; they were united, dead and alive, in some oddball cause.

Ace Lanza was a follower of the Norse god Odin and met weekly with other Odinists in the prison the way Christians and Muslims met with their respective groups. Odinism involved belief, socialization, and protection. In other words, if an inmate started picking on an Odinist, the inmate would be surrounded by the other Odinists in the dorm, ending the conflict.

I was "in" as a journalist who had worked in his area of belief. Lanza offered me suboxone. In fact, I was sometimes given some even when I didn't have money. We sat and talked about Adam Lanza's life and motivation for the killings. Ace had studied several of the school killings, and ticked them off by name: Columbine, Red Lake, Santa Fe, and Virginia Tech. Ace was very sympathetic.

Later, I would learn Ace was an anxiety-ridden hypochondriac. But he was protected by his gang of white nationalists. Why was Ace in this club? Sean McShee who writes for *The Wild Hunt: Pagan News & Commentary*, wrote of the Odinists on July 24, 2018: "Odinism thrives in prisons. The isolation and violence of prison forces most prisoners to need a primary social group for support and protection."

A motley crew we were—Soprano, Gandhi, Ace, and me. We were all Recovery Journal-carrying members of NYASTP's afternoon group in F1. I told Gandhi that when I read the original prospectus for NYASTP, I was intrigued by the words "designated intensive treatment center," and that we would be observed in a rehab or hospital-like setting, not a prison. But we were in a prison just like Collins, only far stricter.

Soprano, who had tasted celebrity before, said when it came to NYASTP, he was "not really there." He was living in the future, doing things that would make him internationally known, tipping his hat to old Rob Base. "I will be earning on TV, on MTV, and I'm going to get me a studio to produce soul music, nigga," Soprano said.

Gandhi commented, "I dream of soul too." But I knew he dreamt of cough medicine, cherry flavor.

It was December 25, 2017, and I was dealing with Christmas expectations set long ago, though I'd spent Christmases of late either stoned or imprisoned.

Last Christmas, I was in the Niagara County Jail. The last few years before that I was in the drunk houses; I no longer saw my family.

When I had a wife and we had a little girl, we had celebrated Christmas four times every year: at our house on Morrow, at my in-laws' house, at my parents' house, and then Christmas night cocktails at my wife's aunt's house. I went from being surrounded by people who loved me to being surrounded by bickering, crack-smoking drunks. I didn't hate myself for it. I just lived like George Plimpton, the participant journalist. If it was like watching *It's a Wonderful Life*, the suicidal guy was me.

Of Christmas at Marcy that year, I wrote in my journal: "Everything feels the same as yesterday, save the new coating of snow. Breakfast was oatmeal and toast. I pocketed bread and sugars. C.O.s would call that stealing, but my father paid his taxes for this food, so I was basically just grabbing some sustenance from home … Home, this wasn't."

I slept that day, went to meds, watched idiots jump the line, and thought about cheeking my Wellbutrin for later. The nurse crushed it and mixed it with water, so I couldn't.

My X-mas present from the folks was money for commissary. I ordered:
- 6 stamps
- 6 beef soups
- 4 Bear Dews
- 5 Snickers
- 3 Jolly Ranchers
- Peanut butter
- 2 writing pads
- 4 black pens
- 2 Shabang chips
- 3 Kool Aid, cherry
- 2 batteries (for Buddha)

My psychiatric counselor at Marcy's infirmary turned out to be more attentive than Mr. P. at Collins. Her name was Elle and she was a cute, round-faced blonde with green eyes. She had what the ghetto talkers call "junk in the trunk," though that didn't matter to me. I needed help. I was still plunging into anxiety attacks and, here at Marcy, there was no way to get away from everyone.

Elle and I reviewed an anxiety worksheet from the Cairn Center. It asked what I was anxious about (obvious), designating the severity from one to ten. It asked about my worst fear, what would happen if the worst occurred, and what evidence did I have to disprove the worst. I later used this form for many situations, and it helped counteract that dark sense of heightened awareness—a menace in the air, someone out there was plotting against me.

The psychiatrist had not met with me, though I did receive an inter-office memo from Dr. Farnum that said she was discontinuing my Wellbutrin. I wasn't sure how she could make this decision without seeing me. The Infirmary was already giving it to me in liquid form (pill crushed in water). By order of the psychiatrist, my Lithium and Haldol were continued. I revised and revised a note to the doctor, finally deciding it might do even more damage than good to send it.

Shortly thereafter, during a discussion on anxiety, Gandhi told me he was a Wiccan. Wicca is a pagan religion developed in Britain during the first half of the twentieth century. It has a number of ritual practices. Gandhi showed me a relaxing meditation where I sat and concentrated on the warm rays of the sun making contact with the top of my head. My feet were connected to roots that went deep into the Earth. My fears and frustrations flowed out the top of my head and were replaced by feelings of peace and calm.

It sounded ridiculous at first, and the skeptic in me challenged everything Gandhi told me about the exercise. However, I needed to work the anxiety out, and the meditation relaxed my mind. I needed to stop using drugs and put myself into that mindset, but what was going to take the place of drugs? There had to be something.

There was a nine-page kick to the nuts called Treatment Standards. Most of the stuff was common sense, yet there were those among us who had no common sense or logical reasoning skills. There was to be no sex, drugs, or violence. There was to be no "bad rapping," lying, racial slurs, profanity, or cliques.

There was to be no horseplay, gambling, stealing, destruction of property, criminal activity, or unauthorized organizational activity.

A summary of when to use phones, restroom, and cooking area was included. No hats, hoods, or sunglasses inside.

The real gem was the line that said, "Nude pictures are to be hung inside locker." There was an officially approved locale for *Buttman* glossies.

On a day in January, we were given an entertainment choice: a documentary about the government's killings at Waco and the David Koresh story, or the reality show "Black Ink." I lobbied my dorm-mates for Waco. "Black Ink" won.

After six months in NYASTP, most students were to attend "work release" in Rochester or Manhattan. The goal was getting users and dealers off the streets and into taxpaying employment. Goals are not always completed, even in ideal situations; in fact, sometimes challenges can improve the final product. Not true in the case of addicted prisoners. The dime-store philosophy of "We knock you down to build you back up" was in use at Marcy. It was said by NYASTP counselors and acted on by C.O.s.

I needed more building up than anything else. I had felt worthless ever since Judge Kloch's sentencing. The Marcy deputy of programs, Mark Douglas, wrote my pre- and post-release treatment recommendations. According to Douglas's report, I "began with alcohol (peer pressure, available), progressing to methadone, heroin, ecstasy, cocaine, and oxycodone (self-medicate, addiction). Began addressing prior suicide [attempt] due to depression and 'great sadness,' relationship between addiction and criminal behavior – 'needing money' and multiple attempts to self-medicate versus developing healthy coping skills. Goals – employment recommendations: continue treatment upon release, maintain abstinence/recovery. Re-integration consists of employment as a writer, mental health and addiction outpatient, and family support."

The part that said "needing money" made me think of all the ways I had obtained my financial bridge to euphoria. First, toward the end, I wrote for J. Fitzgerald Group marketing communications. Then unemployment. I stopped paying rent and had to couch-surf at friends' houses. I lived with two lesbians, a friend named Chuck (who beat his drunk girlfriend), then with Hazlett the drunk, and others. Once unemployment was gone, I assisted with Jim Kane's house-painting business. I did odd jobs for an Italian guy who owned Barone's, the old music store, and I borrowed money all over town, even from folks at the church. A lot of other people paid for my habit, but when I was in the thick of it, I needed more to function.

Douglas's list of drugs was inaccurate. I started with pot, moved to cocaine, and then left that for opiate pills. Ecstasy and methadone were not addictions of mine. I tried both about three times. Alcohol and opiates were my nourishment. And heroin was a flirtation when nothing else was available.

Valefor asked me about my addiction. I told him what had happened and how, eventually, it brought me here. I told him about my family. I was lingering at the bubble, but I didn't care. I needed a pal to chat with me about my fall.

"Are you at rock bottom?" Valefor said.

"There's no such thing," I said.

"Will you make amends? Get back together with your wife?"

"Dude," I said, "once she's sleeping with other guys, it's definitely over."

He laced his fingers, looking like a county judge. "What are your plans?"

"Get out of here. Learn to tango."

He laughed. "And get yourself a smart woman, a good woman."

I thought about that for a few seconds. Then I said, "I don't need the love of a good woman; I need the touch of a great woman."

Valefor said, "She's out there. You'll find her. Just good investigative reporting."

The corrections officers, who traveled the campus roads in battered, otherwise nondescript blue vans, slapped, punched, kicked, and even planned conspiracies against inmates who broke even the smallest of rules at Marcy.

The blue vans, covered in dents and dust, were one of the first things I noticed upon arrival at Marcy. The long line of dorms led to the mess hall, school, and visitors' building, and all in all were about the length of four football fields. Along the stretch were walkways next to the roads. The multipurpose vans demanded to be noticed, especially when speeding down the road, swerving around petrified inmates, while hitting about seventy mph.

The C.O.s ran the vans into snowbanks, and each other, and parked them on the walkway, yelling obscenities at us. They used the vans as drunken teens might use stolen golf carts at midnight at a country club. They drove with the headlights on during sunny days and with the lights off during the blackest Marcy nights.

They transported officers to the dorms so the C.O.s didn't have to share the walkway with inmates or walk during inclement weather, or undertake that long walk from the entrance.

As an inmate, you didn't want to end up in a van. I saw the blue vans streak down the roadway, come to a screeching halt just so the C.O.s could grab an inmate from the walkway, cuff him, and toss him inside. Some vans did not have back seats, so they were obviously trying to hurt the inmate while turning corners at NASCAR speed. C.O.s tossed the inmates in vans after frisks and searches. They sat on the roadway for hours, conducting surveillance.

While I waited in the med line, I saw at least three times when a blue van would roll up to the Infirmary entrance. An officer opened the sliding side door and out would stumble one or two shackled inmates. Either they'd bloodied each other, someone else did it, or it happened in the van. A similar occurrence happened when a van pulled up and two inmates got out, carrying an injured inmate out on a stretcher. One carrier nearly fell on the ice. The C.O. at the wheel did nothing but drive away, spinning tires and fishtailing in the snow.

Unlike Collins, the campus officers at Marcy Correctional were "hands on" and confrontational, meaning they didn't just yell, they got physical. When I arrived, I was headed to the mess hall when I saw officers interrogating and slapping around a dreadlocked young man for taking a grilled cheese sandwich out of the building. They had him spread eagle on a wall, kicking him, punching his back, grabbing his arms, slamming his fists against the bricks, and tossing him to the pavement before letting him go. To limp away.

C.O. Fishe** watched the kid walking and commented, "He'll never come back here again." The against-the-wall frisks I witnessed were frequent and nasty. Each subject searched was suspected of carrying drugs, a weapon, or something illegal. If the inmates mouthed off, moved their arms, or didn't spread their legs wide enough, the fall of a baton could be swift. When a search got ugly or resulted in a takedown, inmates were dealt with behind closed doors in a nearby building. Officers told other prisoners to look away in the case of outside frisks.[5]

5 Corrections Officer Fishe was injured the next week when violence ensued between an inmate and four other officers. Fishe was trying to restrain the inmate who possessed suboxone and was

Ted Conover wrote in *Newjack: Guarding Sing Sing* that officers referred to inmates as "crooks" and "mutts" or "savages." He added, "If a savage dissed you, what did it matter? And if a savage got hurt (particularly due to an error on your part), who cared?" It was a "catharsis" and "thrilling release" for officers "filled with pent-up aggression" to subdue unruly inmates.

The gang mentality—that scary blue wall versus the wall of green—I learned, was prevalent not just among the C.O.s, but also among the inmates. Jack Henry Abbott wrote: "The violence between guard and prisoner is open, naked, and you see a lot of prisoners defending themselves in fistfights with pigs. ...When I speak of a prisoner fist-fighting pigs, I mean that literally: at least five or six pigs at a time." Gang mentality.

We weren't given the benefit of the doubt. We were given the benefit of the blame, and then a slap or two to the head. No matter how prisoners were treated, "A culture of impunity and an 'us versus them' mentality of prison/jail staff created an environment ripe for prisoner abuse," according to the American Friends Service Committee report.

Gandhi was always prepared to offer something poignant when Shit Popped Off (a fight). "That's their job, to stir shit up and beat people. On cop cars, it says, 'To Serve and Protect.' In prison, it says, 'To Harass and Neglect.'"

And the same C.O.s got away with almost anything. My shirt was untucked from my pants one evening when I was on my way to dinner. The tallest C.O. at Marcy stopped me and turned me around, ordering me back to the dorm without dinner. I could have tucked the shirt in right there.

This would not have been so bad if I had eaten lunch. But I missed *that* mid-day meal because I'd forgotten to bring my I.D. Inmates were turned away every day for the same infraction. I missed breakfast one morning when I went to the infirmary for a routine appointment and my opening was delayed because an ambulance arrived for an old guy who had to go to the hospital. My nurse deserted me for him. By the time she met with me, I'd missed chow. In a place like this, it's easy to get brushed aside and forgotten, get snubbed by a vindictive C.O., and wind up having three Ramen noodle soups as meals. Luckily, my friend

kicked in the back by a fellow officer. Fishe was given sick leave at full pay.

Kenny gave me the soups.

Evenings at Marcy were also different than at Collins, where just about everyone went to bed by 11. The F1 dorm at Marcy held a number of younger guys who liked to stay up late. If the C.O. let it happen, these inmates would play tag, wrestle, or talk loudly in their cubes, with radio headphones cranked up. I was in bed early, getting woken, and falling back asleep. It was no surprise that the kids had a tough time with 6 a.m. count. If the evening C.O. was a ballbreaker, the young guys were quiet.

CELL #12

Nothing in the current paradigm measures outcomes, so there is no change, accountability, or measurement of success. Just prisoners, counted daily, which is a measurement of failure. The system's strategy is to blame the victims (prisoners) for the system's own inadequacies. Startlingly, our nation measures the number of annual drug deaths but not the deaths that occur in prison, a system rife with abuses. As H.G. Wells wrote, "There is no intelligence where there is no change and no need of change."

CHAPTER 12

ON SHORT TIME

"As the old maps used to say: Beware. There be monsters here."
—Stephen Hunter, *I, Ripper*

When Gummy and I first met, during my first week at F1 dorm, I did not like him. He was my designated bunkmate until I told the C.O. I couldn't climb because of my 2012 back injury. Gummy was on the bottom bunk. This tall, messy-haired hockey goon from the sticks had a comment or question about everything: "changing cubes was impossible," "who did I think I was?" "Did I know the rules?" He followed me to cube 6 and told me I obviously didn't know how to make a bed. Gummy nudged me aside and made the bed for me. It looked much better than the one I had at Collins Correctional.

Every day, Gummy visited my cube to tell me something I needed to know to survive in F1 and NYASTP. He explained the phone system, chores like mandatory cube-cleaning and inspections, the appointment callout papers on the clipboard, and the movements for chow and school, which were slightly different than at my previous prison.

In a normal situation, these were facts imparted by an official, a counselor, or C.O. But they did nothing to help inmates settle in. Everything, including maintenance, was done by inmates.

Gummy was a grumpy know-it-all, but for some reason he wanted to help me, even though I was never his bunky. I was disturbed by the fact he had no teeth—thus, his nickname. He was about as big as a bear, and I couldn't stop staring at his gums when he spoke with me. I had a new friend whether I wanted him or not.

"Don't ever miss a callout to the Infirmary," Gummy said. "A guy in here got kicked out for doing that. Check the clipboard every day."

I said, "Got kicked out for missing one callout? He must've done more than that."

"Nope. One and he was out."

I didn't question him further, though it sounded like a rumor started by a counselor to keep inmates on their toes.

———————

I had exhausted my reading materials from home. Other inmates had only James Patterson books to offer. So, I tried the miserable little bookshelves in the TV room. After a search, I found a paperback I hadn't seen before. It was a young adult novella called *Freak the Mighty* by Rodman Philbrick.

Ever since childhood, when I got a hold of the *Amityville Horror*, I've "lived in" books, imagining I was a character in them, as moved as they are by the events of the story, as if they were happening to me. This was one of the reasons I became a writer. For an addict like me, the escape of reading provides just as intense of a high as daily living.

Freak the Mighty made Marcy Correctional disappear, even for an hour each day. It was the story of Maxwell Kane, a big kid who's a bit slow, and Kevin Avery, his small, handicapped friend. Kevin is highly intelligent, with a vivid imagination. Upon Maxwell's shoulders, Kevin becomes mighty and leads them both on action-packed adventures. The tale is similar to "My Bodyguard," the 1980 movie, only more touching and magical. And just as unforgettable.

Gummy was a reader too, which surprised me because when I first received his early-dorm recommendations, I figured he might be illiterate. He muscled his way into the Marcy library nearly every week. I recommended *Freak the Mighty* to Gummy and he read it in a day.

"This is us," he said. "You are the Freak."

"And you're the Mighty?" I said.

"Yes," he said. "If we stick together, no one can defeat us."

We had become prison friends. And I probably had a bodyguard if I needed one. I'd met my fifth person who'd get me through this.

———————

Apparently, to show his devotion to our prison friendship, Gummy wrote a small poem about me and my polite power in F1. His writing was like that of a child, but I was touched.

> This is about this
> guy. They call him the Old Great
> One. They should call him
> The All Mighty One. He don't
> look like much. But he
> is master of all. He has
> a mind like no other.
> You might think because
> he is a drunk are [sic] addict
> he makes everything
> around him the way
> he wants it. His power
> is in his fingers.

I got sick of inmates calling me "Stickney" the way the officers did. So, I jokingly came up with a nickname for myself— "Oh Great One." In the 1980s, my mother started calling my father "Oh Great One," because he was a wealthy, globetrotting ad executive. A handle of "B-love" wasn't going to work at Marcy; I needed to be bold. Gummy used the nickname, along with a few others in the dorm (the younger guys). The older inmates looked at me sideways and said, "What's so great about him?"

Gummy had written that I made everything around me the way I wanted it. For Gummy, this was rather profound. From my being so committed to appearing on A&E, to placing Gandhi in the cube next to mine, I did just what Gummy said. I manipulated people, situations, and things to my liking, which like CEOs do—apparently addicts do it too.

Though Gummy and I got along for the rest of his bid in F1, there was some disturbing news. Cigarette ashes were being found all over the bathroom walls, mirrors, toilet seats, and urinal tops. The dorm was up in arms. This mystery smoker would also leave smoke behind in the bathroom, so when the superintendent visited, the dorm got in trouble. This mystery man opened the windows on cold nights, and we all woke up freezing. I thought of the Muslim oils sold in our dorm. They were perfumes, like Bamboo, Ocean Mist, Noontime, and Twilight—oils anyone could use. But watch out when they cut it loose in the dorm. The oils stunk so bad I had to hold my shirt over my nose. It wafted through the dorm and settled on my brain so I couldn't stop smelling that repugnant shit.

I figured out who it was. Yes, all that stuff was done by just one man. Yup! Gummy. First, I saw him spray the Muslim oil. I remained silent. Then he rushed into the bathroom when it was supposed to be quiet time. He came back to his cube reeking of a rollie. I was silent, waiting on the trifecta. That took two days, but I was up late on chineta and saw him approach the east windows. I said, "Hey," and shook my head at him. He gave me the finger and opened the window anyway. I had solved the case. Evidently, a high-paying position with a detective agency or the CIA would not be out of reach for me.

In this NYASTP program, great emphasis was placed on housekeeping, from floor buffing to cube compliance. About eighty percent of NYASTP was dorm cleaning, ten percent was "learning" about addictions/recovery, and the other ten percent amounted to staff days off and forced gym participation.

There were two NYASTP locations, one at Marcy in Central New York and one at Hale Creek Correctional in Johnson, New York. Justin, an inmate who had an opinion on everything, was a Hale Creek reject.

He said Hale Creek had a strict substance abuse recovery program, beginning mornings at five. Inmates were bossed around military-style, forced to run obstacle courses, compelled to carry all their belongings across campus, to follow a rigid curriculum of three-hour meetings, and to suffer other ridiculous punishments. There are no statistics available measuring the effectiveness of this particular program. Thus, no outcome-based management to report to taxpayers.

Mentally and physically challenged inmates were not allowed at Hale Creek. Marcy provided a campus with treatment for mental illness and handicapped accessibility.

In NYASTP, the cube compliance rules dictated tightly-made beds, shoes behind a ruler-drawn line, nothing atop the metal armoire, and one religious book on the small locker. Inspections of cubes were made each weekday by one of our three counselors. The book rule especially bothered me given a constitutionally required separation of church and state.

The sixty men in the dorm were divided into two NYASTP groups, morning and afternoon session. Mondays to Thursdays, class began with an inspirational quote the group would discuss. Jimmy Dean said, "I can't change the direction of the wind, but I can adjust my sails to reach my destination." Norman Vincent Peale said, "Change your thoughts and you change your world." Most members of my afternoon NYASTP group raved about these and other observations. Others commented, "It is what it is."

On Tuesdays, inmates with three months left in the program told their life stories. They usually focused on addiction and recovery. Some stretched their story over several days, to tell us everything about themselves, from birthweight to the number of girlfriends they had waiting on the outside. Still others, like Tennessee, told nothing but war stories about how wasted they were all the time. It was either ugly honesty, like Lonnie hitting his wife and swearing at his kid, or pure fiction, like Tweak saying he made $10,000 a day selling heroin.

One of the more memorable storylines came from Tweak: "My mother met some guy, he busted a nut in her, and later I was born. My father beat my mother, and my mother took her anger out on us. Once I was big, I was mad thirsty, got out on the street, and gave my man his money."

Futz was a pathetic case. I'd swear he got hit in the head too many times in the old neighborhood. Futz was very nice—even generous—to a fault. He didn't want to tell his story and was nervous doing so. "I started then with little pot deals and then some coke," said Futz. "I was thirteen. Once I made money on the deal, I was addicted to the life."

Certain other people in the dorm never admitted using drugs, or if they did, it was "only weed."

All the guys who claimed they were in here for dealing said they were "addicted to the money." It was a cliché and, because these were such small-time players, pretty unbelievable. NYASTP's captive audience laughed now and then, talked over the speaker, and/or fell asleep.

More powerful dealers in our country were absolutely about the money because it put them on the level of today's CEO. Judge James P. Grey of the California Superior Court said, "The major reason why our society is awash in illicit drugs is the unbelievable profits that can be realized in their being manufactured and sold."

I noticed that NYASTP's students had a major concern that went unaddressed in our classes—respect. You weren't a man if you didn't have respect. You were a dead man if you disrespected someone. This was one of my early lessons that told me NYASTP needed to adjust its curriculum for today's inmate. We were different people from those who had limped through here in the '80s and '90s.

Every now and then, counselor Jon Nerber would be left alone with us. The inmates gossiped about Nerber and the other two counselors, Tom Irving and Fawn Trucks. Nerber was the gay one, Irving the cokehead, and Trucks either a junkie or a drunk. Nerber was rarely at work, Irving constantly rubbed his nose, arranging and rearranging his paperwork, and hustling to the staff restroom, and Trucks had that heroin chic look. The last two were supposed to be recovered addicts, though the inmates had their doubts.

When left on his own to teach the class, Nerber had us sit in a circle and have a mini Twelve Steps meeting. The question came up a lot, "How are you?" I had no way to honestly answer that question without getting sent to The Box. Others in the group wanted to talk about "ego." The prevailing thought was that our ego is a bad thing, making us selfish, like addicts. The Big Book mentioned this on page 61. I knew ego because I had looked it up in the dictionary and cited a politician's ego in an old article.

The meaning of ego that I saw was "a person's sense of self-esteem or self-importance." I reasoned that men of power, and artists, must have a strong sense of self to succeed. AA wanted to label drunks as selfish "egomaniacs." Used in home-spun philosophy, and in everyday conversation, ego takes on a negative connotation. With Freud and others, ego was the inner mental power that kept mankind in check. It gave us our sense of reality and personal identity. I didn't bother sharing anything with Nerber's group on the id and the superego.

In the NYASTP meeting room (TV room at night), I overheard all kinds of "wisdom":

-   "Doing crimes is a natural-born privilege."
-   "I'm keeping it whole for you one hundred percent."
-   "I wake up and I just be so loud."
-   "There's a big difference between nigger and nigga."
-   "I just love bustin' through that old lady's front door,
    pointing a gun in her face and getting' money."

When Irving was with us, in class, we concentrated on "character flaws" and read little stories about them. We were told that unless we changed, we'd have two choices: prison, again, or death. If your luck was bad enough, I supposed, you could achieve both!

The short stories condemned us, indirectly, by telling us of fictional people and what their individual character flaws did to them. Flaws included mistrust, believing you can't change, lack of spirituality, powerlessness, denial, gullibility, entitlement, distractibility, laziness, anger, arrogance, procrastination, and grandiosity. There were many more.

Whether you had one or all of these flaws (like me, and were proud of some), that didn't mean you couldn't recover. It didn't prevent you from fighting for the rest of your life to be better. We have the freedom to each of these things. Sober, proper, normal people have many of these flaws, yet they carry on in life and are entitled to the pursuit of happiness, because we are Americans. These character-flaw stories belittled NYASTP students. One even said that if you're not spiritual (religious), you're stupid. Individuals in recovery tend to get on their high horse and tell others they must recover, or else. As writer Benoit Denizet-Lewis said, "Recovery without hope is not possible..." But how can a recovery counselor or an AA member pontificate on religion, or mental health, with students? They're not experts; they have no formal education in these scholarly fields. Thinking that an AA member is an expert is like asking an actor about surgery.

Complaints often followed these "lessons." How could we learn under these circumstances? To answer that question, I'd look to the old timers of AA, who'd say, "Don't question it, just accept it." AA also says the program requires "rigorous honesty," and that you should "fake it 'til you make it." It seemed to me that NYASTP and AA were taking us down a road of self-loathing and confusing, contradictory platitudes. They were doing more damage than good. A number of our inmates wanted to "get better." Prison might not have been the place to start with these lessons. One recovery video was of a guest speaker at some event. He said his professional career was derailed by alcohol. He said God "chose" to save him. So, I guess I finally saw the Chosen One. In response to our questions and laughter, Irving said, "Just do the work."

In December and January, we were punished. The winter I'd feared at Collins had arrived like a never-ending storm at Marcy. Marcy was located in the Mohawk

Valley in Central New York; we were basically a dumping ground for winter's worst. The Mohawks were known as a rugged people; they had to be to live though this. Walking to programs and meals was nearly impossible. The inmates, dressed in coveralls labeled "Marcy Work Gang," shoveled the walkways, and then the plows came along and flooded them again. The wind was formidable, blowing at thirty miles an hour, both ways on the walkway. So, a blinding wave of snow was always at our faces.

I had to go get meds in the mornings as well. Bundled up, we battled the snowy, thirty-mile-an-hour winds and slippery walkways on the way to the Infirmary, only to find twenty people already in line. The Infirmary was small, so most of us had to wait outside in the five-degree weather. There were days when it was minus two, with high winds. Inmates were trying to light their cigarettes and shake off the brutal wind. It went through my coat, pants, and even my boots. The wait in line was often twenty to forty-five minutes. Most of the men in line talked to one other.

I complained aloud. "This is ridiculous," I said. "It's abuse of the mentally ill." Eventually, I filed three grievances, but got no response. The administration must have thought I was right (I thought I was right, so why wouldn't they?). They knew that when spring came, all the complaints would cease. Or the administration thought nothing about it, which is more likely the case. In a perfect example of CYA (Cover Your Ass), the DOCCS handbook noted that the Office of Mental Health declines to address complaints.

But I wasn't giving up. On January 23, I wrote to the New York State Office of Mental Health to share my concerns over this obvious abuse. M. Bernstein, a risk management specialist, responded with a letter that made no sense. He said my letter was forwarded to the Central New York Psychiatric Center's risk management department.

Bernstein added that I had to share my concerns with "facility movement" as they are "outside the purview of OMH," and I needed to contact the appropriate DOCCs medical personnel at (my) facility." So, I went outside the facility for help and got bounced right back. And what the hell was the psychiatric center, nearly a mile away, going to do for us?

They were going to do as much as Marcy's Infirmary would do—*nada.* Granted, this was the same Infirmary that handed out a "Sick Call Procedure," with "floowing" instead of "following," and "availabel" instead of "available," in all capital letters. This document was quite old, the typeface leaning sideways, too light from excessive photocopying.

OMH made it clear they did not want to help ill inmates being abused by standing or sitting in wheelchairs outside for extended periods in winter storm conditions.

Another day, I witnessed an especially interesting incident on the walkway. A female C.O., who looked like popular petite actress Laura San Giacomo, sat in the cab of a state pickup truck near the gym building. Her trail of expletive-laced dialogue could be heard a hundred yards away. She was kibitzing with a male C.O. The woman was attractive, but had a reddish discoloration of the cheeks and nose suggesting she was an alcoholic or spent too much time inside a tanning booth. She was holding a takeout coffee cup, but I wondered what she was really drinking. Then she disappeared, her little area of the morning walkway silent save for inmate chatter. As I wondered where she was. I realized I was attracted to her.

Two months later, I was in the breakfast line at the mess hall and there was Laura San Giacomo, talking to a male C.O. They were at the front of the food line. I poked Gummy next to me and told him to look.

"She's back," I said, excitedly.

Gummy scoffed, "She's a drunk. She got a DWI a few months back leaving the Marcy Tavern (in town) and took out a light pole. Darkened a few streets."

"She has the face … a sexy but drunk face," I said.

"Fuck face! She's a slut. Probably drunk now."

I brought up the subject later with Valefor. He nodded sadly. She was a criminal, just like us.

The other interesting walkway gal was an inmate named Princess. Princess was a transsexual, one of three on the Marcy campus, according to other inmates. I noticed her long hair and her porn star breasts when she passed me near the cafeteria. *There are no female prisoners here*, I thought. Then I realized. She acted classy, talked with other inmates, and was subject of catcalls from the Marcy country boys, who, it's a safe bet, wanted to take a walk on the wilder side of life.

I didn't see the other transsexuals. I felt bad for Princess and wondered why she was here, of all places. She made me recall Easton and his charming meth friends. "Just one little line and I'd be fine."

I'm not a weightlifter, I don't box. And I don't like basketball. Yet I was forced to go to Marcy's gym for Marcy's mandatory recreation, except for bad winter days when the yard was officially closed. Every other Friday was mandatory gym. On the other two Fridays a month, we were forced to clean the dorm, unless Officer Beaver felt like getting rid of all of us and sent us to gym, so he could relax with his crossword puzzles.

For non-participants, the gym had a TV room with hardwood benches too narrow to provide any comfort. Impossible to sleep on. In the same room was a wall with three phones. The ruling party of sports heads made sure the TV was tuned to Sports Center's most annoying show, "First Take" with Stephen Smith and Max Kellerman. One guy was white, and one was black, with polarized views on anything and everything they discussed. Subjects included, "Is Kobe Bryant out for himself or is he a team player?" The way the two men opposed each other led me to believe these were arguments over race rather than sports. Theirs was one of the shows that caused a circle of inmates in our dorm to argue loudly in front of the TV.

Beyond the TV room was the restroom and the airless monstrosity that was the gym. Non-participants here were allowed to sit on foldaway bleachers. They were as uncomfortable as the TV room seats. I sat until I got a cramp, and then I took walks around the basketball courts. There were six hoops in the room, giving us three basketball courts to play on.

Big games of twenty or so players were infrequent. Normally, four to six players, or individuals practicing their shooting, were at three or four of the hoops.

Kenny, who was in here because of four DWIs, and I took walks together, and it felt good doing ten laps around that place. But the warm, humid air adversely affected my breathing, so "100 Pushups Kenny" continued walking after I called it a day.

My first two trips to the gym went well, and I started what could have been an exercise routine. Then came Friday. I was walking past a hoop when a ball came flying at my head, forcing me to duck. A black inmate I hadn't seen before told me I should've grabbed the ball, so it didn't bounce off the wall and roll away. I said, "Okay," and kept walking. I told Kenny and he said it happened to him all the time—balls and bodies flying at him.

The last straw for me occurred under the backboard near the hallway. Out of the corner of my eye, I saw a man in the loud, sweaty game floating through the air and about to land on me. I jumped back, but his elbow clipped my left arm. It was as if I didn't exist—he was the same dude who told me to fetch the ball before. He got up from his kneeling stance at the wall and walked back into the game. No apology, no nothing. I was not surprised—if I'd been a gang member, he'd either have been cut for disrespect, or not bumped me at all.

I told Kenny, "They're doing this to us on purpose."

"Yep," he said. "Why do you think there are no whites in the basketball games?"

The reverse racism was sharply visible at Marcy. Anyone could get dragged into it, especially if you were being taunted.

What had I done to that guy, or the other players? I didn't even know them.

In our dorm was an 18-year-old guy named Milli, but not for Milli Vanilli. It was for milligram. He was a tiny man, as if, only recently, he had exceeded his baby weight, and only just barely. My estimate, he had yet to gain an adult pound. And he had glasses with gigantic circular lenses, which made his eyes bug out.

Milli's appearance on the scene was a kind of foreshadowing. He was one of the first of 150 "youths," aged eighteen to twenty-one, shipped to Marcy by the Department of Corrections. Considering that some of these kids were gang members, and Marcy had the fourth highest cutting rate, I figured they'd fit right in. They were part of the American population who likely had one parent still in prison. The result of more, and longer, drug sentences was a new generation of prisoners. Among the poor, gang affiliated, and mentally ill, they were the population that looked at prison as part of growing up—a rite of passage.

It reminded me of something I'd discussed with Gandhi. My parents were social drinkers. I was part of Generation X, and I grew up knowing alcohol, as did my friends. Because of the subsequent increase in the drinking age to twenty-one, members of Generation Y (or Generation Oxy) experimented with opiate pills and benzos found in their parents' houses or offered for sale by high-school dealers. They rarely drank. The next generation knew prison the way I'd known drinking. A rite of passage.

AA was for those my age and up. NA was only for the kids—you just don't see seventy-year-old men at its meetings.

Just before Christmas, which I knew I wouldn't celebrate, I got a letter from Michael, the pastor who had brought me to the born-again church in Lockport. Between stints in rehab, and during times after I lost my apartment, Michael had allowed me to use his guest room. Along with his wife and six kids, I was considered a member of their family. He wrote, "I want you to know we are thinking of you this Christmas and that you are missed and loved! You have been on my mind and heart a lot the past few weeks—mostly when I see your (rehab arts) bird house dangling from my rearview mirror.

"I know I can speak for my whole family when I say we love having you around, especially at Christmas, and we miss you very much. We remember … that first Christmas Eve service you attended with us after you showed up on our doorstep, and many dinners and stories and random fact contests afterward.

"I remain confident that the Lord has a great and good purpose for you, that he will draw near to you as you draw near to him, and that your best years are yet to come—because Jesus holds the pen. He's seeing something amazing in the pages to come. Hang on to him, Brandon, and I will continue to pray for you and look forward to seeing you next time. You are always welcome at 56 Livingston Place or wherever the Lord might lead us, forever."

Again, I wasn't alone, and maybe there really was a God protecting me and guiding me through this horrific school. Perhaps there was a purpose to all this shit after all.

The 3 p.m. shift started with Officer Valefor. He had a special guest. She was a spunky new officer, a dead-ringer for a 1990s Drew Barrymore, adorned with tattoos of snakes on her hands. Normally, the inmates were put off by new C.O.s, but this situation was going to be different. Valefor gave her the dorm tour and introduced a few of us.

"Are you gonna work in this dorm?" said Soprano.

"Maybe," Officer Winger replied. "We'll find out."

The eyes were on her across the dorm. Inmates did not get a chance to see beautiful women.

When she met me, Valefor told me to tell her about the book I wrote.

She acted impressed and asked me a few questions about journalism that I answered. She said, "Why are you here?"

"Drugs," I said.

"What are you?" she said. "A rock star?"

I just nodded, downplaying the conversation because all eyes were still on her. Inmates couldn't be buddy-buddy with officers because it looked bad to the other inmates. That would have flown in the face of a trust thing. Us against them and all that.

I did not know that she'd make me pay for her compliment.

A couple weeks later, Winger replaced Officer Kelly at 3 p.m. Happiness, even excitement, were the dominant emotions in the dorm. The boys finally had someone to look at, even to objectify, beyond *Buttman*.

Trip O'Donnell visited me—Winger wasn't a no-cube-visiting nut yet—and asked if I had $10. I told him yes and he handed me a small piece of paper. Inside was the chineta. Winger wasn't looking my way, so I dropped the tiny square onto the spoon, added a drop of water, and hid the spoon behind a ragged James Patterson paperback. Ten minutes later, when Winger had to answer the door, I sniffed the chineta.

I was nursing a toothache. Chewing hydrocodone years back had eaten away my molars, some down to nubs, and my toothaches had become more common. Gummy gave me a handful of Ibuprofen. By now, I was in a great mood. Something tempted me to go talk to Winger, but the voice of logic told me: "No way." But my mind said, "She likes you. Go chat." Then: "She's a cop. Stay away."

I strolled to the restroom, giving her a smile as I passed. A new guy to the dorm, Hammer, was in the archway to the can. He asked me if I had any Ibuprofen. I told him I'd meet him at his cube in a few minutes. When back at my space, I grabbed four pills from the pile Gummy gave me. Then I walked to see Hammer and handed him the pills.

I didn't know I was being eyed the whole time. Winger called me to her desk but, once I arrived, just stood there, staring. Nervously, I said, "What's happening?"

"Are you going to tell me what you had in your pocket when you left his cube?" she said.

"Uh, nothing," I said. I was not lying. I was getting very uncomfortable and shaky—I was high. Then I realized what she was talking about. "Oh," I said. "I brought something *to* him. Just a few aspirin."

I was used to her pleasant smile, which was now gone, replaced by a completely different expression. She looked as if she had witnessed a murder or been told she was getting divorced. Her lips were wet, her eyes wide and dark as a shark.

"I'm not sure if we're allowed to share aspirin," I said. "That's why things might have looked shady." I was now as paranoid as I was the first time I'd been arrested in Lockport. The stern look on her face caused my Lithium to stop working, I swear.

"I can check your pockets," she said. "I can check both of your lockers."

"I know," I said. "And you are welcome to. I've done nothing wrong."

The facial expression was unchanged. The questions stopped. I shrugged my shoulders and went back to my cube.

Corrections officers carry radios that have panic buttons. Winger must have pushed hers because, within a few minutes, three thugs in blue rushed in and met her at the desk. She gave them a few words and pointed her long arm toward me.

In seconds, the three club-draggers were at my cube, faces instilling fear, and I was explaining the story to them. I couldn't get my hands to stop shaking. I hoped they didn't see in my eyes that I had a buzz on.

"Your officer said something was going on," said the lead goon in blue.

I explained what happened, again, and the lead guy seemed to relax, so his buddies relaxed. They were no longer in fight stance.

"I believe you," said the lead, quietly. As if he was confiding in me, "She's new. Might have gotten overboard." I thought he meant "overzealous." He added, "We're not gonna toss you or your locker." I was still shaking, but the three guys each said, "Thank you." (First time I'd heard it in prison. Was I dreaming?) They walked back to Winger's desk and shared a few words with her.

It could have ended there. But Winger either had to justify the panic message she'd sent or merely wanted to take the insanity to a higher level. The goon squad grabbed five inmates, seemingly at random, and took them outside to the front porch for questioning on "suspicion" of drug activity. All were put up against the wall and ordered to spread eagle. It was obvious they had the wrong guys. They were questioned, and pushed around, after which the enforcers left F1.

The cop I'd loved turned out to be a psycho bitch. Was she, as the new girl, trying to prove that she didn't put up with shit? That female officers could be tough too? I couldn't know what was going through her head. I felt her staring in my direction, so I spent the rest of the evening in the TV room.

I saw her a couple months later when she came back to F1. She said hello to me, smiled, and was sweet as pie her entire shift. She even said, "Good night" to me at my cube, when she left at 11.

On Wednesdays, I monitored the snowfall through the windows while other classmates read homework assignments aloud. Homework involved writing "treatment essays" when we failed to make our beds properly, left towels lying around, had our shoes out of order, or committed any other dorm room "crimes." There was a Wall of Shame where these transgressions were listed on a paper taped to the counselors' door. From the moment the list was posted, inmates would approach me to tell me of my inclusion.

"Well, Stickney, you're on the wall."

"I know. You're the fifth person to tell me."

"Hey, Stick. Guess what?"

"I bet I already know."

Most NYASTP classes provided no motivation, energy, or interest. They wanted us to believe you could be an alcoholic even though you never took a drink. I worked hard to concentrate and to see if I was learning anything different here than during my countless rehabs. Diversions were a welcome sight, like when Trucks' C.O.-boyfriend came to see her. He was a ruddy-faced, creepy, stalker-type in an officer's uniform. Trucks was not happy to see him; it was like he owned her.

Another distraction were the inmates themselves—their curious sayings and actions, as if they'd never been in a classroom before. The Old Man often had gas, and thereby tortured those of us at his study table. Irving told him to go to the restroom when he was going to let loose, but the obstinate fella wouldn't listen.

Then there was the Spanish dude who brought a porn magazine into class and was reading it while Trucks was teaching. He claimed it was a car magazine.

We were warned to be all business in NYASTP, to follow the program's standards of behavior. Whoever wrote the standards certainly had a good idea of his audience. The guidebook stated, "Feedback, negative or otherwise, will not be tolerated," when an inmate is disciplined in NYASTP. Unacceptable behaviors included "teeth sucking, disrespectful sighs, laughing, or other dismissive noises."

Treatment assignments involved a variety of essays that answered such questions as "How do I expect to change in NYASTP?" Or "One part of my body is suddenly too big for me—which part and what do I do about it?" This Kafka-esque reference was lost on my brethren. To me, a writer, it wasn't so bad to be assigned a 100 to 500-word essay. To others, who hadn't picked up a pencil since walking out of ninth grade, writing such an essay, even at 100 words short, was nearly impossible. They complained, kicked chairs, and whined. They confronted the counselors with "I'm not doing it"; "I didn't do anything wrong"; "I don't deserve this," and such.

A few inmates asked me to write their treatment assignments for them. I did, and I loved doing so because I had to imagine being them. In the case of Cabo Wabo, a Latino fellow with tight hair tied in a ponytail, and a lean build, well, he thought he was Steven Seagal. He was one of those kind inmates—someone you like but also feel sorry for. I had a soft spot for him the first day we met because he told me he was "retarded." And he was serious. He said he took some test or tests that revealed abnormal brain function. I could easily imagine this diagnosis, delivered sometime in the early 1990s, and could understand why it held him back considerably. I did his essays but didn't charge him, as I did the others. I just didn't have it in me to do it. (Of course, he could have been scamming me.) But I felt by doing his work, I was somehow making the world a better place and bringing myself better karma.

Cabo once came to me with a scary situation. C.O. Kilburn had stopped him on the walkway and asked if he was shaving the sides of his head and if so, to knock it off. Kilburn was a Yankees-tattooed slopehead who often stood at the end of the mess hall line, by the spoons, and said "Fuck you" to each passing inmate. He was antagonistic just because he could be. No one was going to stop him.

Cabo's haircut was a style preferred by some Hispanics ever since the '70s. It was not "illegal" at Marcy. *Standards of Inmate Behavior* rule number 110.33 said,

"An inmate wearing hair below shoulder length shall keep his or her hair tied back in a ponytail with a barrette, rubber band, or other fastening device approved by the superintendent." The harassment went on for two weeks and was brought to a head when Cabo went through the metal detector at the yard. Kilburn was there, got in his face, grabbed his shoulders, shook him up, and kicked him out of the yard "for causing a disturbance."

Cabo told me this and asked if I'd help him write a grievance. I had written a few about the service at the Infirmary. Cabo offered two soups and two honeybuns as payment. We detailed each episode of harassment, with dates, times, and locations. Cabo went a little further by suggesting Kilburn was drunk or on drugs. When I'd seen his aggressive conversations with inmates, and assessed his body language, I certainly thought he was on some kind of medication, maybe steroids.

Cabo brought up an excellent point for policing nationally. While the unions have so far been able to quash drug testing for officers, the time had come for regular, across-the-board examinations. Explanation of bizarre police and corrections behavior across our country might be explained with monthly random testing. Why were innocent blacks, Latinos, and shackled inmates being murdered? Why were victims' families winning multimillion-dollar settlements against the police? These drug tests would save lives and taxpayer dollars.

At the end of the form, the grievance asked what the inmate or victim wanted done about the situation. Cabo said he wanted no repercussions, not even an apology—just for Kilburn to leave him alone. He dropped the grievance in the interoffice mail that day.

The Grievance Committee was to receive the claim, review it with the officer, a sergeant, two inmate reps, and others, depending on the nature of the complaint. Then the inmate who filed it was to be called in and the matter discussed with the committee.

When he appeared before the committee, the sergeant accused Cabo of being on drugs during the incidents cited. Cabo denied the charge outright. "I have to pee now. You can test me." The sergeant ignored him and stressed that he had made the outlandish claim that Kilburn was "high." Meanwhile, to intimidate Cabo, there were four C.O.s behind the glass of an office next door, wearing black gloves and staring at him and making other aggressive movements. Where the whole Grievance Committee was, Cabo had no idea. The sergeant then told him he'd get back to Cabo "whenever."

"I don't use drugs," Cabo said. "I told him three times I'd take a test anytime he wanted."

The next time Cabo saw Kilburn, the officer looked the other way. Cabo still feared reprisals from the other officers. There were none. Cabo, it seems, had won a battle few even try.

Officers at all levels in prison can create an atmosphere of fear, so inmate abuse can easily continue. No one in blue got in trouble; yet officers were rather afraid of answering for their irresponsible and arrogant actions—thus the fear they tried to instill in inmates. The American Friends Service Committee report said those pushing for prisoners' rights were targeted when they filed grievances. There's no penetrating that wall of blue.

A majority of inmates take the abuse and, out of fear, do nothing about it.

As it turned out, we never were able to shake Kilburn for good. He kicked us out of lunch early on a Friday, when I wasn't even close to finished. Inmates started bitching and Kilburn shouted, "We're not trying to fill you up. We're just trying to keep you alive."

A week later, Cabo brought me another assignment. I accepted Bustelo coffee as payment. He needed a letter written to the deputy superintendent of programs, Mark Somebody. Cabo wanted his mother, a co-conspirator in his drug case, to be able to visit him.

"I been down fifteen months, padre," Cabo said. "I really need to see her." Cabo's aunt, his mother's sister, had died in April and he needed family around, as did his mother.

The letter I wrote came back two days later with Mark's handwriting. The visit would be scheduled. Cabo was happy and gave me more coffee.

When I was written up for my cube's "disorder," I merely agreed with the C.O. because I either hadn't done what the counselors wanted, or I didn't understand the initial complaint about me. In a legal complaint, if the accused does not understand what is going on, there can be no trial.

I took it as an insult when, knowing my cube was in perfect shape, I somehow earned a "cube out of compliance" citation. Just who wrote me up for that was a mystery. Could've been one of three counselors, or, as I learned in my investigation, it could have been one of our C.O.s.

My cube was near a wall featuring two photos of "the example cubicle"—each cubicle pictured was "in compliance," and what we all should strive toward. I studied it, took a walk around the dorm, and found no one was in compliance with these photos! Everyone's small lockers were on the left side of the cube when, according to the photos, they should have been on the right. The way towels were hung, the location of the large lockers, the beds' relationship to the walls—everything was out of order. Either the photos, which I'd been told to emulate, were wrong, all the inmates were wrong, or both.

I was angry. The write-up had happened on a Thursday. The counselors all took Fridays off, so I had to wait until Monday to straighten things out. Counselors were normally busy on Mondays dealing with all the inmate crap that had happened on Friday through Sunday. My counselor, Irving, took Monday off that week, making me even madder. So, I was stuck with Nerber and Trucks.

I said, "I got a treatment assignment Thursday because my cube, someone said, was out of compliance."

Trucks deflected with, "I didn't do write-ups on Thursday."

I interrupted, "But my cube was in compliance, then and now. I made it match the photos you have on the wall."

Nerber said, "What wall?"

"You have example cubes in photos on the wall near me."

Trucks proved elusive. "Oh, those photos are old."

Boiling over but hiding my anger, I said, "Then what is the example standard that we should follow?"

Nerber said, "Stickney, you should know how to make up your cube. You been here how long now?"

Then Trucks picked up her phone, looked at me, and asked, "Did you write your essay?"

"I wasn't going to." I felt bold in my anger. I was still treating the C.O.s with respect but wasn't backing down.

Nerber: "Why wouldn't you write your essay?"

Me: "Hold a second here. Who wrote this complaint about me? Obviously, there's been a mistake."

Nerber: "We don't make mistakes here. If you're on the wall, you're on the wall."

Me: "If I could just speak with the person who wrote the review. Irving?"

Trucks: "It wasn't him."

Nerber: "Not me."

Trucks, still holding the undialed phone: "Must have been the C.O."

Me: "Which C.O. wrote the report, and which who was on duty, I'm not sure."

Nerber: "That doesn't matter."

Me: "I could clear this up."

Nerber: "It's done. Just write the essay."

Me: "Wait. The cube was allegedly wrong. The wall photos are wrong. Whatever I did wrong cannot be explained to me. So how do I know what not to do again? Or that others will? What is the standard?"

Trucks, dialing: "I gotta make this call."

Nerber (waving me away): "Just hand your essay in. I have to make a call as well."

I was focused on the point I was making, or not making, with Nerber and Trucks. I didn't give a shit about writing an essay. My treatment assignments normally took me five minutes. Or a bit more if I had to rewrite it, legibly, because I have atrocious handwriting.

And here is where I had to break a cardinal rule and trust inmates. No one trusts inmates, especially other inmates. This is why it's so easy for C.O.s to beat prisoners to within an inch of their miserable lives—prisoners lie. "Other inmates beat him up." Or, "We just couldn't control him. He kept fighting us." "He must have strangled himself." C.O.s lie too.

I told inmates for whom I ghostwrote essays that they had to take my copy and put it in their own handwriting. They couldn't hand it in with my sloppy handwriting—the counselors would know who really wrote it. It didn't matter to me if Stingy, The Cosmonaut, or Brain (the other people I wrote for) got in trouble; I only cared about not being detected. I gave them their treatment essays and frequently visited their cubes before class to be sure they were copying my copy in their own handwriting, on their own paper.

But, since I had sympathy for him, I did not check up on Steven Seagal. I had given him the same instruction. We all went to class. Each of us in turn read our essays out loud. I knew something had gone horribly wrong when I saw Steven hold up my folded piece of yellow pad paper and begin reading. The recitation was indescribable. Two words, then an excruciating two-minute pause. Inmates stared at him. A few looked at me and smiled. Three words more. Stuttering pronunciation. Two words. A staggered sentence.

Irving was sitting in the room with us (not looking at me) and finally said, "Okay, let's move on." I was not angry at Steven. My ego was bruised because it had been a damn good essay.

That same day, our group leader shared this from *Twenty-Four Hours a Day*, the Hazelden Edition:

> We must be loyal to the group and each member of it. We must never accuse members behind their backs or even to their faces. It's up to them to tell us themselves if anything is wrong. More than that, we must try not to think bad things about any members because if we do, we're consciously or unconsciously hurting that person. We must be loyal to each other if we are going to be successful. While we're in this lifeboat, trying to save ourselves and each other from alcoholism, we must be truly and sincerely helpful to each other. Am I a loyal member of the group?

A package arrived that afternoon from my parents. We were still working on revising the press materials and PR campaign for my father's October 2018 art show. He sent me Phoebe Hoban's *Basquiat: A Quick Killing in Art*, which I had read years earlier but wanted to reread. Dad also sent *The Autobiography of Frederick Douglass*, and *The War of the Worlds* by H.G. Wells. Mom included cookies, M&Ms, crackers, and cheese. The package room staff had opened the cookies and the M&Ms.

This was frustrating until I heard from a C.O. why food was opened. He said some time, long ago, an officer saw "his favorite chips" in a package and just couldn't stop himself. Inside the bag, to his surprise, he found a package containing 100 suboxone. Since then, package room officers were on the lookout for contraband. I'm a little gullible, so I believed his story for a few hours, then realized it was a creative lie to cover for Marcy staff thieves.

These packages from home made life worth living in prison. They were a distraction that took my mind from what was happening to me. The psychological abuse was interrupted by intellectual endeavor, as with the ten-page Salvador Dali Museum brochure Dad sent to me. On the cover was Dali's "Contemplating the Mediterranean Sea Which at Twenty Meters Becomes a Portrait of Abraham Lincoln." I would get other inmates to stand ten feet away from me and tell me what the abstract photo of colored mini-squares on the cover represented. Most knew it was Abe's bearded face. A fan of Dali since I first saw his work as a kid, I eventually posted the fold-out brochure on my locker. When I saw Lincoln, I wondered if the trip Easton and I planned to the Florida museum would ever happen.

CELL #13

One in five prisoners has a mental health disorder.

Disabilities include schizophrenia, bipolar disorder,

and major depression. The prison society forces

poorly trained C.O.s to care for disabled people,

including the addicted, who they cannot understand.

Inmates are punished and murdered because of their

disabilities, according to a recent New Yorker *exposé.*

CHAPTER 13

EVERYONE KNOWS THIS IS NOWHERE

"Man was born free, and everywhere he is in chains."
—Rousseau

Gandhi and I were discussing treatment essays. A number of their essay assignments asked you to explain who you were without alcohol, drugs, and drug dealing.

"Who are we?" Gandhi said.

"Who we are," I said. Neither of us were convinced we were going to quit just because the court, prison, or NYASTP, wanted us to.

In addition to continuing his Robo-Tripping after prison, Gandhi was convinced he'd resume being a highway drifter after release. I said I was still going to drink. But who I was meant I was someone these other prisoners were not—I was me. It did to me. I wanted to prove it to Gandhi. I took a piece of paper out of my notebook and, seeking deeper meaning, made a list:

- I don't do pushups
- I don't pretend I'm someone I'm not
- I don't tell war stories
- I don't criticize America or my family
- If I don't know something, I look it up
- I get clear directions on a project up front
- I don't let sports rule my world. Life doesn't change if teams win or lose
- I don't overreact to small matters
- I don't seek revenge

I was using Gandhi as a sounding board, trying hard to separate myself from this prison, these inmates, and the staff. "You'll only succeed at this if you stick to it," Gandhi said. Then he started his own list.

A new guy joined the dorm. White, fat, and bald, he spoke with machine-gun speed. "Susan" was tattooed on the back of his neck, which I figured was a BDSM reference. The first thing he did after unpacking his bags was to tape a photo of his black girlfriend to the cube wall. I thought, *okay, he's making a statement*. He claimed she was his "Sugar Mama," or the one who paid all the bills. In clothes obviously purchased from Walmart, she looked ordinary to me.

I hate to sound so jaded, but after hearing for hours that this new guy, Steven "Boxer" Lotto, anyone could tell he was a pathological liar. Steven also tried to get us to believe he was a New York Mafia associate.

He said his photo appeared on the Interpol website (my parents let me know that this was false). Steven said his photo also appeared in the *Five Families* book, but he was misidentified. By the end of the week, so many jokes were circulating in the dorm that even I was embarrassed for him.

"This ain't my first rodeo," said Steven. "I been in an' out of prison since I was sixteen." Something to be proud of. "Okay, Boxer," I said, turning to Gandhi and rolling my eyes.

Rock & Roll Rich, a fellow inmate, said he'd overheard Lotto on the phone a couple times. "The only woman I heard him on with was some old lady at a nursing home in Jersey," said Rich. "He has to practically shout, you know, so she can hear him. Some Sugar Mama."

With Boxer's arrival, I realized I had become a real, obnoxious, jaded, sarcastic, bullying, drug-using prisoner, like everyone else. I was on my way down—the DOCCS system was winning.

That afternoon I met with Irving for my tri-monthly (bi-monthly?) "case plan" update. On the latest report, Irving had written N/A (Not Applicable) for two categories: "client strengths" and "client interests." Okay. Under case plan goals, he quoted me as saying I was outlining my Collins end-of-bid strategy. For the start date, he wrote September 14, 2017, which was a little off (wrong month and year). Irving wrote that I was *still in Collins*, which was a lot off.

The report quoted me as saying I would complete three months of AA, and that I would attend NYASTP. Other milestones were listed, but the mention of

NYASTP was the only thing that placed me in the right prison. Dates of completion were all September 14, 2017, which, again, were the wrong month and year. Irving signed and dated the document as the seventh day of an unreadable month, 2018. So many inmates had told me Irving wasn't doing his job on their cases, and now I believed them.

It was only days after Steven (Boxer's) arrival that the really short guy, Milli, went up to Boxer in the yard and just started wailing on his face, knocking his cigarette and sunglasses to the dirt. Blood began flowing almost instantly.

Running officers were shouting "Red Dot, Yard!" into their radios and preparing for a full-scale riot.

Steven kept saying, "What are you doing, bro? What are you doing, bro?" Milli kept going until a C.O. threw him to the ground and put the handcuffs on. Then Boxer got handcuffed. He was led away bleeding.

After two blue vans pulled up outside the gym, both were taken to the Infirmary. Rumors were flying: Boxer stole from Milli, Boxer was a bigot, Milli was doing the Bloods' bidding, and on and on. "Maybe Boxer really is Mafia," Gandhi quipped.

My anxiety did not flare up. I was surprised. "I just think it's weird that old Boxer is going to The Box."

Evening med run was usually between 8:30 and 9 p.m. Rich was new to the dorm and was one of the obnoxious dudes who enjoyed telling me when I had a treatment assignment. He was six feet tall and lean, with a shaved head and two tattoos on his neck: Motley Crue and the Cincinnati Bengals. Without the tattoos, he looked just like my old lawyer from Lockport, George Muscato. We'd grab our coats and boots to trudge out into the snow and walk the length of two football fields to get to the Infirmary. Rich smoked, but not on the walkway. And he loved to talk rock & roll, coke, and heroin—he was the perfect prison friend for me.

"Kevin Dubrow of Quiet Riot died," he said. "It was years ago. Ten maybe."

"Really? No shit."

"They found lines of coke all over his coffee table."

"Blew out his heart. Like John Entwistle."

"What about Richie Blackmore? Rainbow? 'Street of Dreams' is one of my favorite songs."

"He's still around. You like the Crue?"

"'Home Sweet Home,' yeah. 'Don't Go Away Mad, Girl, Just Go Away.'"

"Ha, ha. I saw them four times. Once in Chicago, once in Tampa, and twice in Syracuse."

"My band is The Who. They played 'Love Reign O'er Me' at a Buffalo show and it actually started raining."

"Ozzy," Rich said. "Saw him three times."

Thursdays were recovery video days. This was a mixed blessing. It gave us a break from Irving's brainwashing treatment—such things as "Your relatives and friends are in prison with you, suffering like you are. You are hurting them by being in prison."

As writer and prisoner Jack Henry Abbott said, prison is all about brainwashing and blaming. "...You are forced to believe that your suffering is a result of your 'ill-behavior,' that it is self-inflicted. You are indoctrinated to blindly accept anything done to you. But if a guard knocks me to the floor, only by indoctrination can I be brought to believe I did it to myself."

Video days involve a popular movie (twenty-years-old "Fisher King," or "Good Will Hunting," for example) or educational DVDs by Delbert Boone, who toured jails and lectured about the dangers of drugs. He claimed to have been convicted of thirteen felonies before he decided to change his life and tour the country lecturing to inmates. When we watched one of Boone's videos, we noticed he had a curious habit of saying "Hmmm?" and "Umm?" when interacting with his audience. This habit made me lose Boone's message because I started counting the hmmms and umms. By my count, he said "hmmm" sixteen times in forty-five minutes. "Umm?" took a close second at thirteen. After a couple days of Boone's videos, all thirty men in my NYASTP class were saying "Hmmm?" and "Umm?" right along with old Delbert, or whenever a situation arose.

So, despite the difference in punishment levels of Marcy and Hale Creek, the NYASTP program was a one-size-fits-all approach. The counselors said, "it's all on you," meaning if you failed, it was your fault. Counseling had progressed since NYASTP was created twenty years ago, so programs themselves were being scrutinized to see how they could be improved and measured for effectiveness.

But not NYASTP. Prison employees took pride in not changing. NYASTP operated as it did at its launch in 1991. On Fridays, counselors were off duty, so prisoners could clean the dorm windows, walls, restroom, showers, tables, chairs, stove, phones, refrigerator, cubicles, and floors. This day was designated "clean-up day" even though inmates were paid fifteen cents hourly, every day to clean all the same things. It was as if NYASTP was trying to graduate a class of future New York state janitors. Cabo joked one day, "I was a drug dealer, making thousands a week. Now I clean floors making four cents an hour."

Why did cube compliance and floor cleaning mean so much to these state workers? Counselors and officers alike answered by repeating this refrain: "If you let the little things go, how can you manage the big things?" Officers and counselors loved to parade these trite slogans and dime-store theologies before us. So, leaving a sock on my floor, or talking during "quiet time," would make my drug/alcohol recovery fail?

The issue of smoking was as bad for me at Marcy as it was in Collins. Lecturer Delbert Boone, whose street name was "the Flim-Flam man," said in a video during NYASTP that cigarettes aren't included in his list of "hard drugs" because they "aren't mind-altering." All the inmate smokers I spoke with said they are so anxiety-ridden they are unable to function without a cigarette. Why Boone would go along with inmates on cigarettes was beyond me. Smokers have eyes that often drift from the conversation or situation when they realize they need a fix. Because that one puff will make them human again.

Marcy, like Collins, sold cigarettes and other smoking products. Unlike Collins, Marcy had a strict restroom smoking policy, which, as in all bureaucracies, made no sense. There was no smoking in the dorm, TV room, laundry room, slop sink room... But there was smoking outside. During dorm time, between meals, programs, vocations, and gym—and in the evenings—C.O.s could either allow inmates to smoke in the restroom or to take them out on the front porch, three at a time, to smoke.

However, the facility superintendent, or warden, did not agree with the Marcy restroom policy that his own employees established and monitored on a daily basis. Thomas Jonas didn't think inmates should be smoking in the restroom at all.

About once a week, Jonas would make a surprise visit to each dorm. When he was spotted arriving on the porch, inmates were supposed to clearly announce, "Microwave," a codeword meaning flush the smokes and get out of the restroom. The superintendent would issue tickets to those caught smoking and to those in the restroom when smoke was present. The latter was harder to prove or enforce, so he usually just busted the cigarette holders.

Upon arriving at Marcy, I had to attend orientation at the school building. The group was led by Superman and Joker, two Jamaicans with thick accents. "Ja, mon!" They played with their dreads and read us the riot act. Most of the time these two inmates were funny because they explained the rules and the way the prison was run (I can't say managed) with those honey- and revolution-dipped accents.

Superman explained the Catch-22 smoking policy, noting that, "All the warden care about is if you blazin' up in his restrooms." I thought he had to be kidding. But no. Other than one meeting of the Inmate Liaison Committee, I never saw Superintendent Jonas until he visited F1's restroom and caught a few guys smoking rollies they'd purchased at Marcy commissary.

As part of orientation, we also had to watch an educational video on sexually transmitted diseases, hosted by a Latino female and an African-American man. They discussed varieties of sex and varieties of people. Now that there are more varieties than just men and women, the Latino host called transsexuals "people with penises."

One of our orientation activities included watching another film, "Omar & Pete," two prisoners facing freedom under parole, which for some can be more difficult than incarceration. In the video, Omar used drugs and got locked up again; Pete stayed clean and free.

Omar's parole officer, a woman half his age, chastised him for using drugs again after graduation from one or two rehabs, including inpatient. This video, and, as I'd learn, the NYASTP literature, were consistent in blaming the addict for his disease and behavior. No science. No medicine. Just opinion and blame. Just the same old "answers" of abstinence and God to bail the addict out.

"Omar & Pete" begins with a sanctimonious declaration from one counselor (unidentified): "We are trying to create a system in which the inmate does not come back." No new system with such a purpose was introduced, identified, or used in the video.

Critical questions went unsaid in Omar's interviews, and with those folks interviewed about him:

-   Did Omar fail his programs, or did they fail him?
-   If all addicts and drugs are the same (a drug is a drug),
    why isn't there an answer to all their problems?
-   And why, because it was first known that addiction existed,
    has no one come up with an answer?
-   Why are some people, like Pete, successful,
    yet an overwhelming majority seem to fail and relapse?

Omar, and millions of other addicts, received "group" treatment through inpatient and outpatient sessions. I attended eleven or more rehabs where I received group treatment. Group treatment is favored by the government because it's much cheaper than individual psychiatric and addiction recovery. Passages Malibu provides an individualized program and is highly successful, according to one-time patient Pax Prentice and his psychiatrist father, Chris Prentice, in *The Alcoholism and Addiction Cure*. This may be the one national program that has measurable outcomes.

Individualized treatment went against AA and NA, and the sweeping statements labeling addicts, and drugs, as all the same. It's my intuition, after many years in AA, that group dynamics are hardly appropriate for sobriety. AA works for some, although its claim to work for all isn't supported by the data.

Individualized care works for some, though the courts, government, prisons, and politicians refuse to admit it. This real solution has supporting statistics. A *National Geographic* article quoted doctors and scientists reporting success in individualized care—addiction treatment specifically tailored for each patient.

Making amends to everyone you believe you hurt seemed like a good idea, but when you really went deep, this step could do even more damage, and even be life threatening. Actor and memoirist Christopher Reeve: "I don't believe in instant fixes. I don't believe we can write an affirmation to forgive our parents and others who have wronged us, and consider it done."

And when you get right down to it, recovery is action, not words.

Lastly, orientation included Narcan training. Not surprising. America was experiencing an "epidemic" of opiate use. Lots of people, including kids, were dying every day. A twenty-seven percent increase in deaths in 2018 (63,600 for all drug overdoses in 2016) caused the government to decide it was time to save Little Suzie, instead of letting Mom and Dad find her with a needle in her arm. The government decided to save everyone, including prisoners, and we received Narcan training in orientation.

After a heavy dose of heroin or some opioid pills, someone might fall asleep so deeply that both breathing and heart stop. To save him, a friend or first responder could give him a snort of Narcan if they are breathing, or from a needle if he is at death's door. The drug, also called Naloxone, wakes the addict up with a start and puts him into painful opioid withdrawal, but it saves his life.

Superman and Joker drew great mirth from this lifesaving scenario. They only smoked pot. "No chasin' dragon, mon."

Joker asked for a volunteer from the class and got a twenty-year-old blabbermouth from the first row. The class noticed that his pants were far too big for him, earning calls of "Rapo," "Baby-fucker," and "Let him die, Superman. Don't save his pederast."

Joker held up a fake demonstration syringe, inducing a class call of "Don't waste the good shit on that faggot." Then Superman yelled for everyone to shut up and the room calmed. Joker took a big yellow cap off the "needle," removed the Narcan container from its handy pouch, drained the Narcan can, and placed the syringe on Rapo's thigh. Then Joker pretended he was calling 9-1-1, and our training to save junkies was complete.

Weekdays, after dinner, we filed into our cubes for an hour of "quiet time," as if we were in kindergarten and needed our afternoon naps. On the daily schedule, posted next to the C.O. desk, "quiet time" was noted as time to work on treatment essays.

F1 dorm was under the control of Officer Hudson, a strangely secretive C.O. who could socialize with just about anyone. But he had a mean streak as well. And he loved to shout whether he was in a bad mood or not. I guess they all did. He loved country and put it on the C.O. radio.

Some inmates complained about the music. At least Hudson knew how to use the radio. When new C.O.s came in, they'd fumble with it forever, until an inmate tried to help. The CD player was stuck on a CD that wouldn't come out: "Midnight Sounds of the Swamp," which sounded a little windy, with water splashing, frogs croaking, and bugs buzzing. Valefor had put it on as a joke but it got stuck in there.

Quiet time seemed to be Hudson's favorite time. Many officers were control freaks about everything. Hudson was a "quiet time" control freak. Lithium controlled my emotions, so I was not suicidal, but it also made me quite thirsty. I had a cup of water or Kool-Aid going from morning until bedtime. As a result, I had to urinate often. If I took a short nap during quiet time, I often felt the need to go to the restroom, but I had to wait a whole hour because, during Hudson's watch, the room was cleaned again. A restroom for sixty men needs to be cleaned often, and it was each day, all day, by the paid inmate porters. You could always tell when the porters were feeling lazy because the restroom would be filthy with cigarette ashes and other bathroom "debris," which likely included the results of cashing-out or getting money.

Hudson appointed four inmates to clean the restroom and two others to sweep the TV room. The restroom was overkill. Due to my location in the dorm, at the north end wall, I was able to get up from my nap and piss into a small plastic soda bottle, near the side of my armoire. I used my left hand to hold the urine bottle, while I looked at a magazine on the locker top and paged through it with my right hand. Disgusting, yes, but no one was the wiser. So that solved the Hudson quiet time problem. I laughed as the inmates lined up at the dorm room door near the end of quiet time, anxious to get to the restroom.

Inmates got bored during quiet time, unless they were sleeping. In pockets and corners of the dorm, some inmates began talking to their cube neighbors. Rather than get up and ask them to honor quiet time, Hudson would shout, "Why are we talking?" from his desk.

When inmates had to use the restroom, other, newer officers forced them to leave their I.D.s at the desk so officers would know where they were. Another petty rule. If the inmate did something wrong, and the officer retained the inmate's

I.D., all kinds of issues were created. For example, the inmate couldn't eat because you had to have your identification to get into the mess hall—in fact, to get in anywhere.

Senior officers pulled that shit too. And it took two weeks to get a new I.D. Trip O'Donnell, who'd run out of commissary supplies, nearly starved to death. Officer Kilburn took his identification when he was subbing in F1 and caught Trip cube visiting, and "playing fuck fuck" with Kush, whatever that meant. He refused to give the ID back to Trip. I talked to Valefor about it and he said officers were not supposed to do that. He told Trip to write to Warden Jonas.

In the *Standards of Inmate Behavior*, stipulation 110.10 clearly stated: "Unless otherwise directed, an inmate shall at all times carry his or her departmental I.D. card and promptly produce the I.D. at the direction of any departmental employee." Our little rule book gave no I.D.-related procedure other than reporting the "loss" in the case of an ID confiscation by an officer.

The best quiet times for me were when I'd sniff a Wellbutrin pill and either chat with Gandhi if he was awake or listen to Buddha's headphone radio. Music transported me back to better days and gave me inspiration for the future I knew I'd have after prison. Former MTV VJ Nina Blackwood's hits of the 1980s show proved a tonic to me. She spun "How to be a Millionaire" by ABC, bringing me back to drunken weekends with my Regent Street friends. Then she switched to "New Moon on Monday" by Duran Duran.

I'd sit in my chair at the corner of my cube and look out at the gathering dusk on the prison soccer field. In the distance was the Central New York Psychiatric Center, and I'd focus on the red light blinking at the building's façade. I had no idea what the light was for, yet it relaxed me. Hudson was talking to inmates, so he wasn't yelling, I had nowhere to be and my worries had been dulled by the Wellbutrin. The noise box inmates were out watching the Black Entertainment Television. I could tune the prison out almost completely, especially when "Kokomo" by the Beach Boys came on, with two references to Florida: Largo and the Keys.

After daily anxiety attacks, it was the only serenity I could achieve.

If they can, inmates often push things to the max. Knocc was a Baby Huey-type. He claimed he was a Blood, though he did not leave the dorm for any reason, unless it was mandatory gym, but I think he got out of that somehow. Knocc had dealt me suboxone on a few occasions and I owed him some commissary. He seemed cool to wait until I could catch up. One week, my commissary money didn't arrive on time, so I couldn't pay my debt.

During one quiet time, Hudson appointed Knocc to work the restroom. This was before I had the bottle idea. I stood in line with the rest. When it was my turn, I went to the urinal and Knocc started calling my name. We were the only two in the room and he started pushing a mop handle into my ass. "Cut it out," I said, and he laughed and kept poking. He was an angry bully, with some sick sexual shit going on. I owed him money.

Now I was angry. I could:

-    Turn and punch him in the face, risking getting beaten and expelled
-    Scream "rape"—PREA would ensure Knocc would disappear
-    Finish pissing and walk away, pretending the incident never happened

I was in NYASTP, concentrating on getting out. The smartest thing for me would be to diffuse the situation and not allow anyone such an opportunity again. I finished at the urinal and pulled the mop from his hands. He laughed. I walked out, leaving the mop next to the bubble. Hudson wasn't looking at me.

Most weeks, Hudson worked three afternoon shifts in a row, 3 to 11 p.m. He wore tinted glasses, the DOCCS baseball cap, the standard C.O. uniform, and expensive hiking boots. Hudson was a hunter/trapper, and I often saw him with a *Rifleman* magazine. I counted on him the way I counted on Valefor to be sane and approachable.

Despite his heroic friendliness, Valefor also had a sinister side. Inmates often did not know their exact leave dates, and that was the case with Yum-Yum. At nine on the dot, Valefor got a phone call at the bubble. He said "okay" a few times and hung up.

"Yum-Yum, pack up your shit. You're outta here!" Valefor bellowed.

"Yes." Yum-Yum made a fist and then stopped himself. "Today's Wednesday, Valefor. Niggas go home on Monday."

Valefor said, "I don't make the rules. Pack your shit. Let's go. Let's go."

Now Valefor and Yum-Yum were practically buddies, something that's not supposed to happen in prison, on the officer's side or on the inmate's side. That's how drug deals, prostitution, and escape plots start. They ignored their critics, talking with each other all the time.

Yum-Yum had been in the dorm a month longer than me. We were all on short time. He'd been awaiting this day. The only thing was, no one was believing it.

An inmate can be written up and lose privileges by ignoring a direct order, so Yum-Yum was packing up, but not with the enthusiasm of a man just told he was being set free.

Gandhi helped Yum-Yum with his bags and then Valefor walked them out the door. There was tension; I could see it. Valefor, normally everybody's trusted, predictable officer, had something up his sleeve. We watched them pace up the walkway. Prisoners who've been freed have a certain walk, and Yum-Yum didn't have it here. They stopped. Everyone watching at the window let out a collective, "Woooow."

Some things you just don't do, no matter who you are. Torture or death by officer is worse than what Valefor put Yum-Yum through. Yum-yum folded his arms and shouted a couple times at Valefor, who was in hysterics. There was an hour left in his shift and Yum-Yum said everything he could without getting in trouble, which was a lot. Valefor had pranked him. Just watching Yum-Yum unpack was agony for all of us.

A week passed and Yum-yum was called up again. A different officer was working that Monday. Finally, Yum-Yum walked the walk of a free man.

But I wondered how Valefor and Hudson could be employed in the same place where the other C.O.s saw us as animals. Writer Jack Henry Abbott explained, "We have been handed over to policemen, to be dealt with in any way it pleases them."

No two officers were alike in the four prisons I saw. There was a *Policies & Procedures* book that C.O.s followed, sometimes. But their applications of the rules differed by officer, mood, day, time, dorm, weather, ass-kissing, and every other factor. No wonder inmates got in so much trouble every day, C.O.s made up the rules as they went along.

Now inmates had to be careful when approaching the C.O. desk. If you were seen there, other inmates imagined you might be a narc, you might accidentally say something incriminating about yourself to the C.O., or a sergeant might come in and ask why the hell you were always talking to the C.O. Hudson made it tough on inmates because, though friendly, he was also a slow-talker.

A slow-talker is a person who listens to you quietly and then, when it's his turn to speak, will offer a few sentences, take a long pause, and then tell you more and more and more what they think about the same subject. You try to quickly change the subject and they look at you, pause, and go on talking about that same subject.

Now I'm a fast talker, blathering on quickly about many subjects at the same time, interrupting myself, cracking jokes and carrying on, in a normal voice. Don't confuse a fast talker with a ghetto talker, noise box, or loud talker. So, needless to say, it was impossible for me to have a quick talk with Hudson. All around, inmates would be listening. The saying in the dorm was, "If you don't want to get in trouble, stay away from the bubble."

I met Hudson and all the other F1 C.O.s on first arriving at F1 dorm. They gave me cube 6, right next to the C.O. desk. At first, I was happy with the arrangement. Other new F1 inmates had to bunk in the newbie section across the dorm; the C.O. on duty, Ortez, wanted to give me a top bunk. After the 2012 car accident and the six-hour shackled ride in the DOCCS van, I did not want a bunk. Cabo, the Latin dude, was already in cube 6, and overheard my car accident/back injury conversation. He volunteered to take a bunk and give me 6. The C.O. just shrugged his shoulders and Cabo got packing. What the C.O. did not know was that Cabo had been moved to 6 because he was deemed a "behavior problem," and at 6, the officers could keep their eyes on him. Cabo knew he was pulling a fast one.

The next time I met Hudson, he peppered me with questions. I told him about the drug sale sentence and that I was an author and journalist. "Uh huh," he said. I had to learn how to talk to him, but I had experience—my father is a slow talker and I'd been trying to tell him a million things since I was a kid (I'm only up to three hundred things that made it through).

Hudson turned out to be quite funny. He loved to antagonize, not provoke like the monster officers. Hudson liked to create situations that got under people's skin, like the quiet time shouting. When March Madness arrived, Hudson told the dorm that NASCAR was going to be on the TV those Sundays. Inmates made angry comments at the start of every game/race and started an argument or two—any one of which could have sent them to The Box. Hudson also told us there would be no MTV, VH1, or related stations on the TV. Those stations featured shows like "Black Ink," which Hudson said contained too much arguing and violence. Soprano complained, "But it juss like that at my crib!"

Marcy housed an inmate called "Canada," an unknown hip-hop song writer and guitarist. He was Canadian but had been living in North Creek, New York, a hamlet outside of Lake George. Canada admitted to seeing UFOs and an alien at a Lake George campground, and having other bizarre experiences. He was selling acid at North Creek where he got busted.

He served a year or so, then joined NYASTP for early release, but figured ICE was eventually going to deport him. He had lived all over the United States touring with his mother, an unknown country singer. Canada still had a Canadian accent—this combined with his outrageous stories made inmates want to pull up their chairs and listen to his "fireside" chats.

Hudson seemed to love Canada and would politely interrogate him for hours as the prisoners looked on and listened.

"What color was the alien?" Hudson said.

A serious Canada said, "Red. A glowing red."

"How old were you?"

"Thirteen… Ah, no, fifteen. I was still a virgin. That was the summer I lost my virginity at the KOA campground."

"What was his name?"

"Whose name? The alien?"

"You lost it to an alien?!"

"Oh, my virginity. A big gal named Honey. She did fortunes. Predicted the future."

"Taking your virginity and fortune telling," Hudson was smiling big. There was inmate laughter around the bubble. "What'd she charge for that?"

"Twenty bucks," Canada said. "My mom paid her."

"To lose your virginity? Plus, the fortune?"

"No—"

"You paid her twenty. She told you your fortune, that you were going to get your first fuck." Unlike the other C.O.s, Hudson rarely said "fuck."

"Uh, ha, ha," said Canada. "The other way around."

"I'm confused. How was the sex—"

"Real good, ha, ha."

"What was your fortune? That you'd see an alien?"

"No. The alien was, ah, first."

"That you'd lose your virginity to an alien. Was she an illegal immigrant like you?"

"Hudson, I'm serious."

"Okay," Hudson said. He was laughing. "I'm... What was your fortune?"

"The fortune. Oh, I didn't get that done." A collective groan from the inmate audience.

"Twenty to bang a fat girl at a KOA? That's a rip-off. I'd pay five, tops. Maybe only two."

"No, she was nice. She nearly suffocated me."

"What?!"

"Her—she was a big girl, not fat, like not a beer gut. Honey was taller than me. I was skinny, and she had huge tits—my face was in them. She sat on top of me. I was sitting in a chair outside the camper. She climbed on, ah."

"She nearly killed you? Why were you outside, in front of all the other campers?"

"We took the chair into the woods."

"Did your mother watch?"

"No! And I had to stop early. Couldn't go all night."

"Why?"

"Nasty headache. Earlier, at the camp's pond, I dove in and hit my head on a rock."

Laughter.

"So, you were okay?"

"You see me standin' here, dontcha?"

Canada and Hudson could go on like this forever. That same evening, around 9, Hudson asked Canada if he would sweep the TV room, "Now." Canada was involved in a conversation at his cube with the Cosmonaut and Gandhi. A few newbies on the bunks were listening. Canada had an audience. Reluctantly, and with an eyeroll, Canada said he would sweep. It wasn't as if he could say "no." That could result in a ticket for disobeying an officer's order.

Unlike Collins, stuffy Marcy had a rule against cube visiting. The rules—no talking in the dorm, and no cube visiting—were enforced by most other C.O.s. Hudson let those two rules slide most of the time, as long as the noise boxes weren't getting out of hand. Otherwise, all conversations were to take place in the TV room or restroom. If an inmate broke a rule, they'd be written up in The Book of Death, a black ledger kept at the officers' desk. Earlier, I had been written up by some mysterious C.O. for having my cube out of compliance. To this day, I do not know what was wrong.

At some point while Canada was sweeping, he made The Book of Death. Hudson could be your friend one minute and then stab you in the back the next. Canada got his ticket for cube visiting. Hudson had struck again.

Finding out the next day that his name was on the Wall of Shame, Canada was furious and refused to write his essay. "I swept that floor for him and he pulls this shit?" Canada wound up meeting with his counselor, Nerber, during NYASTP class. Nerber apparently listened to the story (it was hard to tell when or if a NYASTP counselor was really listening) and told Canada to write the essay. On the Wall of Shame, I saw that Canada and nine others had been written up for cube visiting. The essay was, "Why do I cling to deviant behavior?" I told him I'd write it for him for some commissary donuts. He said he'd do it himself—Hudson had broken him.

Hudson enjoyed his time with The Wizard as well. The Wizard was the ideal African-American Santa Claus. Seemingly ageless, The Wizard came into the dorm with all kinds of tall tales.

- He wrote a book with the "Star Wars" screenwriters
- He had a lot of money, and plenty for suboxone
- He was a graphic artist
- He made holiday cards for inmates for commissary
- He never used drugs

His early lies were almost convincing, even to long-time prisoners used to being surrounded by liars. I imagined that The Wizard believed his own fairy tales. What made me skeptical was his assertion that he had written a book immediately after I told him I was an author. He wanted to one-up me because a book about Star Wars would be much bigger than a book about the Oklahoma City bombing. I asked my parents to search on Amazon for The Wizard's books. He also told me he wrote another book, under his real name. "It's simply called 'The Wizard,'" he said. My folks said they'd look up both.

In the meantime, Hudson came on shift and got into a conversation with The Wizard. The Wizard said that he'd been clean his whole life and had never sold drugs. His drug-related conviction, he said, was all a set-up. This was believable because many prisoners' original arrests are indeed the results of legal or police entrapment, pulled off either to fill jails or to get DA's re-elected.

Hudson said, "You never even tried marijuana?"

"No," said The Wizard. Then he smiled, revealing a gold incisor.

"Never?" Hudson was on the case.

"Okay, yes, I guess, when I was comin' up."

Hudson took The Wizard through pot, cocaine, acid, ecstasy, and even meth. The Wizard backpedaled on every one of them.

"I just don't have a real good memory," said The Wizard.

Undaunted, Hudson asked him if he had a girlfriend at home.

"Many, many ladies," The Wizard said. "Gotta pencil them in my calenda."

The two dorm dealers who had already fronted suboxone to The Wizard were also present, listening closely. They looked horrified, knowing their deals were dead. And, days later, when The Wizard had no money on his commissary account, they knew the truth.

"Oh, my father be stealing my money again," said The Wizard. "He done this before."

But the fuming dealers couldn't do anything to him, or they'd get kicked out of NYASTP and have to serve their entire sentences.

No C.O. was like another. All officer training took place in Albany, and though they all attended the same classes, it was as if they had been trained in different worlds. Each C.O. followed the rules and administered punishments in whatever way they saw fit. No other government branch seemed to allow this behavior. Imagine if military soldiers did whatever struck their fancy.

Hudson had a unique personality. Some officers were robots, some had no personality. Some were worse criminals than us. Some were impossible to figure out. A few challenged inmates to fight them. Some were friendly, while others gave the impression they hoped to shoot you one day at the prison's gun range. Walking outside, I often heard the sickening pops at the range. I couldn't help thinking of *Night* by Elie Wiesel.

CELL #14

Due to my character defects, I was sent into this prison society. I saw a minimum of good and an overpowering wave of ugly. I participated in prison habits, was exposed to several cultures (to which I had been alien), was known as "17-B-1378," "B-love," and "Stickney," was mentally abused, force-fed estrogen, and used my journalistic training to create a report that might open your eyes and move you to support needed reform. You can bet that, somewhere in America, a handcuffed, mentally ill addict is being beaten by corrections officers with clubs.

CHAPTER 14

TOUGHING IT OUT

"I have striven not to laugh at human actions,
not to weep at them, nor to hate them, but to understand them."
—Spinoza

Her name was Officer Lupon. Never in my life have I met a woman like her. She must have weighed in at about 220. She wore heavy makeup, with slashes of rouge on her bubble cheeks. Lupon had a spare tire at the waist and her uniforms were always too tight, as if she was trying to emphasize her breasts and ass. Since her breasts did not stick out as far as her stomach, that didn't work. And her pants' seams were always screaming.

"Shut the fuck up," Officer Lupon said, entering the dorm. She handled the 3 p.m. shift when Hudson was off. "I don't want to hear it. I shouldn't hear a fucking sound in this dorm all night. If you want to talk, if you want to visit, take it out there [the TV room]. I don't want to hear you out there either. If I do, you're going in the book. If I can't get you to calm down, I'll call in some guys who will, and it won't be pretty."

She had everyone's attention. Inmates around me spoke under their breath: "Ok, Officer Tampon" (Soprano); "Officer Loser" (Ghandi); and "Fuck you, you fat fucking bitch" (Canada). Nacho called her "The Titanic."

The guys she referred to were from the goon squad—C.O.s who'd run to Lupon's rescue, just as they had with Winger—and rough us up for insubordination. At a moment's notice, these Dudley Dorights stormed into the room, tossed cube stuff all around, and made threats, basically because they were chivalrously showing off for their female cohort.

The dorm inmates started their rumor-mongering, which could destroy anyone. Lupon:

- Had six kids, the oldest was in county jail
- Was divorced. She stabbed him with a blue pen.

- Had maxed out her credit
- Drank
- Smoked pot
- Only liked black dick
- Also went both ways

She must have known the inmates labeled and defamed her. A quiet voice monitoring you can be heard in a riotous crowd—you hear it with your mind, not your ears. So, she must have heard us. I just kept thinking, and saying, "She's obviously miserable. Why does she work here?" Reasons folks take corrections officer jobs, according to the inmates, included:

- Got bullied in high school; wanted to even the score
- Couldn't get hired anywhere else
- Altruistic—wanted to do good where there is bad
- Sadomasochist—wanted to hurt and get hurt
- Great pay, greater overtime: needed the cash (couldn't get it this good anywhere else with his/her low level of intelligence)
- Stepping-stone to better things
- A job he/her could keep forever, no matter how good/bad they behaved (union protected)

A fellow named Chap introduced himself to me. He was twenty-one. Half Chinese and half African-American, he had rather light skin, curly black hair, and was solidly built. Weightlifting had turned his body into an almost perfect T. As it turned out, he was the dorm's young saint, never speaking ill of anyone, and rarely complaining about anything.

We talked about books and art. Chap called me "Oh Great One," telling others to do so the same. He was interested in writing but was afraid to put pen to paper, other than his journal. He was well-spoken, though he said he'd been in and out of juvenile homes because he was always dealing pot. Chap's link to the intellectual world was through his uncle, a professor at Columbia University. The uncle sent him books and copies of The New Yorker.

I borrowed his copy of Catch-22 by Joseph Heller, the hilarious book I'd enjoyed in college. As I got back into it, I was reminded of the bureaucracy I was currently living in. It was still funny, but now it was aggravating—these were the people running my life.

***

Though the F1 floors were spotless (cleaned so many times the top layers of wood had been stripped away), the NYASTP office had needed a cleaning for quite some time. Nerber, Irving, and Trucks worked in a room that had a window in a wall from which they could observe goings-on in the TV room. NYASTP class met in the TV room. We were required to wear our green uniforms, white socks, and big black boots.

F1 was the only NYASTP dorm. There were eighteen dorms on the Marcy campus where things weren't as strict. However, they were general population dorms where you take your life in your own hands. Every inmate in NYASTP, from Canada to Soprano, wanted to go home as soon as possible. Completing NYASTP meant, in some cases, shaving years off our sentences.

NYASTP was basically run by us. The counselors created a schedule of what to do each of the four days a week we had NYASTP class. Nothing had changed since 1991 when the program began, including the lessons and contents of the glass-walled NYASTP office. Breaking one of three rules—no fighting, no drugs, no sex—meant getting kicked out of the program. Chap was appointed to direct our daily meetings.

There was some good NYASTP news. Irving handed out a paper, "Enhancing Qualities of Addiction." Our disease meant we had the following qualities:

- Perseverance
- Diligence
- Creativity
- Communication
- Perception
- Humor

There was supposed to be no fighting in NYASTP, though other dorms mixed it up regularly. When a fight occurred, or "Shit was Poppin'," the announcement "Red Dot" came over the C.O.'s radio. Officers ran to a certain dorm. A short time later, handcuffed inmates emerged, escorted by officers to their vans. There was certainly potential for a battle in F1. When and where would be decided in time.

Rock & Roll Rich got sick, with muscle aches, had a lump under his arm, and couldn't sleep. I had seen an episode of "House, M.D." where a girl had a lump under her arm. I jokingly told Rich it was the plague. He went to the Infirmary and the medical doctor told him it was the flu and to "tough it out."

Then Rich got more lumps and started sleeping all day. He declined to eat. After a few more days of agonizing visits, the Infirmary finally sent him to a hospital in Syracuse. The C.O. packed up the contents of his cube as if he wouldn't be returning.

To look good in Irving's eyes, I signed up for AA. Our sessions took place in the school. Meetings involved six guys, two of them were in wheelchairs. We'd have an AA meeting whenever someone said they needed to talk to sort out a problem. On other days, we watched movies. A kind C.O. left them in a file cabinet for us.

AA folks have little clichés they say and put on bumper stickers, such as "One Day at a Time," "Let Go and Let God," and "Easy Does It." One group member was talking about how he'd been in prison too long and was going crazy. The black guy in the wheelchair said, "Easy Does It." The complainer shot back, "You remember bending over and displaying your ass at reception? That was 'Easy Does It.'" He brought the house down.

The Big Book explains AA in its first 164 pages. The rest of the book consists of life stories by alcoholics who dropped the bottle and got well. There are no fails discussed in this book. Like *Dianetics*, the AA book is an advertisement for itself. Chapter 5, "How it Works," declares that for drunks to succeed in AA, they must embrace God. Then it says, "Half measures availed us nothing. We stood at the turning point." Since 1996, I had heard these two lines read to me at meetings, and I still believe there was something missing.

I hadn't drunk in many months and I really didn't feel any different than before. I was not withdrawing from opiates, which made life easier. God became more of a mystery; I was closer to God when I was high—opiates being the absolute truth. I had not prayed in prison. So many find solace and a future by chasing faith in prison, whatever religion it is, and I saw them engaging each other in spirituality.

So, I could not embrace AA's Higher Power or even G.O.D., "group of drunks." Another AA cliché, "Fake it 'till you make it" seemed a desperate lie to me. One of the worst AA clichés: "When I was young, I never said I wanted to grow up and be an alcoholic." Pretend I believe in God until I believe? But some alcoholics were that desperate. Of course, some folks had led such horrendous lives, with terrible families, that they escaped into the bottle. AA was the only place they had to turn. I had no issue with these people—anything that would help.

I had to tolerate the NYASTP and AA meetings. Tolerance, not acceptance, was the way out for me. At meetings, I admitted I was an addict. Addicts feel guilt and denial, though I no longer felt either. I had been more of a hedonist, someone enjoying himself and being right out in the open about it—happiness was the most important thing in life. Until I got caught.

For those unfamiliar with hedonism, it's a way of life, of living for today. It had been celebrated by the hippies of Woodstock while standing against war and oppression. It's about freedom, though today's Republican moralists would say people like me were selfish. Some of hedonisms's tenets include:

- Fall in love
- Live life to the fullest. No regrets
- Surround yourself with beautiful things and people
- One day at a time (sounds like AA!)
- Make your life what you want it to be
- Laugh
- Read. Get away from technology
- Live without materialism

Officer Hudson and I developed a scholarly relationship based on satire. He'd call me over to his desk and act as if he had something serious to say, as if I'd done something wrong. Then he'd speak.

"I have an idea for a book. How about *Fingernail Clippings: Garbage or America's Premier Natural Resource?*"

"We could stop global warming." I said, nodded, and pretended to contemplate the idea by placing a professorial hand to my chin. "I think it's brilliant," I said. "How about if I pen the introduction?"

He'd grin but not burst out laughing, but I did. *"Transsexuals: They're Not Just for Men Anymore."* It was another of his book suggestions. Most C.O.s were politically incorrect—Hudson was intellectually and politically incorrect. Just about every shift Hudson had (three per week), he'd strike up a conversation. I had to be careful because he could be a long talker. What I thought was going to be a brief, funny exchange could turn into a half-hour lesson about fishing or NASCAR, with me as the pupil.

When my people sent packages that included M&Ms, I'd bring some to Hudson. Normally, C.O.s refused gifts, yet Hudson accepted them. I'd laughingly say, "Here's your graft." Valefor always declined when I offered the same, which made me a little sad… well, that was his way. These guys were the only C.O.s I offered anything to except Lupon. It didn't seem to give me an "in." I did give her a James Patterson paperback my mother had sent to me. I felt guilty that we were all making fun of her. I noticed Lupon liked to read Patterson, so I thought, *What the hell?*

Luckily, the inmates didn't see me do it.

***

Gandhi and I were at the sad little bookshelves in the TV room, looking at the latest collection. Every three months, Marcy's librarian (or assistant librarian) visited each dorm to take the old battered books and replace them with new battered books.

This time there was more Danielle Steele, Lee Child, and Patricia Cornwell. There were more Spanish Bibles, a Jack London story collection, a couple of Eastern philosophy paperbacks, and a bunch of authors I'd not heard of before. I grabbed a hip-looking noir by Andrew Vachss called *Shella*.

Gandhi made a hushed sound and held up a college textbook, *Psychology*. Having found the Dead Sea Scrolls of prison, he opened it, and we looked. One page had a large multicolored pyramid labeled "Maslow's Hierarchy of Needs." I remembered it from some college course.

The bottom floor of Maslow's pyramid was man's need for physiological well-being—satisfying hunger, thirst, sleep, and sex. The next floor up was safety, including stability, protection, and strength.

The middle floor was acceptance—love and belonging. Second from the top was esteem— the need for prestige and reputation.

At the top of Maslow's hierarchy was self-actualization, or self-fulfillment.

"Does NYASTP, or Marcy, help us with Maslow?" said Gandhi.

"Let's test it," I said. "How about physiological? My need for food, drink, and sleep are, at best, accidentally covered. But I still need sex. Oops, T level only 200—no need for loving."

"Stay away from me," said Gandhi. "How about safety?"

"Do you feel safe here in NYASTP?"

"I feel safe from inmates and war, but I do not feel safe when it comes to my own mind or correctional officers."

"Me neither. C.O.s are angry and scared … of us. Fear is the most dangerous threat to safety."

"Acceptance?"

"I don't feel love, except when I look at *Buttman* magazine."

"Belonging?"

"I don't belong here, no. You do."

"Okay. Esteem. I'll tell you now that mine is in the toilet."

"Mine too, brother. Mine too."

"You have a reputation for not bathing."

"Only among those of the Latino persuasion."

"Now, we have made it to the top of the pyramid. Self-fulfillment."

"Self-actualization. That's what NYASTP's for!"

"They should tell us—the counselors—that we're working toward self-fulfillment."

"No, that's the guys who take a towel, Vaseline, and a *Buttman* to the restroom."

"Then what's self-actualization?"

"Do I have to believe in God or a higher power? Or thump the AA book?"

"Let's look it up," Gandhi said, flipping pages. "Expressing one's creativity, quest for spiritual enlightenment, pursuit of knowledge, and the desire to give to society."

"Deep, brother," I said. "I'd rather express my creativity, encouraging others to give to me."

"That's quite Zen," Gandhi said. "The student becomes the master and hears the one hand clapping."

On Tuesday at NYASTP, Irving polled the class on what we wanted most in a sober life. Several inmates offered obvious and mundane answers. A few simply didn't know.

Clearly bored, Gandhi raised his arm, "I want to fly," he said.

"In a plane or helicopter? Or fly a kite?" said Irving. The two of them already had a bit of contention in their relationship. Mainly, it was because Gandhi failed to be as serious as Irving. And Gandhi was never going to stop Robo-Tripping.

The highway drifter had already confided in me about his hobby—wanting to fly without technical assistance. He'd run in a field and jump, hands out like wings, and expect to fly. He had small scars on his forehead from when he landed on his mug.

"No, I mean fly, myself. Going into the sky," said Gandhi. "Fly past birds, over planes, and into clouds. I can fly."

Irving's face went blank. "You really believe you can fly?" Irving was probably thinking this NYASTP student needed psychiatric help, or he was just fucking with the teacher. That pissed Irving off.

"Stop it," I said to Gandhi. "Or you're going to get in trouble."

"I know I have the power," Gandhi said.

"I will call the Infirmary right now," said Irving. "No one wants you to hurt yourself."

Other inmates started telling Gandhi to desist, right now. Amazingly, Gandhi complied. After class, the two men met, and Gandhi wound up writing an apology for disrupting the class. It was either that or disciplinary action. Irving was no joke.

Later, I borrowed Gandhi's astrology book, looking for The Big Answer. Gummy told me to read "Proverbs." The truth was elsewhere. Gandhi's book said, under Leo, "Among your most striking characteristics is a refusal to be hampered by petty rules. Day-to-day routine quickly leads to boredom and makes you desperately unhappy. Your unhappiness won't last long because you simply won't put up with it."

I know a lot of folks no longer believe in astrology, but, true or not, I have respect for it. Sometimes it picks the right words out of nowhere and applies them to your current situation, as it did in this case. "You feel you have an important role to play in life and you're going to find it."

I was saddened to find out later that author Woolfolk had died in May 2013. Her book seemed so alive. Her death gave the book's contents a more mysterious quality.

I rarely ventured from the dorm at night, except for meds. But something possessed me to head out to evening rec in the yard. There was a lot of dealing going on. Shivering, I took a walk around the track—I didn't want to be accused of staring at a gang.

A kid who looked like Gummy, only with teeth, caught up to me on the track and started talking. He said he was in G1 dorm and the "homies" ran the place. The gang members were making shanks, he said. Also, when inmates received packages from their people, or home, "the homies are on them like a pack of wolves. They beat people, and no one will stand up to them because there are so many."

Gummy 2 continued, "Last night a guy dumped a fresh container of hot coffee all over another guy and burned his chest. A bystander got it too."

And that was it. He moved onto the soccer field. I had no idea why he spoke with me. Must've needed to tell someone.

Fighting, sex, drugs—inmates regularly bought it by involving themselves in any of these three activities. The first time I saw it was during a gang-related attack in January 2018. Graveyard was a dark black man with tight cornrows and what looked like hundreds of tattoos. His skin was so black you couldn't tell what the tattoos were. It just looked as if he had veins on the surface of his skin.

I only spoke with Graveyard once, during a University of Buffalo basketball game in the TV room. UB is my alma mater, and the only reason I was watching basketball. Graveyard took the empty seat next to me. I was told he was a Blood and the reporter in me thought this might be a good time to gather some facts. As we watched the game, I formulated questions I'd pose.

In prison as in life, the blacks hung out with the blacks, the Latinos hung around the Hispanics, the Aryans had their own kind, Native Americans, etc., kind of like the Crips and the Bloods, only with fewer gang rules. I'm Irish, Italian, German, Welsh, Dutch, and a few other things. I identified as Jewish in Elmira. My uncle claimed we have Spanish blood on Mom's side. I didn't fit into any prison category, so I never knew what was going to happen when I talked to anyone. I had no gang to identify with or make instant friends among. Usually people like Gandhi and Officer Hudson opened up to me because they liked the way I spoke—as if I didn't belong in prison. I didn't really feel I was better than anyone, unless they insulted me.

"You been down a long time?" I said to Graveyard during a commercial.

"Nah," Graveyard said. Then he said a whole sentence that was in ghetto speak. I had no idea what he said. But I wanted to know. Then he met my eyes hard, as if waiting for a response.

"Yeah," I said. "I got two years for selling my prescription." I shrugged my shoulders. "Are you glad you got in here, NYASTP, to get a bit of time off your bid?"

Graveyard nodded in earnest. I thought, *Oh, boy, I broke through.* Then Graveyard said something about "a brother" and "he got a body," which I knew meant a friend of his had killed somebody. Of course, he could have said anything—I couldn't be sure.

"I see. Wow, man," I said. And the game came back on. He got up and engaged with Stovepipe, another Blood, and that was the end of my great interview.

A few weeks later, I saw Graveyard get stabbed. We were on the walkway, on our way back from a dinner of crap poured over rice. There was a silver sky, snow on the ground, naked trees to the left, and snowbanks to the right, in front of each dorm.

As I approached F1, I saw a flash, though I had no idea what I was seeing. It was quite beautiful actually, like a ballet dancer. A man hurtled the snowbank in front of our dorm. Then I saw a screen of green inmate uniforms, gathering and bouncing like a football fight. When we got closer, we saw blood on our porch, and C.O.s everywhere, yelling, running, and pulling up in their blue vans. Night sticks raised, the C.O.s shoved inmates to the ground. We were herded into the dorms and told to get to our cubicles.

"Graveyard got shot," said Soprano, breathless.

"Shot?" I said. I wasn't sure what had happened.

"Stabbed, man. They cut his face."

I had witnessed a cutting. As Soprano explained, cuttings were rather complicated. The gang had to have a "beef" with someone, then pick a day and time to attack. Always the attack involved a team of three—a lookout, a fighter, and a cutter. The fighter picked a fight with the victim to distract him while the cutter swooped in and did the deed.

Graveyard had been taken to the Infirmary. He had been cut from his right eye down his cheek to his throat. After the Infirmary and likely an offsite emergency room, he was sent to The Box. Both the instigator (if caught) and the victim went to The Box in prison fights. Needless to say, Graveyard was no longer in our NYASTP class.

Officer Valefor was talking to a few of us the next day. Of all the prisons in New York State, Marcy, he said, ranked fourth out of the top five in cutting frequency. The others were Bear Hill, Greene, Wyoming, and Fishkill. "It depends on the young guys," said Valefor. "The more young, the more cuttings. It's the Cut Culture."

Inmates who didn't bathe were despised because of their odor. Despite the daily housecleaning, the dorm was so dirty that dirt jumped onto us and clung. Mental illness and depression would cause a person to let himself go. It happened in every prison, especially those ill equipped to serve the mental health population.

I felt like I was a rebel, but maybe my refusal to shave or get a haircut was more a sign of a chemical imbalance in my brain—depression-induced sloppiness, apathy, or anger. I had my hair cut once at the inmate barbershop and once in the Marcy bathroom. That was twice in the eight months I was locked up. There was no one here of importance for whom to "look good."

I did begin showering every other day, depending on how much environmental dirt clung to my skin. Despite the daily scrubbing, the dorm was sullied. It dirtied us all.

As at Collins, the phones were monitored at Marcy. The Global-Tel-Link surveillance workers who listened to our conversations would provide tapes to the administration and the cops. Stupid inmates allowed their calls to outsiders—about drugs, murder plots, and conspiracies—to be tapped. Smart inmates involved in criminal behavior spoke in code to their people.

The Wizard earned a name for himself when speaking with one of his "many girlfriends" by saying things like he "knew where the bodies were buried" and so did his "gang." The Wizard had a sense of humor and was likely trying to make his girl laugh. He didn't have gang tattoos, or flash signs, or run with a set. He was in for a money-laundering conspiracy.

But the words he used during the call were enough to launch an investigation. On a Wednesday morning, The Wizard was called down to the administration building. In an empty room, save for a desk and two chairs, A C.O. introduced him to a state police investigator. The cop grilled him about suspected gang affiliation and other matters for about an hour, likely figuring him to be a lying moron. The Wizard was allowed to resume serving his sentence after the interview was completed.

The phone behavior was a glimpse into what these inmates' home lives were like. Walking past the phones one day, I heard a guy barking into the phone, "You only stressed out because you don't listen. You on some bullshit." I knew about this prisoner's personal life and I thought: *No, dummy. She's stressed because you're in here and she ain't got drugs, or money, or anyone to watch your six kids.*

Some inmates yelled at their mothers. Others screamed at wives who'd just sent a package, and even shouted at the kids. Besides recovery, I figured that a lot more education was needed.

My friends and family supported my commissary account. I wanted to work my money-earning craft as I did at Collins, helping Cougar and Bear with their book projects. Other than The Wizard's claim, F1 had no would-be book writers or really any creative convicts. In fact, few in Marcy believed me when I said I was a published author.

My father had to buy a copy of *All-American Monster* from Amazon and mail it to me. When it arrived at the package room, I brought it back to the dorm. Gummy grabbed it from me, compared the real me to the author photo on the jacket cover, and then took the book around the dorm to show the ten or so nonbelievers. Within a day, the difference in the way the majority of F1 treated me was measurable. I received even more respect from Valefor, Hudson, Kelly, and Bebitt, and even recognition from our cast of C.O.s.

Gummy, who took the McVeigh book to Nerber and Trucks that day, said they didn't believe him until they saw the author photo. According to Gummy, Nerber looked at the photo, then said, "This was him before the drugs." Some people just aren't worth the effort.

The C.O.s we liked were the ones who treated us with respect. The officers who weren't our regulars would often come pounding into the dorm, order us around, and yell for no good reason. Our dorm moved in unison when the jerks took charge. We were disruptive and disrespectful until the C.O. was ready to explode. We pushed things until he threatened tickets or write-ups, and then we pushed it further: cube visiting, talking, smoking wherever, yelling in front of the TV.

One winner, a young, blond dude who looked like the Terminator, came in for the 11 p.m. shift. He stood at the bubble, staring at all of us. We took it as a signal to be quiet. "I'm not putting up with any shit tonight," he said. "Predictable," I whispered to Gandhi.

"I want it quiet. One inmate at a time to the restroom. No smoking. And if anyone disagrees with that, wants to try me, come on up here now."

This was at best a hollow threat because, if anyone did challenge him, he'd just call in the goon squad and they'd beat us down. "He must be scared," Gandhi said. "Afraid of us. C.O. trying to look tough."

Ace handed me a piece of chineta that night that I decided to save until morning. For me, merely possessing it was my slight to the new tough guy. No matter what he said, we were going to do what we wanted.

C.O.s' differences were something I chronicled in my diaries because, even though they were in a prison, and had a union, they made their own rules. I asked Valefor about a C.O. named Blosat who came onto his shift disheveled and sweating. He was a regular substitute for those who had days off. Blosat was a bulky, friendly jock.

"He had just gotten into a fight," Valefor said.

"With an inmate?" I felt bad for the inmate.

"With another officer."

"What!? I thought all you guys were friends and protected each other. Wall of blue?"

"No," Valefor said, chuckling. "This is kind of like any other workplace: people you like, people you hate, people you tolerate."

Of course, the workplaces of my past did not allow fighting among employees. Surprised at Valefor's candor, I felt my mind change—nasty conflicts existed behind even the wall of blue.

Ace, who took to wearing a do-rag, dealt to the new guy, a bread truck driver named Green Lantern. He was in Marcy for selling cocaine. Dealing to the Lantern, Ace soon found out, was a mistake. Green Lantern had every excuse in the book as to why he couldn't pay.

Ace decided to have a "sit down" with the Odinists, who agreed something needed to be done. Ace said he didn't want to cut the guy—what if his money did show up? So, Ace met Lantern in the dorm before dinner. Ace was holding a white athletic sock that "tonight will have a lock in it." A lock in a sock, or "slock," meant it was going to connect with Lantern's head when he was asleep.

Lantern, a rather big dude, begged Ace to hold off, to give him three more days. Ace agreed to wait, much to the chagrin of the Odinists (gangs can be bloodthirsty). Three days passed, and Lantern handed Ace his commissary sheet. The debt was paid.

We had a NYASTP class on preparing for the Parole Board. I had a June Parole Board date, but Irving said NYASTP would satisfy my requirements. Also, he said, I was a nonviolent criminal, and the board was normally concerned only about killers, shooters, and deadly sex maniacs. I was glad I hadn't forced the suboxone on Israel because I then could have been charged with a violent crime.

We examined a list of absurd questions the board might pose. To me, the questions were rather funny:

-   Where did you get the gun?
-   Why did you have the gun?
-   Why did you think you needed the gun?
-   Why did you sell drugs?
-   Did you think selling drugs was a victimless crime?
-   Do you think drug dealing is a non-violent crime? (Now this was a sticky one. The board wanted this answer: "It could be violent if violence is caused by the deal." This question was to see if the felon had any morals.)
-   You said, "If it weren't for your drug use, you wouldn't commit crimes." Why do you do drugs?
-   Why do you drink alcohol?
-   Why were you robbing people?
-   Why did you have to kill the man (woman, child)? You should think long and hard about this question, if you have not already done so. Whatever you say, do not say that you had to kill them because they could identify you.

There were several more questions related to these. Inmates often came back to the dorm from their Parole Board interview angry, agitated, and confused. Irving said the board purposely frustrated inmates to see how they'd hold up under pressure. Those who cracked or gave insane answers had their parole requests denied. They could not make it in the real world, the board reasoned, without going right back to their bad habits. They would be community risks.

The rejected inmates should have taken the preliminary advice we received:

"Dos and Don'ts at a Parole Board Hearing":

- Accept responsibility for your crimes. (All of them?)
- Be clear and concise. (Only one-third of Marcy inmates knew what "concise" meant.)
- Direct your answers to all the commissioners and make eye contact. (But don't stare them down.)
- Don't say "I'm sorry." Find stronger language to express remorse. (We live in an age when few apologize or express thanks.)
- Don't say "I made a mistake." You were convicted of a crime; it wasn't a mistake. Own up to it as a crime. (In an unrelated point, what if the inmate was wrongly convicted? In a police state, individuals must admit to crimes they did not commit.)
- Don't be intimidated. (It's only your life in their hands.)

Before falling out of society and losing employment in a trade for daily pills and Four Loko drinks, I had worked for The Partnership, Stand, and J. Fitzgerald Group, all Western New York advertising agencies, serving as a copywriter. Our clients included Volvo and Becton, Dickinson. Even at the time, I felt the irony in working for Becton, Dickinson, one of the largest syringe manufacturers in America.

If no one was an author in F1, maybe there were some businessmen who needed a brochure, news release, or website copy written. Ad agency stuff. Inmates did have lives and businesses (other than drug dealing) outside the prison that they'd go back to soon. I could even write letters to help inmates with administrative matters. NYASTP was a "going home" program even if my date for that was still eight months away.

I listened closely at the NYASTP meetings and talked to a few businessmen, offering my writing services. I found Kenny, an older fellow in the delivery business. Back in Manhattan, he had managed a high-end document courier service for attorneys, stockbrokers, and others. Kenny was here because of four DWIs, so he didn't lose his business the way others had.

DWI guys like Kenny just didn't belong in prison. Maybe county jail. But prison? Maybe if they had killed someone. But because of Mothers Against Drunk Driving, the nation treated drunk drivers like minor murderers.

With his wife, the Cosmonaut owned a greasy spoon restaurant in Corning,

NY. He was the main cook.

Finally, there was Guns. He had a boring common name in real life, like Bill, Don, or John. Guns came from the hip-hop star, as most handles did. Guns' wife was a home-care aide in Brooklyn. There was a lot of competition in her field and she wanted to stand out.

Kenny, the delivery guy, was skeptical about my offer of services because, he said, most of his work came from referrals. For brochure text and a sample layout, I said I'd charge him $10 in commissary. That way I could afford suboxone without cutting into my own food budget from my people. I didn't tell him that. In fact, Gandhi said no one knew I got high, except for Trip and Kush, and one other dealer.

The Cosmonaut gave me peanut butter, a pack of chocolate cookies, and half a brick of Bustelo Coffee in exchange for a brochure about his restaurant.

Guns said his wife was practically desperate. Two longtime clients had died of old age and she needed to ramp up. He offered me two packs of Newports, knowing I had a habit. This made me feel angry at the law for locking me up—that's addict thinking. But I felt really guilty doing drugs with money. Indirectly, I had taken from old people.

Plus, as things looked, as long as I didn't fail a drug test, I'd get released from prison in a few months. Then what would I do, on parole, looking for a fix? If I tested positive multiple times for drugs while on parole, I'd be sent right back to prison to serve out my parole time—two years. I felt clean time coming soon.

Kenny kept putting me off on a date of when we could interview him for his brochure. The Cosmonaut's took a few days and he was happy. Guns and I sat down several times, made revisions, and after about a month, I delivered the final product. Both the Cosmonaut and Guns paid me immediately. I left the door open with Kenny even though he didn't have the courage to tell me he was no longer interested.

On the other hand, I found out that the big reader Gummy was challenged when it came to writing. He asked for letters and love poems to his girlfriend, a birthday letter, and a Mother's Day card (Wizard was the card designer).

Gummy was a dishwasher to many of the inmates who ate in the dorm rather than the mess hall. As payment for cleaning their dishes, Gummy received dinner five nights of the week. They gave him so much food, he shared some of it with me as payment for the letters.

Stuck when it came to the love poem to Gummy's woman (I hadn't been in love in fifteen years), I borrowed a couple of lines from Pete Townshend, "...There's a place you walk where love falls from the trees." That line from "Who Are You" was enough for a poem, though I padded it with Gummy-centric facts and ideas to personalize it.

Guns came to me with another opportunity. He and his sister had been pulled over in a bad neighborhood by two female cops for failing to signal. One cop, Officer Hand (here comes the irony) asked Guns, sitting in the passenger seat, to get out of the car. Without telling him anything, she began a full search of his person, which was way beyond what a frisk would entail. She wound up finding a decent-sized bag of cocaine in his pants.

They were both hauled off to jail and Guns, represented by a shitty attorney, was convicted after a quick trial. I was familiar with that. The assignment was to write an appeal for him. That would mean a lot of law library work. Knowing the money I could make from Guns, I was enthusiastic.

We had to meet about the legal papers he had, plus the LexisNexis criminal law documents. He also had a book on appeals. We met in the TV room, but Officer Hudson kept interrupting us with stupid questions. Inmates are not allowed to provide legal aid to other inmates, according to the *Standards of Inmate Behavior*. Hudson suspected us, but I told him we were writing Guns' biography.

Guns also gave me two legal books and I studied *Miranda* and improper search and seizure decisions. I found case law in the library and studied other prisoners' appeals. In three weeks, I had written my first legal appeal. We revised it together and I was rewarded with $20 in bricks.

Spider, a Latino don, left the dorm one morning. He was always bragging that his son "got a body" and was in prison too. Spider drove me nuts. Morning, noon, and night, we were treated to his daily whistled versions of "My Way" and "Greensleeves."

It was so nice when he was sleeping because the dorm could be a little more quiet. Spider was at least seventy, so he likely had about nine years left on the planet. I got so tired of him I yelled across the dorm, "Please stop whistling!" Spider kept going, so I said it again. He stopped. "You don't know who you're dealing with," he said.

I wasn't afraid of this poser. His life story was as fake as they came (six wives?). At least he stopped whistling that day. He told me on another day they were going to make a movie of his life called "The Last Don." I said I'd watch for it.

I always tried to watch my words around these criminals. Gandhi reminded me that, as a Leo, my words "motivated some people to violence." Other people's words were simply ridiculous. Tennessee told me his life story. When he was in high school, he claimed, he "had mad weed, mad coke, and mad meth," and always took the prettiest girl home.

I spoke every other day with my parents in Florida. With them, I verbally reviewed my days, good and mostly bad. How can you have a good day in prison? My mother, the saint, raised what she called a "wild child" who grew up, got married, had a child, a house, and a job in finance. The dream was deferred by drugs, and as things fell apart... Well, my parents were there for my partial recovery and the sobriety that followed. The post-prison plan was to move to Florida and join the nation's 4.5 million people on parole and/or probation. I wrote a Plan B as well, just in case the administration screwed me over and turned down my interstate transfer.

Plan B (staying in New York state) involved staying with Rachael. We became drug friends in 2006 after meeting at the Locust Street party house. Or I could stay with Pastor Michael. I also had an outpatient and mental health facility lined up. I'd reconnect with my AA sponsor. Plan A included all the same things, except for friends. Still, it was better than Plan B, where I'd certainly have issues with Niagara County Parole.

One person made repeat appearances in my dreams—my crusty old editor at the *Union-Sun & Journal*, Dan Kane. He was an Irish intellectual, a father to seven adult children, a mentor, real estate mogul (of sorts) and, I was told, an addict. I knew he drank whiskey now and then, but I never saw him use drugs. When he'd hired me, I was twenty-two and he was about sixty. He had been a boxer and still had the strength of a young man. I had three mentors: author Geoffrey Giuliano, editor Dan Kane, and my ad exec father. Giuliano and Kane taught me how to question people, and my dad taught me how to question life.

I was in jail the first or second time, twenty years after leaving the newspaper, and Dan Kane's ghost showed up in a midnight dream about the newsroom. I knew he was dead. But he was alive in my mind, and I was feeling like a failure because I'd only been once to "The Show" —when an author goes on a national book tour. My second book, seven years later, was a regional publication.

I was about to leave the dream newsroom when Kane grabbed my sleeve. I stopped. "So that's it?" he said. I woke up feeling ambitious and pleased—I'd gotten to see an old friend and mentor who had an important message for me: My career as a book writer wasn't over.

I can't say I was addicted to suboxone in prison. I used it twice a month for about four months, just as I had at Collins. I came close to addiction and realized I had to cut myself off for a spell. I was waiting for Trip O'Donnell to deliver to me that day and in my anxiety, I became obsessed, watching his every move: *He's getting it now. Nope, now he's going to the restroom. Now, he's lighting a cigarette. No, he's going to get it now. Now, he's just sitting down. He hasn't gotten anything yet. Who is his connection in this dorm? I should already know that. We had a deal. He made a promise. Now I'm fucked. I'm pissed. This is the third time these guys have lied to me. This is bullshit. He's talking to that guy. They'll talk forever, God damn it!*

My id was taking control over my ego and this was not good; I'd have to quit it. *They're just seeing how far they can push me without doing something about it. What's he gonna do? You want a piece of me, Trip? You got it.*

I rarely saw Collins drug test anyone, so there was no fear for me at that facility. Drug testing was much more common at Marcy, a hands-on prison where Supt. Jonas' men were always trying to catch us breaking the rules. NYASTP was particularly strict.

Irving told us we'd be tested soon after our arrival, once mid-stay, and once before our sentences were up. That schedule did not include random state-ordered tests, or tests for "suspicion." Suspicion meant you were acting weird, looking glassy-eyed, or having an "episode" in front of staff or a C.O. Sometimes, when an inmate was furious with another inmate, they might exact revenge by telling a C.O., or handing in an anonymous note, that this guy was using. I was lucky the Latinos weren't that angry about my shower outburst because otherwise I could have been turned in.

Trip O'Donnell didn't like me when I first arrived and met him at F1 in December, and it was reciprocal at the time. He had a name like a college kid. He bunked directly across from me in 16 cube. Trip's father owned a string of garages in upstate New York—they were car guys, or gear heads. Seeing Trip for the first time, a burly guy's-guy with tattoo sleeves on his arms, I didn't much like him either.

Trip was one of the ones who, after he saw my first published book, became a believer. He started talking to me more, offering a cup of coffee in the morning and even a cigarette now and again. It took him a few times before he figured out that I didn't smoke. He had a good sense of humor, which made me like him.

Next to Trip was a bi-lingual Korean-Latino thug. His handle was Tip, as in Hollow-Tip, the bullet that kills cops by going through body armor. Tip and Trip? Well, let's just say they weren't friends. Trip eyed me one day and nodded toward Tip, who was talking to Cabo in Spanish. There would be a sentence or two in Spanish, and then Tip would end a sentence by saying, "My nigga." My nigga means my brother or my friend. Then Cabo would say something in Spanish and end his sentence with "my nigga." They bumped fists and Cabo walked away. Trip leaned over toward me and said, "My nigga? Doesn't it translate?"

Trip was friendly with Red the Kush, another Irishman. (Kush is a kind of pot.) Trip and Red were a team. They obtained Westies and sold suboxone together. Like heroin, suboxone will put you into withdrawal if you use it heavily and then cut it off suddenly. I could tell there was no suboxone around when Trip and Red were walking around with flu-like symptoms and/or sleeping a lot. Unlike others in the dorm, I didn't need or want to be high every day.

Getting high took the mind out of prison, made neighbors tolerable, and was the ultimate "go to hell" expression to authorities who seemed to enjoy imprisoning us. Suboxone provided an enthusiasm for life not normally found here. I could understand why other inmates might need it every day, considering that their lives outside of prison might be even worse.

CELL #15

Prisons are notorious for many reasons, including censorship. What happens in the local prison, including riots and killings, is routinely kept from the media. When guards are arrested for their own lawbreaking behavior, news of such an event is even kept from the inmate population. Writers and correspondents who are incarcerated have their mail censored whether it's incoming or outgoing. When something happens, the administration quickly snuffs out the word. Prisons are funded by taxpayers. Other public entities face media scrutiny, but somehow the prisons don't. That's the way the superintendent likes it.

CHAPTER 15

HIDING MY BANANA

"The human brain, a three-pound mass of interwoven nerve cells
that controls our activity, is one of the most magnificent—
and mysterious—wonders of creation."
—George H.W. Bush

When Irving called me into the counselor's office, I thought the jig was up. I entered feeling quite paranoid. "Got something for you," said Irving. "You're in good standing here, you're in AA, and they've got an opening at the school, Transitional Services, if you'd like to claim it." Transitional Services helped inmates "transition" from prison life to the outside world.

I was relieved and shocked—though I was university educated, Irving hadn't done anything solely for me all these months. Now, he seemed to be telling me to go to the school and meet Mrs. Victoria to learn more.

As I was leaving the dorm, Hudson met me at the dorm with Chang, the new Chinese inmate who spoke no English, only Mandarin, although some said he was faking to get out of NYASTP assignments.

We were both walking to the school. Apparently, Irving had tapped him too.

I asked him a few questions. Chang just shrugged his shoulders.

"You have good computer skills? That's what they want at Transitional Services."

"Computer?" he answered,

"This is a joke, right?" I asked.

"Irving likes to play games."

She explained that I'd help with the files of inmates, providing them with addresses of living centers, colleges, workplaces for felons, and social services aid throughout the state.

Inside the back of a classroom with a bookshelf divider, she showed me the thick info books they had on every county—the college admissions documents, and the Transitional Services section on the 1995-era computer. Mrs. Victoria sternly warned me not to use the computer for personal purposes because "the director" checks it often and "clerks have been fired before."

I started Monday morning typing labels for files. Inmate customers came to me individually, by appointment with Mrs. Victoria, and I typed their resumés and created cover letters for their businesses.

One agitated inmate looked around in all directions. "I'm trying to go home," he said. "But that director won't answer my requests to come in here."

"Let me get Mrs. Victoria." I was creeped out by this guy. There was something really wrong with him. I went to Mrs. Victoria's office next door and told her about the man. She walked back with me and when she saw the inmate, she gave me a look of horror and shook her head no, then went back into her office.

I felt like I had done something wrong. I started shaking, the adrenaline seeping in. I went back to him and said, "She's really busy right now. She said come back later, with an appointment."

"Yeah," he said. "That's her." He made a motion to punch the wall, stopped himself, and walked out.

Five minutes remained before my shift ended. I sat at the desk and meditated on positive things back home, just so I could calm down.

Over the three months I would serve at Transitional, I saw the "girls in the office" meet with many prisoners about their goals and end-of-bid planning. Mrs. Victoria seemed to be doing the best she could with what she had—all her resources were out of date. That was frustrating to the inmates, many of whom were starting with nothing. It became clear to me that inmate planning was not Marcy's priority.

Former inmate and writer Michael G. Santos echoed my sentiment. Some prisons "lack the resources" and "lack the vision to appreciate the advantages that come with management through the promise of incentives rather than through the threat of punishment... The prisoner's preparation for release is of secondary, and in some cases zero, importance."

As my office work days passed, I learned that the administration really didn't care if inmates were doing their post-sentence planning or not. The priority was issuing dire warnings, and imposing discipline and punishment, as it was in the other departments. Other than GEDs, which Marcy received grants to offer, the prison didn't really care about higher learning. And anger management didn't count. But the prison was not solely to blame—Congress eliminated college grants in 1995.

Having places to live and work were the top priorities for outgoing inmates. In my experience, Marcy fell short on meeting both priorities. Many inmates relied on Probation to help them secure group home and halfway house placements. Others, like Soprano and old Easton, had family or money to secure a domicile. The sad cases had nowhere to go.

An eye-opening report from citylab.com by Tanvi Misra said formerly incarcerated people were often homeless, thereby drawing the attention again of police. Misra wrote, "Thus starts an unrelenting cycle, through which people are tossed back and forth between jail and the street." I was part of that horrifying cycle when I was owned by Lockport Drug Court. When I went to jail, Social Services stopped paying my rent, my landlord was angered, and I eventually lost my apartment on Washburn Street.

The citylab.com report said the rate of homelessness among the formerly incarcerated was ten times that of the general public. "It suggests that prisons in the United States aren't helping people reintegrate," said Lucius Couloute of Prison Policy Initiative.

The report urged "...states and local governments to develop a coordinated inter-agency approach—something like a department of re-entry—that provides short-term and long-term support to the formerly incarcerated." I may be jaded, but in my limited experience, no one in Niagara County government, or at Marcy, was sophisticated or liberal enough to entertain such an idea. And few people in New York state are flooding their local representatives to help the formerly incarcerated—the prison population is a "not in my backyard" proposition.

In fact, the priority at Marcy, at least so far as I was concerned, seemed to be micro-managing office volunteers. A memo I saw circulated by Deputy Supt. Laird Strassmeier listed the things office clerks were not allowed to do, under penalty of expulsion. Photocopies had to be approved by a counselor, there would be no "personal business," "sleeping," or "giving the appearance of sleeping," and no leaving your post to wander the building.

Strassmeier must have inspected the Transitional Services computer once a week. He had fired people for writing letters to their families, resumés, jokes, and all kinds of other crap. Of course, the computer had no internet, the house music had been deleted, and other clerks seemingly enjoyed watching over your back while you were typing.

The clerks were narcs and the counselors were petty tyrants. Rather than helping men leave prison and succeed, it was more important to catch them doing something wrong.

A banana nearly interrupted my illustrious career at Transitional Services. Unlike other foods, apples, oranges, and bananas provided at the mess hall were considered "carry out." I slept through breakfast one morning and took my leftover banana to the school in my pants pocket. I wasn't frisked. This was the second time I had done this.

Deputy Supt. Strassmeier saw the banana on a table near me and flipped out. He raised his voice and pounded around the room, getting everyone's attention. A guy with class would have quietly told me, "Don't do this again." But Strassmeier had to bully me about it. In overkill mode, Strassmeier went on and on that if I was a diabetic, I'd need a doctor's note to eat here— "verified documentation." I gave him some "yes, sirs" and "I forgots."

In prison, when you have an exceptional behavioral record, like me, the staff rewards you with things, such as Transitional Services (instead of mandatory rec). Then, once you're in, the staff takes those things you are given, and twists them into additional punishments, because this is prison.

It was my day for it. In addition to Strassmeier, a new officer was on duty at the school. He, too, had been trained in pettiness. I had to use the restroom twice in fifteen minutes. Hey, I was fifty years old. The officer lit me up with, "Whattaya gotta go to the bathroom seventeen times for?"

I shut him down with, "Urinary tract infection. Very painful."

He added the last word, "All these fucking people wandering around in the hallway. I gotta watch them all."

The guy had so irritated me that I'd forgotten my Zen outlook. When I got back to the school room, I purposefully misfiled the new orientation packets. Then I left for the day. It was 9:30 a.m.

I expected inmate aid, education, and transitions to entail much more than a few filing cabinets and a lot of confused prisoners. Why did I expect this? Because prison is what the state spends billions upon annually, and because I'm an optimist.

The three counselors, who were all smiles on my first day, turned out to be control freaks and two-faced misanthropes.

I avoided them and did my clerk work, then went "home." One summer morning, my back was killing me from the 2012 car accident, and I had no Ibuprofen. Bed rest was the only solution until I could barter for pills.

Knocking on the door to the office, I saw that Mrs. Victoria and the two other counselors were there. I'll call them Miss Takes and Mrs. Clinton. Mrs. Victoria waved me in, and I said hello to all three.

"Mrs. Victoria," I said, "I'm having some pain in my back and I can't concentrate. May I go back to my dorm and lay down?"

Mrs. Victoria did not get a chance to answer because Mrs. Clinton cut in with, "You're walking alright. It doesn't look like you're in pain to me."

Shaken but not dismayed, I treated her as any other inmate would whose ire was raised. I said, "And which university is your doctorate in medicine from?"

That's basically what I said to rude inmates who threw their medical and hygiene-related advice at me … "And your medical degree is from…?" Because I knew most of them had no degree. They had drug money, guns, and cars with big silver rims, but no degree.

The school room went silent. Most inmates would have said "Fuck you" and gotten the goon squad pounding on their head for disrespecting a female staffer.

I went the intellectual route and talked right over her head. I couldn't get beaten up for that.

Mrs. Clinton eventually replied, "You're not supposed to talk back. You're supposed to just take it and keep your mouth shut." Her words made me imagine she was holding a riding crop. ﹀

And that was it—in just a few words from a Marcy counselor, the institution's overall educational philosophy was expressed. Marcy gets to pound us into the dirt, and the staff is safe because we are not allowed to fight back.

So, my initial suspicion was wrong, I did indeed learn something that day. The Marcy education program was a top performer.

"You can go," Mrs. Victoria said, returning to her paperwork.

Back at the dorm, I eliminated two prison problems—the Latino bullying and the opinion among my brethren that I was not really an author. Another issue was staying creative in a place where, if they could, they'd burn books and destroy precious works of art.

To battle my own losses, I kept notebooks of daily happenings, composed poems no one understood, and wrote essays on everything from the effectiveness of NYASTP to what it's like to know a sex offender. I used suboxone to see if it would improve my idea generation or my writing. Suboxone made me want to go socialize with friendly inmates. It also improved my essay revision work. I wasn't more creative, but I wanted to work longer and harder, borrowing Buddha's radio.

I met with The Cosmonaut first, figuring his brochure copy would be easier than Guns'. At first, The Cosmonaut was reluctant to talk about Road Trip Café. He suggested that an essay by him on working your bis, tris, pecs, and glutes might be better. He suggested the title "Don't Pout, You Gotta Work Out." He said, "You know, to get people off the couch." Then he held his arm up and made a muscle. "You should be working out with me, Stickney." I told him, "I want to lose weight, not gain." Then I decided my whole brochure idea was silly. But my old "project management" training kicked in and I smoothly told The Cosmonaut that he was suggesting three projects:

- Road Trip Café brochure
- "Don't Pout" brochure
- Our workouts together

"Why don't we do one at a time?" I said. "Café first and the others after we're done with that."

Entranced with the look of his arm, The Cosmonaut said, "My father started the Café when I was seven."

I had my notebook with me and jotted this down. In about twenty minutes, I had the history, average clientele, menu, interior design, and a few customer comments that The Cosmonaut retrieved from memory.

I found what I thought was Jean-Michel Basquait's finest looking painting in a paperback coffee-table book. It was "Riding with Death," a take-off on Albert Pinkham Ryder's haunting "The Race Track" (Death on a Pale Horse).

The horse in Basquait's work was walking bones. Riding the horse was an abstract version of Basquait, the background pale gray. It's considered to be prophetic because the artist died shortly thereafter.

Feeling close to him because of art/drugs, and my readings years ago of his works in *Artforum*, I redrew Basquait's painting with colored pencils on 8x12 paper. At the top, I wrote "Nothing to Be Gained Here," "Nothing to Be Gained Here." It was my preliminary goodbye to a place that had given me grief in my blood and tried to take my soul. I posted the work on my locker. Chap said it was "mad good" and offered to buy it. Suddenly, I had a patron.

Officer Bebbit, a chubby, jolly, tobacco-chewing local, worked at F1 only four days of the month. Yet he started his shift today with a bang, ordering us to our cubes for standing count.

We all waited, watching him. Bebbit stood before the bubble with that Copenhagen smile of his.

"This is probably the best-behaved dorm in Marcy. I been here a long time, boys, and have seen no fights in the dorm, no busts, not even a real argument. Maybe a minor flare-up. That's it."

Bebbit let that sink in: "But you don't have a good reputation because a few of these bored C.O.s whine too much: signing out, messy beds, pissant shit that the dorms out there see and turn away every day because they got bigger problems: shanks, theft ... you know." He stopped talking and we started with our celebrations—fist bumps, "right on," "way to go, nigga," and laughter. We never got compliments.

Nor had I ever heard a C.O. disparage his brothers in blue before. I took these words to heart, scribbling about the historic event in my notebook.

Rock & Roll Rich finally returned to the dorm. He had been transferred to

Syracuse University Hospital, where they had treated him with strong antibiotics and painkillers. I had my med-run friend back. I told him two other inmates had gotten sick after him and they were both treated with pills at the Infirmary. One improved and the other was transferred somewhere. Prison made men vanish.

He didn't tell me whether it was MRSA or not. Admitting it would have made Rich "MRSA Man" for the duration of his Marcy stay. He just claimed it "was a bad infection."

A C.O. had come looking for Rich two days after he left for the hospital. Marcy apparently did not know the location of one of its own. Thinking of it, F1 should have been scrubbed down, and Rich's bed disinfected or thrown out if MRSA was even suspected. Nothing was done to protect the rest of us.

Rich got two bits of bad news upon his return. One was he had to make up the month of NYASTP that he missed. The other was Irving telling him he had to take ART (Aggression Replacement Training). The curriculum included moral reasoning, anger control sequences, styles of anger, and defense mechanisms. The ART guide said the program helped inmates use "alternative methods of addressing violent situations." Rich complained, "I don't mind the class—gets me out of mandatory rec. Then again, man, I've got to sit in class with a bunch of rapists."

Rich lent me a book called *The Dirt* by Motley Crüe, a fast-paced, highly entertaining look at the band members' turbulent lives before and after wealth and fame. I was afraid for Vince Neil, who killed his friend in a drunk driving accident. Drunks like me say, "What if it was me?" I was happy I'd kept drinking but ceased driving.

The Dirt was a typical jail book, in this sense: It was held together with tape, and pages 188 and 189 were missing. For me, it replaced *The Gargoyle* by Andrew Davidson, a smart story where the main character had his penis burned off. I just couldn't think about that in F1.

During the evening med run, the darkness seeped through every crevice of the Marcy campus. Rich, me, and whoever else was walking with us checked out the big valley sky, looking for UFOs that might want to abduct the Canadian.

Gazing at the lonely stars and a big light that we speculated was Mars helped guide us on our walk. The sky was interrupted, not by UFOs, but by thundering airplanes and aces from the nearby Air Force base. These specters resembled brightly lit flying cities. The busy blue-black skyline took my thoughts to beyond the prison, flying to wherever my new home would be. Who was deciding? Me?

My Higher Power? The big empty? No one? I figured it was me.

Marcy felt like purgatory. Inmates started bids here and exited for other prisons or home. But it really felt like no one ever left, that we were stuck in a place where time was frozen. There were ten months of winter, and the only change we knew was when Marcy's own bumpkin home-towners came here to pose as C.O.s. The only other thing to change was the weather, and the coming spring, which brought out a heavenly crescent moon.

Irving walked into the dorm to chat with Officer Beaver. Irving looked exactly like David, my former father-in-law, only twenty years younger. Even their voices were similar. It was another time, halcyon days, when David was in my life.

But now only Irving was left. Gandhi walked up to me to say Irving was cold, distant, and calculating. "He does not care about us at all," Gandhi said. "He doesn't care what happens to us." *Did I want to believe this darkness?*

Beaver, one of our most notorious corrections officers, was on duty the day I interviewed The Cosmonaut. Officers often walked outside on warm, sunny days, leaving us alone in the dorm. It had to be some kind of a violation of internal policy or state law to leave sixty prisoners alone in a dorm for any length of time, considering the 2015 escape of murderers David Sweat and Richard Matt from Clinton prison.

Beaver was about sixty, balding, and usually upset. He had the personality of an old lady who's just had her purse stolen. He would shout and stomp and bitch when we weren't doing exactly what he wanted. Missing a pinky on one hand and a thumb on the other, Beaver was the subject of various inmate rumors. When things were quiet, he'd listen to Rush Limbaugh on the little C.O. radio at the desk.

He eyed me on my way from The Cosmonaut's cube, ready to explode, and I diffused the explosion by offering, "Dude just wanted a few sheets of paper."

"Get the fuck back to your own cube," Beaver said. "No visiting." He returned to his daily crossword puzzle.

Beaver was normally a Saturday C.O. When we wanted to sleep in, he'd bang pots and pans and order us to get up and clean up our cubes. One time, when Beaver tried the pot trick, one of our guys yelled, "Fuck off."

That got Beaver hopping like popcorn. "I can hear," he yelled. "I know what you said. Hey, I give this dorm a lot of leeway—more than other dorms. Get your goddamn cubes in order and keep your shit to yourselves."

Beaver also prohibited smoking in the restroom. That was why I liked him. I'd have a whole morning without a second-hand smoke! Instead, he took the smokers outside, three at a time. They stood in a line near the door, fiddling with their unlit cigarettes, anxiously waiting their turn.

This officer did not like cigarette smoke, but he hated cigar smoke even more. Some inmates received cigars in their packages from home. After the smokers were done, Beaver walked into the restroom, looking to catch someone. He came out looking like the character Anger from Pixar's animated movie "Inside Out." He blew his top, shouting about cigar smokers, dancing about, pointing fingers and making threats. "One of you swingin' dicks lit up in there. Someone's gonna get it before this day is over."

Walking by my cube and Tip's on the way to the restroom, Kush said, "Damn. Every time he turns around, someone's puffin' on a Cuban."

In the end, just before the 3 p.m. shift change, Tennessee was the one to "get it." Tennessee had just woken up from a nap and was walking to the restroom, wearing his evening cap. Beaver had strict policies against smoking and against hat-wearing indoors. Prison policy prohibited do-rags in the dorms (guys still donned them).

Beaver saw him and told Tennessee to "lose the hat." The inmate was a wiry shrimp who had rage issues, just like Beaver.

"Fuck you, Beaver," Tennessee said and kept walking. Beaver jumped from his desk, grabbed the inmate, and pushed him into a wall. Tennessee promptly pissed his pants, ending the physical confrontation. Beaver continued to verbally abuse Tennessee, making him grab a mop and bucket to clean the floor. The officer wrote Tennessee up, recommending that he be removed from NYASTP.

Beaver told the story to Hudson, who was coming in for the 3 p.m. shift. Tennessee was ordered to stay in his cube for the remainder of the day. Feeling sympathetic, Hudson let Tennessee leave his cube to watch TV around 8 p.m.

I kept busy that afternoon with The Cosmonaut's brochure, finishing a first draft, under duress. The conflict had gotten my anxiety going and I had to meditate on how this particular fight had nothing to do with me. Paranoia came for a visit, but by meditating, I let it flow out. *Good things were happening*, I told myself. *The months were ticking away. And I could write—the one thing they could not strip from me. Could I really make it in the world after this?*

———

I received a piece of mail from the director of temporary release. I had told Irving I did not want Work Release, because it was basically another six months in jail and a halfway house, surrounded by annoying inmates—the perfect situation for my depression to flare up. More shackled bus rides, more C.O.s. trying to make me break down. Irving shared my feelings with the director. But Marcy was not going to let me make a decision for myself. *Who's running this jail Stickney? You or us? You try to reject us, but we reject you, nasty like.*

In the form of a memo, they issued a reminder about "selling illegal substances to another." My reply was that the substance was not illegal, the sale was.

They said I was "originally sentenced to probation for this conviction, but subsequently violated it, resulting in your current term." Technically, I did not violate probation—the court did not give me a urinalysis to prove I was using.

"Criminal history," the memo continued, "includes prior convictions for attempted petit larceny and DWI." I did steal that Four Loko. There was no "attempted" about it. And my DWI occurred in 1996, twenty-one years earlier!

The memo continued, "Your willingness to introduce illegal substances into the community renders you a risk to public health and public safety." Now this was quite a STRETCH. I didn't "introduce" substances. Suboxone was invented in 2002, so someone out there introduced it long before I did. Moreover, I didn't introduce anything to the community. The suboxone went to a police informant, a narc, who then gave the shit to a drug task force investigator. And don't forget the doctors who prescribed suboxone every day.

I did not want Work Release, as I had told Irving months ago. So, don't try to body-slam me after the fact.

To add insult to insult, Collins wrote to me on November 17, 2017, saying that I was accepted for Work Release, as long as I completed NYASTP, which I did.

———

Then came the day of Gov. Cuomo's "mock escape drills." Because of Sweat and Matt, those two dim bulbs from Clinton who escaped in 2015, our governor thought we should practice not escaping.

For most of the day, we remained in the dorm and did standing counts. I did go out in the morning, but the whole campus went back to the dorms by 9:30 a.m. The officer on duty, Oritz, was cool about the whole thing, doing what he was ordered to do, looking at our I.D.s and counting us, over and over.

Then they did "cross counts," where they'd go next door and count those inmates. The C.O.s from next door came to count us, then compared figures.

We had C.O. escorts to and from chow. NYASTP, work, and school were all canceled. I hope all the effort on my part, and those of my brethren, prevented future escapes. After all, who'd want to leave here?

Marcy's rules, regulations, and schedule gave inmates plenty of time to be bored and depressed. Whenever things got dull or sad, Gummy would begin to entertain me and whomever else was watching by telling brutally corny jokes. I had to pretend to laugh so he was happy.

Some of Gummy's jokes were terrible in any circle: "They gave me a date rape drug. But all I got was raped. No date. And they left me in the parking lot."

And, "That was when I spray-painted my false teeth gold and sold them to my drug dealer."

Then Gummy made his old-man face, which resembled the character from the 2009 animated movie, "Up." Gummy had no teeth, so he could collapse his face and make it scrunchy happy, angry, or sad. Soprano said Gummy had an "elastic face."

I said to Gummy, "Every time I look up, I expect to see Pamela Anderson, but I see you." When he was obnoxious to me, I'd slay him with: "In my mind, I've killed you many times."

Gummy also passed on gossip, like who was a narc, who was gay, who was going to get kicked out, and who was going home or to Work Release next. I tried not to listen because the gossip was either true, and I didn't care, or it was gibberish. Gummy was normally right about who'd be expelled and who was going home.

Kenny was supposed to go to work release at Lincoln Correctional in Manhattan on Monday, July 2. He'd satisfied his NYASTP requirements, and the paperwork had been signed by him and Irving. July 2 came and went with no phone call at the C.O.'s desk about his departure. When he asked Irving what was happening, Irving said he'd look into it.

I cared about Kenny because he reminded me of some of the managers I'd worked with at Mercedes. Like me, he knew about corporate speak, measurable outcomes, project management, and crisis communications. And he told me when we first met here that his bid began at Rikers Island, where he was caged together with rival Bloods, Crips, and Latin Kings so they'd fight. Kenny said fights were broken up with pepper spray, but innocents like him were also hit. "There were three different occasions," Kenny said. "On the third, I finally learned to lay face down on the floor and pull my jacket over my head to stop the contact." He added that C.O.s held "blanket parties" to beat inmates.

Days went by, with Kenny getting more and more agitated. Irving then informed him that his medical documentation had yet to be completed. This was the typical bureaucratic subterfuge that nearly everyone encountered at Marcy Correctional. Kenny went to the Infirmary and signed the papers, but another two weeks went by with no phone call.

Back home, his daughter had already begun calling Superintendent Jonas. Kenny spoke with Irving every other day. No one had any answers, and they pointed the finger at anyone from the Infirmary to Lincoln itself. Twenty-one days passed after Kenny's leave date, and other inmates bound for Lincoln had left the campus.

The superintendent called Irving one day and said it'd be another week. Kenny didn't believe it. One of the administrative buildings posted a weekly list of inmate leave times. Gummy was a cleaner in this building and told Kenny he'd look for his name on the wall. Kenny would be in the yard when Gummy was getting off work in the building.

Gummy would pass the yard on the walkway and give Kenny a hand signal as to whether or not his name appeared. Inmates in the yard weren't allowed anywhere near the fences; inmates on the outside weren't allowed to talk with those inside, or they'd risk a beating.

I was friends with Kenny and wanted to show support (he read my essays), so I went to the sun-splashed yard with him and we stood beyond the basketball court, near the furthest cement bench. It was a few minutes before we saw Gummy's distant figure emerging from the building near the Infirmary. Gummy also had to be careful—his hand gestures could be mistaken for gang signs. I guess I had been stupid to involve myself in their communication because guards could think I was in on it. Gummy got near and flashed a thumb's up on the side of his leg. Kenny let out a holler—he was going home days from now. I congratulated him and felt excited about my own leave date.

Writing treatment essays for others turned out to be rather rewarding. In addition to the coffee, honey buns, and soups I was paid, my reward was going deep on the creative side.

One assignment was like Kafka's "Metamorphosis." We were told: "You wake up and something about you has changed. What do you do?"

Three inmates asked me for help. I turned the Chinaman into Elvis, and he sang. Cabo woke up with a basketball for a head, and he went outside looking for a pickup game. Ace didn't feel like doing his essay, so I gave him the sound of an electric shaver for a voice. He became a sought-after commodity in the dorm.

I would have had more assignments, but Gandhi caught on to my act, and he also started writing essays for others. I let it go because he was poor.

The time of the Insulin Jerk had come. Nightly at 7:45 p.m., Rock & Roll Rich visited my cube and reminded me to get ready—med time was upon us. The call came between 7:45 and 8:45 p.m., which was a huge window of time for something we did every night, especially when adding in the ten minutes of walking both ways and waiting in line.

We just wanted to get down there, cop, and roll (get our pills and go). After getting ready, walking, copping, and walking back, without any interruptions, our patience was tested. We were tired from another long day in prison. We had to wear our state clothes and boots—we were sick of these greens by day's end.

The diabetics were called separately to the Infirmary before us, at 7 p.m. or so, for their shots and pills. They had a full hour to get their shit done because it took longer to check their sugar and get the shot. The nurses didn't want to clog up the med line with diabetics.

The Insulin Jerk, a light-skinned fellow with plastic glasses, waited for the med-inmates (us) so he could go through our faster line. We'd leave our dorm, and Rich would say, "Ho, there he is," walking ahead of us. The Insulin Jerk couldn't cop and roll. He took FOREVER checking his sugar level, chatting up the nurse and being an overall nuisance.

We were onto his game and we grumbled about him, loudly.

It wasn't just at meds that he got under my skin. The Insulin Jerk with a motormouth showed up at orientation at Transitional Services so he could explain maintenance work to the new recruits. He showed the new guys how to use a floor buffer, saying his friend lost a toe operating a buffer improperly. He glided through the motions, rocking on his banana feet, as if any fresh inmate to Marcy was hoping to immediately start cleaning floors.

"You could strangle yourself with this cord," he said, the cord draped over his shoulder. Now, the suicidal inmates had an alternative way to do it.

We were concentrating on the movements of Insulin Jerk in his natural habitat. We were shocked when a van came speeding up the road, skidding to a halt right next to our med line. The side door slid open and a nurse stepped out on—one sexy leg after the other. When the other leg appeared, she fell from the van, flat on her face.

As the nurse was trying to get up, despite her one lame leg, two inmates walked toward her. The van spun its tires and was gone. "Are you okay?" "Are you hurt?" Then the officers came out of the Infirmary, staring the inmates down. The nurse got up and a C.O. brought her inside.

The line was all voices about the incident. Why did the driver take off? Was he drunk? Were they both drunk? I wished for a few seconds that I was drunk. If the nurses and officers didn't care about me, why would I care about them?

Walking back, me and Rock & Roll Rich bumped into Hip-Hop, a friendly, "slow" kid from G dorm. Rich asked him if he passed his Anger Management tests. Hip said he didn't know—he hadn't received his grade yet. Hip was a slight, soft-spoken man with a thin mustache and red sneakers. He did a complicated handshake with Rich and went on his way.

Rich watched him head toward the Infirmary and said, "There goes a pathetic case." With acute cognitive impairment, Hip was the target of daily C.O. abuse, as if the officers were schoolyard bullies. I can't imagine if their Albany training included how to abuse slower folks, but they seemed good at pushing Hip down, calling him "retard" and "dummy," taking his sneakers and I.D., ripping his pants, and harassing the kid at meals and in the gym. But Hip took it all in stride, as though it was a normal part of the prison experience. And that's what infuriated the officers. They wanted to see fear on his face. I expected they were going to hurt him badly someday.

Obviously, none of that behavior was appropriate. Some of the C.O.s who bullied Hip had gone through a mental health training course created by the state. The course detailed how C.O.s are on the front line and should be helping the mentally ill and challenged with helpfulness and respect.

On July 3, I completed my morning work at Transitional Services and was headed back to F1 when I passed Irving, carrying his paperwork and going the other way. I asked what was going on and he said the dorm was evacuated and inmates were sent to the gym/yard at 9 a.m.

"The drug-sniffing dogs are in there now," Irving said, hustling away. "Go to the gym." I almost laughed when he said drug-sniffing dogs. I made it to within one hundred feet of the dorm, and there they were. A cop was standing near a police K-9 Unit SUV, holding the leash of a German Shepherd. Irving told me the raid had started at 9—why was this cop/dog team still outside? I felt like Marcy was playing with my brain.

It was absurd overkill—maximum control in a medium-security facility. The officers had raided us two months earlier but found nothing of substance. Two sets of surprise urine tests had been administered in the past two weeks. Now dogs? I thought dogs worked the airports, bus stations, and federal buildings. No one dealt in kilos here. I didn't see anyone that high.

On my way to the gym, I felt a little nervous for our dorm. Yet I was also outraged. A drug dog raid for sixty guys? Those dogs, their keepers, and transportation didn't come cheap. Nearly $30,000 for the dog, $45,000 for the SUV, plus the cop's salary. These costs don't include training, food, vets ...

I did begin to feel a little paranoid—if something was found, we'd all get punished. Was there anything, even a wrapper, in my locker? Nah. There was always a bad egg, but we were NYASTP—not perfect, but trying.

In the gym, the scuttlebutt was we would be strip-searched after gym time. I could tell that was a stupid rumor. The gym was where the dealers and users met up year-round. No one was bothered by the raid, or, if they were, they weren't showing it.

Gym ended at 11:15 and we paraded back to the dorm. Beaver confided in somebody that the dogs came up short. One at a time, inmates began complaining of finding dog hair in their lockers and in their beds. The Police State sure loved its mind games.

I felt like I was watching *Goodfellas*. It was lunchtime on May 18, and F1 was called to the mess hall. Geese were in the yard. So was the occasional dove. Well-built men with short hair, lots of gold, and gorilla arms spread out throughout the walkway, shaking hands and gabbing away with the officers. The journalist in me realized it right away. These were union guys, making their presence known on campus. I recognized the logo on the pins they wore on their open-necked Oxford shirts. The union guys got into and out of Marcy vans. They were even at the mess hall, buddying up to the C.O.s.

I had covered union negotiations for state, county, and school workers in Lockport. In those five years, I never saw union reps on county or school property. When I saw the gentlemen, I could not help but think that they didn't belong on campus (as visiting civilians, what if they were injured by inmates?), that there was something clandestine happening, and that they were seriously distracting the C.O.s from doing their job. Why were they really there? Did this happen all the time? Were contract negotiations going on? There was certainly a lot of money at stake. Maybe it was just because, as they said, they were "friends of ours." I laughed when I remembered Rich telling me "union guys who love overtime are called clocksuckers."

It was that time of year, spring here, and summer coming. The dorm's double-hung windows were open. The snow was gone, and we could smile again. Other dorm inmates were out in the yard, playing softball. Every time I heard the aluminum bat connect with the ball, I thought of summers past, and I knew I was closer to my goal.

Nate West was a criminal and drug buddy who I knew from Lockport. When I first arrived at Marcy, I did not know he also was here. I knew only that he'd been sent to State for a burglary he orchestrated right in our neighborhood, on Spalding Street, off Washburn.

"Brandon Stickney," I heard on the walkway, looking in the direction of the voice. No one knew my first name at Marcy. There was tall, bulky Nate, standing in front of dorm C2.

"What a coincidence. You okay? Anyone bothering you? You need anything?" He was obviously happy to see me. I was happy to see him as well, because, as a prison inmate getting no visitors, you're thrilled to see someone from your hometown. Even if it was Nate West. I first met Nate when I was high in a bar called Pat's Place. The mold spores of Lockport went to Pat's for cheap drinks and games of pool. Patrons could also smoke inside the bar after the 2004 New York State ban.

Nate was the white-haired man next to me at the bar. He was about six feet, 200 pounds. I offered him a shot from the rum bottle I was holding. It was a cold winter night and I'd been walking the streets and drinking. He looked at the two girls standing with him and then motioned for the bartender. "He's got his own bottle," Nate said. I was busted and kicked out. I'll never understand why he did that, but thinking of it now, thinking of Nate, I figured he just wanted to create drama.

I knew the name because of the number of times I'd written him up in the *Union-Sun & Journal*'s police report. Petty theft, fights, possession. We did not become friends, yet he did become one of my drug buddies on Washburn Street near the end of my run. Nate told me he could get some good crack. Others told me he was the type to take your money and run. Crack was his obsession. He'd stroll through the 'hood, babe on his arm, on the way to or from a crack house, and wave me over. A year after the bar bottle incident, we learned to appreciate each other—I had money and he had opiate pills. He sold his pills to buy cocaine.

A hairy-handed-Joe named Nappo lived on Spalding Street, next door to Nate's mother's house (he lived with his mother). Nappo was an out-of-work tree trimmer. No matter where they live or journey, addicts will always find each other. The biggest scar on my left arm is from Nappo when he gave me a morphine injection with a used, bent needle.

Nate hung out at Nappo's house, where there was always drug activity. Nappo's father was rich and had purchased the home for him; Nappo's income came from the couple in the small front apartment. The cast of characters in and out of there were either from jail or on their way to prison. We used coke and meth and drank a lot of booze. The cops raided Nappo's place and found him and several folks in possession of meth. I wasn't there that day. On my next return visit, the manufacturing equipment had already been taken down and dismantled.

The rumor was Nappo was working for the drug task force, got the main meth cook taken down, and skated away with a six-month jail term. We were all headed to jail before long. Nate and I wound up in the same facility.

"You ever have a problem here, tell me," Nate said. I believed he'd "take care of it," as he said. Nate West was big enough that most inmates would think twice about messing with him. Nate also said that he had many bricks if I ever needed them. He meant cigarettes to trade for chineta. I got paranoid, though—I didn't want him finding out about me just yet. I told him, "Thank you," and he winked, walking into his dorm.

NYASTP, and other rehabs I attended, pounded me with a bunch of rules and consequences and fostered an antagonistic relationship with patients/customers, as in "Do what we want or else." In the spirit of making the situation better, and rather than complaining, I designed what I thought would be a better rehabilitation/treatment model:

- Help with understanding sobriety (few knew what it really meant)
- Positivity
- Group acceptance
- Mental health – day-to-day support
- Spiritual
- Clarity in direction (This was about "cube compliance"
   —how can I fix it if I don't know what was wrong in the first place?)

NYASTP had none of these things. And I wondered how anyone could recover from addiction in this atmosphere. It was like telling a bum he'd go to jail unless he cleaned up his act. There was something critical missing in NYASTP's prison recovery model—mental health.

With NYASTP, despite its many flaws, I knew I was at least moving toward an eventual release date. A recent inspirational quote made me laugh: "You can't be a silent tap dancer."

I was attending AA, basically trying to be a good inmate, and decided to join the Inmate Liaison Committee. Though Bear had said I seemed to be in a daze, a dreamy wanderer, it was the ILC that woke me to the real politics of the administration and the abuses of officers against inmates at Marcy.

CELL #16

Former C.O. Ted Conover said that in the 1950s,

the state advertised to officer candidates that they'd

have opportunities to help "counsel and reform

the prisoner." During Conover's C.O. training in

Albany, "nothing like that was ever presented to

me... Today's C.O. would only laugh." Punishment

is the law of the land. Recent reports indicate

ongoing abuses of American prisoners by staff: sexual

violence, humiliation, unsanitary conditions, extreme

temperatures, inadequate medical care, psychological

torture, racism, extreme force, and much more.

CHAPTER 16

NOTHING TO BE GAINED HERE

"The weak are always anxious for justice and equality.
The strong pay no heed to either."
—Aristotle

The sign I saw for the ILC said "advocate for your dorm and your fellow inmates." I'd seen C.O.s abusing us, and our dorm had all kinds of problems, from a broken hotpot to leaking toilets. Then there were those in-between issues we couldn't get answers for, including green baloney in the mess hall, and commissary's inability to keep popular items in stock, like soups or lighters. These all might seem like insignificant issues, but they are critical in a prison when a Ramen noodle soup is the only happiness you may get in a single day.

Commissary was staffed by civilian women. Mouthing off to them meant swift punishment. A black inmate named Antwon complained to a clerk about summer sausage being out of stock, then said "Fuck you" to her. The C.O. at the desk roughed Antwon up in the corner, frisked him, and put him outside to stand against a wall in frisk stance. I'm not sure how long he had to stand that way, but his chin was right up against the cement.

I needed three votes from the dorm to be elected F1's representative on the ILC. No one else wanted to sign up. *Fear of retaliation*, I imagined.

Kush and Tennessee heard about my candidacy. They met me at my cube. Neither would sign my petition. Kush said, "You fuck up on that board and a C.O.'s gonna toss a shank under your mattress."

"That's a nice bullseye you got on your back." Tennessee said.

Buddha, Soprano, and Canada signed my petition. They were encouraging. Word travels fast in prison. I got permission from Hudson to deliver my signatures to the ILC room at the school. I wasn't even out the door and inmates were rushing up to me asking for better movies, more time for dominoes, a new toaster, less retribution when filing grievances about C.O. abuses, and healthier foods at commissary. "It's all sugar and starch," said The Cosmonaut. Other inmates continued trying to convince me I was a dead man.

I "won" the election; no one else from F1 entered. The ILC wanted one rep from each of Marcy's dorms. The ILC's first meeting was at an office next to the gym where we met our civilian leader, Dean Dyoyo. He was a former college athlete of merit; also, an adviser to the gym. I thought, *How could a gym need an advisor? A guy who told the administration when the gym needed new soccer balls or backboards for basketball, or about a leak in the yard's urinal?* Turns out it was a full-time position—and Gov. Cuomo said he was going to eliminate the fat from the state budget.

I had big expectations coming into this forum. As a newspaper reporter, I was used to community organizations, legislative bodies, and board meetings being run properly. I had attended hundreds of them and was familiar with Robert's *Rules of Order*. The ILC was unlike any committee I'd ever seen.

There were only seven ILC members, meaning more than half the dorms failed to send a representative. I met a cool, old black dude named Fig. I sat next to him. Fig handed out pieces of hard candy to all of us. Refusing the candy, Dyoyo sat before us fingering through the contents of a manila file. He delivered a speech to us about *his* ILC: "You guys can get together, talk things over and stuff. Just don't bring anything to me." At this point, I thought Dyoyo was kidding. He said, "The dorms will give you all kinds of stuff they want done. We have, like, limited resources, you know? Listen if you want, but don't bring me anything. I don't care."

With that, Dyoyo gathered himself and left the room. We were left with the Marcy ILC president, a Hispanic inmate in sunglasses, and the VP, a very white African-American man. The latter two started a ghetto speak conversation with the others. I recognized the president as the inmate who ran "Click-Click," the photography service for inmates to send snapshots of themselves to friends and relatives. Months back, I had asked Soprano why they had the stupid name Click-Click. Soprano explained that the inner-city kids of today, with cell phones and computers, had no idea what "photo" or "photography" meant. "It's an ancient word," he said.

Fig and I were ignored by the board, and I had no idea what was going on. Fig told me "this ILC be running things wrong." I told him that was obvious. According to ILC's governing body in Albany, each prison ILC was supposed to have its own office for meetings, not a borrowed classroom or gym space. There were guidelines and rules that governed all New York State ILCs, as well as meetings, that Marcy was obviously ignoring.

The ILC was supposed to be the voice of the inmates, on all dorm-related issues, including C.O. abuses. Fig said, "Those two up there," meaning the president and VP, were close with the administration and the sergeants. With Dyoyo, the veeps kept the ILC quiet, "so no one could rock the boat," in return for certain favors. If this was a mute board, I asked Fig, then why was he on it? "For change," Fig said. "Someone gotta start it. I'm gonna."

We were supposed to meet quarterly. We were also supposed to have regular and ongoing communication with Dyoyo. But he effectively hid from us. Then, though we were given a callout for a meeting, Dyoyo failed to attend. We waited three months for the meeting with administration that was supposed to be held regularly.

The object of Marcy's inaction was to get inmate members frustrated enough to resign our positions. Why make waves and get yourself in trouble? Especially if you only had a few weeks left in your bid?

New York State's revised 2017 directive on ILCs said the superintendent at each prison "establishes an ILC" to advise on the general welfare of the inmate population. It also said Dyoyo was responsible for our day-to-day operations. We were supposed to be given office space along with desks, typewriters, stationery, and supplies to conduct our work on behalf of the inmate population.

After a couple of meetings, we had a list of agenda items, from the "time of lights-out" to "frisk procedure questions," that were forwarded to the administration. Dyoyo actually showed up for this meeting, as did Supt. Jonas, Deputy Supt. Kim Colon of Security, and a few others.

Seeing Jonas at my own table, I was surprised I had no dislike for him. Yes, he was in charge of this Kafkaesque summer camp. Yet there was something about him—a short man wearing a moderately expensive suit—that made him less threatening. He even seemed approachable.

We got off to a bad start. We weren't sure who invited him. José, a young Latino kid with a wiggly blow-out, spoke first with no prompting. He said he had been roughed up at chow by a couple of corrections officers and he wanted something done about it—his message was mainly delivered in ghetto speak. José wasn't on the ILC and we hadn't invited him, yet it was clear someone had invited him to make the ILC look stupid in front of the superintendent.

State ILC rules said the ILC was to entertain the needs of the inmate body, not individual inmates. Unfortunately, no one could get him to shut up. Jonas sat there and grinned, and José ate up twenty minutes of our allotted hour. It was plain why José had been roughed up—his disrespect. Knowing the meeting had been sabotaged, Fig looked at me and said quietly, "This is Dyoyo's doing."

We had prepared a full agenda of issues for Jonas and the administration:

- The Maintenance Department had an abundance of unfulfilled work orders, including leaky toilets and broken washing machines
- Commissary wouldn't meet with the ILC about out-of-stock food items
- The state movie night schedule was posted but not followed by the staff who prepared the schedule
- There was no allowance for the ILC to visit other dorms to gather information on our issues
- Officers conducting dorm raids were throwing inmate food away and leaving cubes a mess (Directive 4910 mandated officers to make sure dorm quarters were in the same condition as they were prior to search)
- Out-of-town visitors to inmates were having their visits terminated early

There were many more issues to be discussed. Those listed were the only ones the administrative committee had time to entertain. Still distracted by the ghetto speak kid, the committee approved a request to have "lights out" at 10:15 p.m. rather than 11:15 p.m. Other items were briefly discussed but unresolved. I knew Dyoyo had picked up his administrative style from somewhere.

Overall, I didn't like the way things went with the ILC. All of its defects were as a result of administrative malfeasance. I did some research and found the office to contact and request change. I addressed my missive to James A. O'Gorman, Acting Deputy Commissioner of the Department of Corrections and Community Supervision:

In addition to not meeting regularly or sharing minutes with the inmate population, Marcy's ILC does not have a published budget, does not have its own office, and does not meet regularly with the administration. Basically, the ILC exists, but it's a totally ineffective body with a civilian leader and an inmate president who do nothing. Without effective leadership, our board can't even host meetings. We have not been apprised of our rights as an entity, and, therefore do not know what we are doing. So many dorms and inmates ask us for help, and we cannot help them because we don't even meet.

I mailed the letter after I resigned from the ILC. I would be leaving, but the ILC would still be here, stumbling along, unless the state intervened. I held my breath for just a little while.

The bookshelves in the NYASTP meeting room had an odd collection of Bibles in English and Spanish (I didn't see any ghetto speak Bibles). I found a few newly delivered gems like the short stories of Nathaniel Hawthorne and a biography of Zora Neale Hurston. Luigi Pirandello was there with *Six Characters in Search of an Author*. Hawthorne and Thurston had not yet been enjoyed by my brethren. The other books were beat all to hell, with broken spines and missing pages. I found a book by Andy Rooney with a missing front cover, a broken spine, and a back cover with a circular scorch, as if someone had set it upon a burner.

I avoided the Marcy library. When I first arrived, there was no librarian, so the library was closed. I filed a grievance to get it re-opened. Some substitute teacher from the town of Marcy was brought in and it re-opened. But to get into the library, inmates had to leave the dorm when evening gym was called, had to be wearing boots, and had to get through the metal detector line fast enough to be one of the first twenty to arrive. No more than twenty inmates were allowed at the same time. Twice I tried to get in. Twice I failed.

But the Andy Rooney book stuck in my craw. Not only was it severely damaged, but it had been given to F1 as a source of education and entertainment. As a bibliophile who once owned more than 2,500 books at my Morrow Avenue house, I had had enough of the Marcy library. I wrote "a kite" to the librarian, noting: "Maybe distribution can be more careful in the future. If the book is destroyed, so is the story."

The reply to my kite came from P. Rundle, Sr. Librarian. P. Rundle stressed that F1 should not count on special treatment from the library and that our inmates should "donate books to the library when they (inmates) are done with them so that the dorms can have immediate access to a further selection of reading materials." *What of Andy Rooney?* No mention. It occurred to me that a top DOCCS position in Albany was well within P. Rundle's reach.

NYASTP gave us a "Handout #14" assignment to write about who we were, using a Mad Libs-style worksheet. The format was an obituary. Here lies Brandon M. Stickney. He was ... seventy-eight years old. When he was young, ... he enjoyed soccer, The Who, KISS music, '80s music, girls, friends, hippie values, and love.

If he could change one thing in his life, it would be ... the felony. To change that mistake, he would ... have had better friends. He was happiest when ... reading and writing. If he could have left one thing to the world, it would have been ... a book people loved. His advice to those still living? ... Seize the day.

For good behavior, F1 was rewarded with a raid on May 8. The goon squad pounded in after breakfast, led by a dude who looked like Jeff Bridges in a white cowboy hat, sergeant's uniform, and cowboy boots. The goons came in, yelling, swearing, and knocking things about—toppling the little bookshelves and flipping NYASTP tables. Cowboy Bridges said, "We can do this the easy way or the hard way. You won't like the hard way."

We were ordered to strip, stand in front of our cubes, and place our hands behind our backs. The guards dispersed throughout the dorm. The guard who stood next to me was a friend of Valefor. He looked at me and offered me a small grin. My anxiety was instantly eased. The officer focused on my wall, where I had hung my father's paintings. "Those are really nice," he said. "Yours?" I said, "No, my father's a painter." He nodded. "Very nice."

The officers ordered us through the same sequence as the previous time—until we heard, "Got one." Everyone looked to the east of the dorm, where they were handcuffing a young man from Buffalo, whom I had not had a chance to meet. Cowboy Bridges said, "You're in NYASTP?" The handcuffed kid said he was. Cowboy Bridges said, "Well you better quit because it's not working." I wondered who wrote his scripts.

Then the C.O.s took another guy out. A degenerate card gambler, Slopper was from New York. The officers walked him through their X-ray, and it started ringing. Then they took him out on "suspicion" of having a weapon hidden inside his body. He wound up in The Box's plumbing-free cell, or "dry cell," so officers could wait for him to defecate and then examine the feces for metal pieces. I couldn't fathom being a C.O. on that assignment, waiting hours for a grown man's bowel movement and then sorting through it. Slopper returned to the dorm two days after the officers found nothing.

While this raid was longer, because they "caught" two people, it was also meaner than the usual. The officers threw all the food from the fridge and freezer on the floor. Opened the NYASTP counselors' office but barely touched anything. They were treating us as if we were all guilty. I was lucky I had the guard who liked Dad's artwork.

My mood crashed. No anxiety. Just depression. Another May day spent in prison. It used to be that I came alive in May. Spring was here, all over my tree-lined streets and in me. Regent Street, Morrow Avenue, Willow Street were gorgeous at night, the moon casting shadows on me and Bill Hannigan's faces as we shared a bottle of Irish Whiskey, talking of John Knowles, J.D. Salinger, Jack Kerouac, and how the world would know our writings too someday. America got to know a little of me when terrorism came to Oklahoma. Old Bill became a state trooper in New Jersey.

Rachael popped into my mind with, "Don't worry about it, man. You're doing your best." The Lockport Molson Summer Concert Series—Rachael sharing a pint of rum on the way to the show. Brett was there. So was Gary McGranahan. And I almost died there—during my drunken romantic lost-love opiate suicide sunset summer. "Don't worry about it, man."

Buddha loaned me his radio because I looked "gray." I put the headphones on, and The Ramones were singing "I Wanna be Sedated." I felt sorry for myself because nowhere is home. How long does a dry drunk last?

Dad came through that month with *Jekyll & Hyde*, *The Portrait of Dorian Gray*, and *The Time Machine*. He forwarded the final version of the art show news release and color reductions of three new paintings. I got some tape from Valefor and became the only inmate to have original Hobo Hieroglyphics artwork on his wall, by his father no less. Though my depression had left me, I still needed an ego boost. This did it. Did I feel better than the other inmates and the officers? Yes. I was given so much in life, and those I stayed with were not so lucky. I guess I didn't feel better than my inmate friends, but I did feel better than the mean inmates and C.O.s. In the package, Mom included M&Ms, a *Rolling Stone,* and a *Wall Street Journal* magazine.

Reading Robert Louis Stevenson, I identified with Hyde, of course—addicted, lusting after a drug that does not exist, and seeing his body and mind slipping into ruin, all while Jekyll stalks him like a cop, like a truth, like a rejection of the drug. Impossible. Inevitable.

The warmer weather signaled an uptick both in gang activity and in C.O. activity. Claiming they were looking for drugs and weapons, the C.O.s parked themselves strategically along the walkway and had a van posted near the gym entrance. As inmates walked to a program or to dinner, the C.O.s would grab them and order them to stand against walls or the van for pat down.

Deputy Supt. Colon, a bulky, big-boned woman with a Q-Tip-sized head, called these pat downs "frisks." She was either purposely lying or did not know the legal definition of frisk, which is a rapid pat down of the body, searching for weapons. What they were really doing was a "search," meaning putting their gloved hands inside pockets, down men's pants, and inside shirts and jackets. Prosecutor's court cases have been lost because street cops did not know the difference between frisk and search.

One C.O. seemed to enjoy search a little too much. Officer Andersen, his cap pulled down tight, wore reflective sunglasses and leather gloves, as if trying to hide his identity. But he was on a mission. Andersen did "credit card swipes" on prisoners—he put his hand down the back of the pants and swiped his hand over the testicles and through the ass-crack. This move can be very painful to a man—the testicles are sensitive. Why any C.O. would want to feel other men's balls was beyond me.

But some of the searches made sense. There were hundreds of newly 18-year-old punks and street kids in this prison. Ghetto-speak was their primary language, and they were always up to something—stealing, harassing people, fighting. They carried drugs and shanks.

Each one of them got a reputation, and the officers gave them a hard time on the walkway. It was common for the officers to corner one of these kids near a dorm and search them. Then the C.O. would shred their state-issued pants from hip to ankle. The kids would scream, and the C.O. would rough them up some more. Letting the officers know you had a bad attitude was a foolish response.

My release date drew near, yet everything seemed unresolved. I told other inmates, and they blamed Irving. "He fucks up everyone's time allotment and we go home a few months later," said Soprano. When I talked to Irving about my time, he hid behind a veneer of Chevy Chase-type reactions and one-liners.

I'd be completing NYASTP on June 6. To begin my parole, I planned on staying with Rachael or with Pastor Michael in Lockport. My parents in Florida asked that I stay with them, and I mused: *What a fitting end to my incarceration—retirement near Palm Beach.* While I had not been a perfect angel in prison, I hadn't drunk alcohol for nearly two years, ending my strongest and worst addiction.

But I still could not get an answer about when I'd be released.

I called my parents on May 31. Mom was excited because they had just received a call from Florida Parole. The officer and Mom set a date for the officer to visit them and inspect my future house.

Irving and the rest of the automatons at Marcy told me zip about this important development. They either didn't know, didn't want to tell me, or had some other lame excuse. To me, my revolution of one was moving forward. I kept it in a continuous loop in my head—to leave prison and retire at fifty-one in Palm Beach. Not half bad. *Cautious optimism.*

On June 4, I met with Irving, who said he knew nothing about my interstate contract. He was accurate about knowing zero. The next day, I went to Mental Health in the Infirmary to sign end-of-bid paperwork.

Trip and Kush, the suboxone brothers, carried on their drug dealing unabated.

One night, Kush was subjected to a urine test, along with six other inmates. All passed. The secret, Kush explained, was water. It was an old but effective trick. Drug tests were normally given after dinner, around 6:30. The Infirmary would call our C.O. around 6:15, paging inmates who had been "under suspicion," or chosen by a counselor to be tested.

The dummies got called a lot. These were the guys who'd use a piece of chineta and start thinking they had it all together. They'd stand there at the bubble, glassy-eyed, and talk a mile a minute to the C.O., somehow pretending "I'm high and he doesn't know." Most of our C.O.s were veterans who could easily see when an inmate was stoned. Toxicologies were held about every three months, right around the time of drug/weapons raids. Why does The Man refuse us our euphoria? There were 71,568 opiate-related deaths in America in 2017, but we aren't all suicidal like Kurt Cobain, or overdosing like sweet-sixteen Suzie Q's from the suburbs.

Trip obtained his chineta most often from Smooth, a black dude who looked no older than twenty. Smooth reminded me of one of the Cosby kids. They met up at the gym, or outside at recreation. Then Trip used Western Union to pay Smooth. I didn't know how deep Trip was until I visited Kush's cube and saw Trip sniff a piece off a spoon that was the size of a quarter. I took pieces as big as a period. Trip inhaled and then began coughing and choking on the wet suboxone. His dose was enough to keep me high forever. I didn't buy or use anywhere near that much.

Inmates have little to look forward to, so when Trip promised his customers, including me, that the stuff was coming today, we waited with great impatience. Trip had other dealers besides Smooth. You never knew when suboxone was in the dorm until you saw a bunch of people walking around with too much energy. In my hurry, I visited both Trip's cube and Kush's cube, and kept a close watch on Trip's every move, hoping he'd walk my way. Waiting was agony because other than writing or talking to Gandhi, I had nothing to do. Others gossiped while they waited: "He isn't getting nothing" … "His bill is too high" … "He missed the handoff" … "He's getting a boatload this time" … "It's only two milligrams" … etc.

I nearly got caught one time when I had a toothache. The infirmary took two months to get to dental issues—prisoners here and across the country had no recourse when treatment was withheld, according to prison abuse reports. I had scoured the dorm to trade for antibiotics, Ibuprofen, salt for saltwater gargling, anything. Everyone seemed to come up empty, so I had to hold ice cubes against the infected molar, even on the way to and from meds. That numbed the pain until each cube melted. I tried numbing it with toothpaste and grinding up aspirin and putting it right on the tooth. Trip offered me a $20 piece of chineta, and, in desperation, I agreed. Suboxone has painkiller properties, though it isn't used as such, except among addicts. It can also lessen the desire for alcohol.

I wetted and took the suboxone. The euphoria nearly made me forget about the throbbing dental pain, and I became social. I still had to use the ice cubes, but then an inmate finally provided me with some tiny salt packets, rarely distributed in the mess hall. The suboxone piece had been big—bigger than I normally sniffed. Mixing the salt with water in the bathroom, I began to hallucinate in front of the mirror, falling asleep for two seconds and then talking to myself. Inmates were watching me. I had become very tired from the pain and the drug. Suddenly, I felt a hand on my shoulder. It was Trip.

"People are talking about you," he said. "Let's walk to your cube and you can lay down for sleep before Officer Kelly sends you out for a urine test." I wigged, did as Trip said, and went to bed for the night. The pain was there for another day. Continued use of the saltwater helped and the pain finally ceased. Luckily for me, I was not harassed about the incident.

Then Trip's father died. His parents lived somewhere near Utica. Trip had told us he used to party hard with his father after he was eighteen. Cocaine and booze. Trip Senior was only fifty-six. Trip was in a daze for a while, right up until the wake. Marcy administration granted him a two-day leave to attend the funeral.

What I didn't know, until much later, was that the younger Trip was in debt to a few Marcy people, including the Bloods. He was sad and happy when he got back from the funeral because the C.O.s had let him alone with his wife. They did it in the men's room of the funeral home. Trip said if he knew the officers were going to be "so cool," he would have had the wife slip him a bunch of suboxone. He wasn't even strip-searched upon his return.

The O'Donnell family was moneyed. However, Trip's mother was not as generous as his father. So, Trip couldn't call in a Western Union order to make everything better with the Bloods. You could see the worry on Trip's face. He'd skip meals and gym, hiding in our dorm. I saw Smooth on the walkway and he said, "Hey, get Trip out to chow tonight. We need to talk."

Ace Lanza became the new chineta guy for the dorm. He'd throw me a free piece now and then because he wanted me to help him with a screenplay about Sandy Hook. He had a great idea—Adam Lanza and friend Bob Tether talking in Bob's bedroom, about bullies, teachers, growing up, and a revenge plot. The whole movie was to be set in flashbacks and end the day before the massacre. With my journalistic background, Ace felt I was the ideal partner. He also offered to make a shank for me, but I declined.

Trip still had to leave the dorm for meds at the Infirmary. I didn't walk with him because he was a smoker and walked very slow. Rich and I went to the Infirmary together, Rich keeping me entertained with rock folklore and tales of his own concert trips. The wind had died down and the days were getting just a little longer.

It was still dusk for med run. On the way out of the infirmary, Rich and I saw Trip holding his face, standing in the line. I asked what had happened and he waved me off. Back at the dorm, Ace told me one of the Bloods punched Trip in the face when he was passing the school. "They want their fucking money today, not tomorrow," said Ace.

Kush, Cabo, and The Cosmonaut were all called up for Work Release. Early one morning, they packed their belongings, gave away a few things—like books and clothes—then left via bus to Rochester Correctional, where they spent the next two weeks, after which they were allowed to work some pre-selected job for about six months. If they proved themselves trustworthy and in recovery, they'd only have to spend weekends in prison.

Somehow, despite almost daily drug use, Kush had made it through Marcy and NYASTP without failing a drug test. Trip, it seemed to me, had a tough time, initially, after Kush left for Rochester. Most relationships among men in prison, I observed, were less than surface. Hardly anybody missed their prison friends when they left; in fact, it was like the person had never existed. No one talked about an inmate after he left. On that important day, with bags packed, the inmate would walk out of the dorm, past the NYASTP class. The class would do the obligatory clapping, and that was it.

I offered to be Trip's "replacement Kush" so he would have a reliable friend.

Trip laughed and said no, he was okay. It had only been a few weeks since his father died, and he seemed to be doing remarkably well. He'd gotten a new friend, some tall blond dude named Green Lantern who was a housepainter. Trip began using him to run his errands, so he could avoid those out to get him. He became very unreliable, making promises he wouldn't keep, asking to borrow commissary credit "in exchange," and taking whatever chineta he got for himself.

Mister High Strung, Ace became the main purveyor of prison gossip: "They are testing us tonight..." "Tomorrow will be a raid" ... "The counselors know what's going on and have a list of users." Ace still dealt, though he was nervous all the time. Either he was making me paranoid, or I needed to clean up to graduate, or both.

CELL #17

Criminology professor Elliot Currie writes:

"The prison has become a looming presence in our

society to an extent unparalleled in our history or

that of any other industrial democracy. Short of

major wars, mass incarceration has been the most

thoroughly implemented government social program

of our time."

CHAPTER 17

THE BIG EMPTY

"Life can only be understood backwards, but it must be lived forwards."
—Soren Kierkegaard

On a sunny day in June, Officer Beaver decided that we were all going outside. On clean-up Fridays, it was up to the C.O. whether to keep some of us back in the afternoon or make us all go to gym. I had been told my leave date would be August 28. Even though it seemed like a year away, I was counting the days. I wanted to get out to the yard and celebrate future freedom. Clearly, I was feeling a little better.

Ace said he was bringing bricks to the yard. "It's happening," he said. On Ace's behalf, I had borrowed a pack of Newports from the Chinese kid. A package had just arrived from my parents: M&Ms, summer sausage, sharp cheddar, crackers, and more! Buddha, Gandhi, and I were going to have a feast after gym.

The line for the yard wrapped around the walkway. I tried my best to avoid breathing in the cigarette smoke and to ignore the rapid ghetto talk. I passed through the metal detector. Luckily, Valefor was working the line, so I didn't have to answer any moronic questions or get yelled at by the metal detector. On the other side, I saw Nate West. I yelled to him because this was rare. He was on the "other side" of the campus, so our dorms were rarely in the yard at the same time.

We decided to walk the track together rather than watching softball. We talked of people we knew in Lockport, of growing up there, and of the crimes that had brought us to Marcy. Michael Clines died of a heroin overdose. He was Nate's cousin whom I had known since second grade. David Henry shot himself. Nate got crack from him, I bought suboxone. Others had been arrested, or moved, or who should have been dead from drugs but were somehow still alive.

"I can't wait to go home and get a Four Loko," I said.

"Now, why would you do that after all this clean time?" said Nate. I thought he was going to agree with me. He spent his adulthood in bars, jails, and crackhouses.

I couldn't imagine Nate ever being a voice of reason. He was sounding like Cougar, back at Collins.

"I miss it," I said. "I miss being drunk, sniffing pills." TV personality Craig Ferguson said in *American on Purpose* that he was a reformed alcoholic who still entertained ideas of taking a drink. Ferguson: "Alcohol ruined me financially and morally, broke my heart and the hearts of too many others. Even though it did this to me and it almost killed me, and even though I haven't touched a drop of it in seventeen years, sometimes I wonder if I could get away with drinking. I totally subscribe to the notion that alcoholism is a mental illness because thinking like that is clearly insane."

While 500,000 mentally challenged people are housed in America's prisons, that number would be double if alcoholic prisoners were formally declared mentally ill as well. However, there seem to be as many definitions of alcoholic—arguments over who is and who isn't—as there are definitions of "rock bottom," and what's involved in hitting it.

Ferguson, the Americans with Disabilities Act, and the National Institute on Drug Abuse all agree, as late as August 2018: Addiction *is* a mental illness. The Institute reports, "Addiction alters the brain in fundamental ways, changing a person's normal needs and desires and replacing them with new priorities connected with seeking and using the drug. This results in compulsive behaviors that weaken the ability to control impulses, despite the negative consequences, and are similar to hallmarks of other mental illnesses." Unfortunately, Social Security does not consider addiction a mental illness.

Nate said drinking would be a bad idea for me. "Brandon, you look better now. You sound better. Start over with this clean time you have built up. Or do you want to come back here?"

"No," I said, "I don't want to come back to prison. The good thing is, I can't lose anymore—there's nothing left to lose. I'm starting fresh. But I want my grape Loko. I want good times again."

We were walking the cinder track, passing the soccer field. Inmates deep in ghetto speak walked past us. It was hot. Nate took his shirt off. He was also a non-smoker, unless it was cocaine.

"I just love that feeling." I said, "It fills the emptiness."

"Fill it with something else." Nate said. "Write another book. Get a girlfriend. Imagine having money and spending time with your daughter."

Nate made me feel guilty and, I admit, made me long for a sober life. Time with my family and friends who weren't wasted all the time or living off the system. Sticking it to The Man… Was that so important that I had to lose my life doing it?

I did not tell Nate that Ace was scoring in the yard as we walked, that I was going back to party in the dorm. But I did think this could be the last time I'd do it. When I got out, I'd have to follow Parole's stipulations and if I fucked up, I'd be right back in prison, for two years. Or, if I failed a piss test, I'd be here after my current release date. NYASTP time wouldn't matter anymore.

The letter from my daughter. The phone calls with my parents. Nate's talk. It was finally sinking in. I wasn't William Burroughs or Hunter S. Thompson. The bad-boy writer thing wasn't working; maybe it had never worked. It just took away from what I was capable of, and it made my mental illness worse.

As we switched to another subject, the C.O.s called us back to the clubhouse. We lined up with our dorms by number and got harassed by a sergeant who wanted "straight lines" of inmates. Then we were released to go back. I wondered if Ace had scored, and whether I should bother with him at all.

Had I really changed here? Sobriety did hold some kind of promise, a romantic mystery that I had not known in nearly thirty years.

At my cube, I looked for Ace. We made eye contact and he gave me a slight nod. "I'll see you in a minute," he said.

I looked out over the dorm. Nearly sixty guys. In my mind, I saw the web of crimes they had committed before prison. I estimated fifty to a thousand because no criminal or addict commits just one crime. I also imagined how, in this dorm, we were all linked, if only for six months of our lives.

I asked Buddha to take my cheese from the refrigerator and microwave it over some Club Crackers. I told Gandhi we were having a cheese and cracker snack, on me.

Ace arrived and handed me a balled-up tissue. Inside was a very tiny piece, much smaller than what I should've gotten for $10. I set in on my plastic spoon and poured in a tiny drop of water. I looked over to the C.O. desk a few times, to see if Beaver was watching me. He wasn't, as usual. I sniffed, hoping that I would have the will power to make this my last time. The signs were adding up since Trip's dad died: he went broke, my family contact, Nate's message, and Ace turning out to be a rip-off artist. Then a letter from Uncle Mason: "I don't know if you can see the changes in the way you think, but it's amazing to read your letters and see how differently you look at your life. You don't sound like a victim anymore."

Hudson came in for the 3 p.m. shift. Buddha, who all but radiated Zen, made the crackers with melted cheese. When Buddha and Gandhi were near, I felt an unspoken tranquility; we thought alike, we'd been addicts, and we were different from the other inmates and from the fascists who ran this prison camp. The suboxone made me aware of a God-like presence of compassion that said we did not have to physically battle our captors—we only had to tolerate and rise above them.

That night, Buddha found a huge bug on his locker. We were fascinated. It was as large as a Praying Mantis, had green eyes, long legs, and what looked like green shoes. No one knew what kind of bug it was or had ever seen it before. Always up for a dorm adventure, Hudson captured the bug in a cup and set it free on the front porch. That was nice because I thought one of these Neanderthals was going to squash it. Buddha said he took "the whole bug experience" as a positive sign.

Before bed, Gandhi and I shared cookies, and had a wide-ranging conversation about Mars, space exploration, communes, the 1960s, Benzedrine, *On the Road*, cough medicine, and he read me a poem he wrote. The poem went thusly:

Positive affirmation

Prostitute application

Gravity, synchronicity, randomness

Mistakes, corrections, erasure

I live a shoulder above the competition

But do nothing to completion.

The next morning, four C.O.s barged into F1 after breakfast. They called out four names, including Trip and Green Lantern. My heart was beating quickly. But no more names were called. The four inmates were manhandled on their way to the gym, with about eighty others, for urine tests. Three guys refused the test. Within two days, Trip, Green Lantern, and one other who'd refused the tox test were kicked out of NYASTP and sent to general population dorms. The one guy who didn't refuse, Travis, was branded a narc. Ace said, "Avoid him at all costs." Easy for me to do. I didn't even know him.

—————————————————————————————

My graduation date for NYASTP came and went. I expected a ticker tape parade, celebrating ... as Leos like to do. My journal entry from that day: "Apparently graduating from NYASTP isn't as important as starting the program. I didn't even get to sign paperwork saying I was done. Maybe Irving gets paid more for keeping us in the program longer?

"Is graduation not an achievement? Where is my certificate? Something to show the judge and employers. We have three counselors (well, one just quit) and thirty students, yet nothing happens on the six-month completion date. Something shady is going on. I had to raise my hand and tell the class and the counselors I was done, and no one reacted in any way."

—————————————————————————————

My parents told me they spoke with my parole officer, who said I am "welcome in the state of Florida." Instead of flying me down, my folks sent information to the prison and to Parole saying B.E. Chamberlain, my old neighborhood friend, would pick me up in his F150 and drive us to Palm Beach.

In a moment of end-of-bid levity, I composed a list of things I should be doing as my leave date approached:
- Skipping group
- Giving more people the finger
- Eating off others' trays
- Stealing Gandhi's right shoes (I really did this when he was napping)
- Shouting "One Love"
- Picking my nose in mess hall
- Reading Oscar Wilde aloud at 3 a.m.
- Dancing and shaking my sexy ass
- Staring Gandhi dead in the eye and saying, "I smell chloroform."
- Not giving a fuck (courtesy of Soprano)

I had been writing notes to administration and anyone who would listen that I had been passed over for my original leave date. Irving told me that there was some rule (not listed in my NYASTP booklet) that said even when you are finished with NYASTP, you still have to attend group.

It had been nearly eight months and NYASTP was only a six-month program. By giving me an August 28 leave date, they were treating me as if I had never taken NYASTP or failed the class. It was well-known among the prison population that if a prison keeps you beyond your official leave date, you are entitled to state payment of more than $100 per day because—on the theory that, if the prison had not made such an error, the inmate could have been out, working and making money.

My complaints were floating around out there. Every time I tried to get an answer from Irving, he turned into Patsy Cline: "Please release me. Let me go." He sang in frustration, certainly, since ten different inmates likely came to him each day asking about their leave dates. Instead of making fun of inmates, he should have been doing his $80,000-per-year job.

I was about to write to Supt. Jonas himself, I was so angry. As I was walking to the intake building, I was smoothing my hair, which was quite long, as was my beard. *Was I really going home earlier? Did they realize their mistake? I finished NYASTP June 6. I should have left a long time ago. And I was entitled to about $3,000 in compensation. To get it, I'd probably need a lawyer on the outside.*

Then, on July 27, two days before my fifty-first birthday, I was paged to the intake room—where I had not been since December 6—for a new I.D. The C.O. said, "A new I.D. means you're going home very soon." My release date was August 28. That was not soon enough for me.

There, inside the office, was the last C.O. I'd ever meet. Of course, he was kind of like all the others, raising his voice a few times, trying to get me to "stand right" in front of the camera. I stood before one of the police posters that measures how tall suspects are.

"I'm supposed to go home August 28," I told him.

"Let me see," he said. "No. This says August 6. You got ten days left."

I smiled; I could've kissed him. He handed me my new I.D. and I floated out of the office to the walkway, staring up at the poplar trees and the starlings fluttering around the fence line. The sun was beautiful. The black crows looked splendid. A song on the breeze played in my heart. There was finally real, solid hope. I just had to live ten more days.

At the dorm, I found a letter from Rachael, wishing me a happy birthday and telling me to stay positive. Rachael wrote, "…And remember your saga continues when you are free. This is not the end, my friend."

Isn't it curious that my prison story was framed by Sartre? The famous French philosopher and writer, Jean-Paul Sartre, was one of the key figures in the school of existential thought. Before all this began, back when I was released into general population from the county jail's isolation SHU, I was awaiting transfer to a state prison to serve my two years. Seeking a book, I found a big black hardcover of prison fiction. Me without a book is like a man without food. In the table of contents, my finger landed on Sartre's "The Wall." A rare find, indeed. Published originally in 1939, the tale from the Spanish Civil War concerns three fellows—Pablo, Tom, and Juan—spending the evening in a prison. They have been sentenced to death by shooting at sunrise.

The prison is a war-damaged building. The room the three are housed in has a hole in the ceiling, water running about, and no heat. The narrator, Pablo, is asked by an interrogator the whereabouts of anarchist Ramon Gris. Pablo claims ignorance. The fact of their pending death in the morning eats at the minds of the three men. Morning arrives, and Tom and Juan are taken to the wall outside and shot.

Pablo meets with the guard again. After smartly revealing the information he knows about Ramon, he is set free. He begins laughing "so hard that I cried." Though Pablo lives, the unfathomable loneliness that the story conveyed ate at me and magnified many events to come, including when I left. Some well-meaning inmate set a copy of Sartre's play "No Exit" on my locker. Did it mean that I wasn't leaving after all? Translated into English, the French title means a private meeting, behind closed doors.

Regardless of meanings and inferences and intellectual impossibilities, I couldn't have had a more brutal, and trustworthy, guide in my journey.

"The Opioid Diaries," a masterwork of photojournalism by James Nachtwey, appeared in *Time* magazine with a syringe ready to ease into a man's arm. The special issue included quotes and photos of addicts on the street, and law enforcement not only intervening in the lives of the homeless, but picking up the dead as well.

A ranking officer at a sheriff's department compared the number of opioid deaths to terrorism and wondered why the nation was not as frantic about "doing something" as they would if a terrorist killed ten Americans. My answer would be that the sick and dying have a right to painkillers, just as anyone with severe pain does. Some people choose to put needles in their arms. There's nothing to "do" about it. Opioids are nirvana—people will always use them. And there will always be casualties.

The best quote in the issue was by social worker Angela Davis, who expertly answered the question of what we should do: "If your family member is struggling with addiction, love them. Don't fight them, don't judge them. And for the love of everything holy, pray for them."

The prospect of leaving prison soon gave me pause for reflection—that goes without saying. Every time a C.O. said this was his dorm, his gym, his mess hall ... Ownership of anything had been lost to me at least five years ago. Prison is a kind of homelessness as jailors strip everything from you.

My journey was certainly Eastern in my mind; I had given up American materialism. I had given up clothes—I wore the robes my overlord had lent me. I gave up friends and was urged by Marcy's old Rev. Dunmore to pray. I had a few filled notebooks, some coffee, and a desire to go see what was beyond my hometown and my prison and live the second half of my life.

Writer Scott Gutches described similar feelings, "Possession ... is alien and familiar at the same time, and I doubt I will resume it when I leave. That's ironic in a way, because it's an implicit requirement for parole—work, buy, consume, possess."

One of the hundreds of media appearances I made for *All-American Monster* was with Jack Ford on MSNBC's "Inter-nite." Timothy McVeigh's trial was about to get underway in Denver. I was given tickets to fly to New York that afternoon for the show. I changed into a jacket and tie in the Lincoln Town Car as the friendly driver eased us through Manhattan traffic.

Once inside NBC studios, I was rushed into makeup, and made small talk with Jack as we sat next to each other. I had already done nearly 100 newspaper, radio, and TV interviews, and I was ready for MSNBC. Interviews had gone on for nearly five years. I was the main non-lawyer expert on the panels, wined and dined from Seattle to Denver.

Then I was hired by Mercedes-Benz Financial. The more money I had for my little family, the more I drank and chased coke. I stayed in journalism while I was in marketing. I just couldn't give it up. I penned "Person of the Year" stories, local color pieces for magazines, and op-eds, locally and nationally. Even while suffering the worst part of my addiction, I still wrote for the news, and completed a biography of the Seven Sutherland Sisters.

During prison, I gave up nearly everything, including the ghost. Alcohol now seems far away now, a backwards road. I can't imagine myself buying pills in Palm Beach. It wasn't AA, NA, NYASTP, Marcy, Collins, my judges, fate, my pastor, a best friend, or my family that made me want to stop drinking, one day at a time. I can't give the credit to God either. It just happened. Comedian Richard Lewis testified to successful sobriety in *The Harder They Fall*. He wrote: "It was clear to me, even in very early recovery, that the only people who ultimately saved themselves and seriously entered recovery … knew that they needed it, but also wanted it." For a long time, I didn't really want it. I wanted the bohemian-me back. For me, sobriety just happened.

You'd think that during an experience such as prison, the inmate would learn a few great lessons he would take home and use. From what I saw, C.O.s too often use their criminal and addict thinking. Most C.O.s are good people doing a tough job, and don't want to see anyone hurt. However, the bad eggs are front and center, flaunting their power.

Bureaucracy and confusion are the two chief features of our prisons, not the administration. Inmates learn nothing in prison, unless it's from each other. There must be a change for our 2.3 million prisoners if we are to help make America great again. Considering inmate families, the number involved in prison is closer to 17 million because families are so deeply affected, and forever changed. And it continues to baffle me why violent offenders are housed with the nonviolent.

Mainly, though, it was the officers' culture that was the most disturbing because C.O.s protected the prison, not the prisoners. According to writer Gary Cornelius of Corrections.com, there are eight primary reasons a C.O. could get fired:

- Theft or improper use of property
- Mishandling or theft of inmate property
- Personal substance abuse
- Accepting gifts
- Discrimination
- Abuse of authority
- General boundary limitation (such as sex with an inmate)
- Violence or excessive force

In my experience, these rules were broken with the arrogance and brashness of career criminals. They put inmates and the mentally ill at risk. C.O.s often said, "You're not running this prison. This is my dorm." A true statement. It is their prison, not that of the administration, the government, or the taxpayers. This army of officers fights the American people every day.

Looking back on NYASTP and its theft of ideas from similar failed group activities, I questioned the easy category labels we use, like alcoholic, addict, disease. As expert Benoit Denizet-Lewis asked, "Is addiction a disease...or is it a malady of the spirit? Why do some recover from addiction, while others die from it?" If these questions cannot be answered—other than some inmates simply need abstinence or are weak-willed—things will remain the same in this intoxicated and remorseful world.

My own denial told me I was never a drug addict. Addiction means being "physically and mentally dependent on a particular substance, unable to stop taking it without adverse effects." I was an alcoholic who used illegal and illicit narcotics for about twenty years before I broke the law and was forced to stop.

If I was a true addict, wouldn't I be on the streets, looking and doing anything for the next high? Or the next drink? I was an alcoholic who was heavily involved in drugs for a while. There was no every day, or every other. It was whenever the situation presented itself, as it often did. I didn't go through withdrawal in prison. And I haven't had an alcoholic drink since April 23, 2017. AA has so many arguments to convince a drinker he is an alcoholic. This is where Dianetics cult behavior comes into play… Why is being in AA a reason to convince others of a disease, especially since you are not a medical doctor, scientist, or psychiatrist?

Back to the definition of "addiction," this time according to Merriam-Webster: "Compulsive need for and use of habit-forming substance (such as heroin, nicotine, or alcohol) characterized by tolerance and by well-defined physiological symptoms upon withdrawal." For me, in denial, I was neither physically nor mentally *dependent* on any particular substance. I was able to stop taking alcohol and substances without adverse effects, other than mild withdrawal from opiates. I wanted more, sometimes, though I never robbed banks for drugs. And I never holed up in my apartment for a week, using. Drugs and alcohol made me social; I was rarely at home. My hospitalizations were bipolar-related. My denial was almost as powerful as my addiction.

So many addicts confess that they've always been addicts, of sex, of power, of money, of music, of material things. As a kid, I collected comic books and Matchbox cars, yet I didn't grow up to be a superhero actor or one of those pudgy guys on Discovery's "Street Outlaws." I wasn't addicted to any of those things, except maybe reading. Some out there seem addicted to addiction because it gives them an identity (or personality), when they'd normally have none.

I may have lost everything, to alcohol, and wound up in prison. But, until the definition changed, I did not suffer from drug addiction. I gave up alcohol the way many do—being forced to by circumstances. It seemed I'd tell myself anything to keep going.

Journalist Pete Hamill gave up the bottle without anyone's help. "I didn't join Alcoholics Anonymous. I didn't seek out other help. I just stopped." Alone. Not with a doctor or counselor. Not in a group. When will the courts and purveyors of abstinence and recovery understand that there's more than one way to stop? Different things work for different people.

RELEASE

EPILOGUE

The morning of my last day in prison, the C.O. told me to pack up. I gave away my possessions except the clothes I was wearing and my prison uniform. The uniform items had to be handed in at State Shop. An Aryan Nations guy volunteered to help carry my bags. We walked from the dorm to the infirmary (to grab my med supply) to the visiting area, where there was a fence. I thanked him, and he walked back. I wanted to say something to him, like, "You'll be out soon too." But he had four years to go.

This may not have been *The Odyssey*, but I felt the end needed some marker to show the horrible history that had passed here. Considering my company this year, and some personal change, I couldn't think of a more appropriate coda than "This then is my story," the words Vladimir Nabokov wrote for the character Humbert Humbert in his famous tale of forbidden love called *Lolita*.

"I have reread it. It has bits of marrow sticking to it, and blood, and beautiful bright green flies. At this or that twist of it, I feel my slippery self-eluding me, gliding into deeper and darker waters than I care to probe."

A few other soon-to-be-former inmates were also waiting at the gate: a fat guy in a wheelchair, a withered alcoholic, and a Latin king. A sergeant took us through to a waiting area, where we were given our "outside" clothes and handed in our prison uniforms and boots. The outside clothes included a long-sleeved, white Corcraft shirt and khaki pants. I was allowed to keep my prison sneakers.

The sergeant took us outside to a cage with a gate. He unlocked the gate and led us into an upscale reception area—the nicest room I'd seen in months. We stood in line at a counter where they gave us identification papers and $40. Me and the alcoholic dude sat in comfortable chairs, waiting. I could see Chamberlain in his Ford truck. It had been nearly ten years since we had last spoken.

After picking up my money and I.D., I sat back down again. The C.O. at the counter said, "No. You're free to go. Just walk out that door." I got up, walked to the door, and went outside into a moment I had been waiting for, talking about, envisioning, and thinking would never happen, as if I was walking through the "Field of Dreams." Mentally, I looked back and saw the faces of Bear, Pastor Mark, Gummy, Gandhi, and even officer Valefor, and I wished them the greatest gift I could imagine—inner peace. As radio host Mark Maron once said, "Taking responsibility is one thing. But does everyone deserve to be destroyed forever for anything transgressive?"

My mind racing, I knew that old voice urging self-harm had been silenced. I walked toward the Ford as Chamberlain got out, looking bigger and tanner than when we'd last seen each other.

This moment was not how I thought it would be. I was calm but anticipatory, and more afraid than I knew. The weight of Parole came down on me, springing my ugly paranoia, and I'd only been out of prison thirty seconds.

I greeted my friend and wanted to tell him everything—all my thoughts as they came, my last several months, the good times we had in college, and my sorrys over our falling out. I had to tell him all of this, all at once.

Instead, I simply said, "I have a lot to say."

PRISONER'S BILL OF RIGHTS

Inmates, whether in jail or in prison, have basic rights protected by the U.S. Constitution:

1) The right to humane facilities and conditions

2) The right to be free from sexual crimes

3) The right to be free from racial segregation

4) The right to express condition complaints

5) The right to assert rights under the Americans with Disabilities Act

6) The right to medical care and attention as needed

7) The right to appropriate mental health care

8) The right to a hearing if prisoner is moved to a mental health facility

ACKNOWLEDGEMENTS

This was the most difficult book for me to write. Thank you to those who made it possible: my parents; my daughter; Mason Arrigo and Philip Barragan; Mimi; the readers of my "Couch-surfing" on Facebook; Brett and Carol Chamberlain; N. Frank Daniels; Brett Vaughan; Rachael Norton and Sam Lasky; Jim Kane; Randy Reese; Patrick O'Neil; Michael and Megan Foster; the folks at White Deer Run; Madeline Wolf, my exceptional literary assistant at Bancroft; and especially the five prison men who broke through to me and made me want to live.

BIBLIOGRAPHY

Abbott, Jack Henry. *In the Belly of the Beast* (Vintage, 1991)

Alcoholics Anonymous, *Big Book* (AA World Services, 2001)

Auster, Paul. Invisible (Thorndike Press, 2009)

Bauer, Shane. *American Prison: A Reporter's Undercover Journey into the Business of Punishment* (Penguin, 2018)

Butterfield, Fox. *All God's Children: The Bosket Family and the American Tradition of Violence* (Avon, 1995)

Bunker, Edward. *Education of a Felon* (St. Martin's, 2000)

Burroughs, Augusten. *Dry: A Memoir* (Picador, 2013)

Cleaver, Eldridge. *Soul on Ice* (Delta, 1999)

Cheever, Susan. *Home Before Dark* (Washington Square Press, 2015)

Conover, Ted. *Newjack: Guarding Sing Sing* (Random House, 2000)

Currie, Elliot. *Crime and Punishment in America* (Holt, 1998)

Davis, Angela Y. *Are Prisons Obsolete?* (Seven Stories Press, 2003)

Darnton, Kate et al. (Editors) *Peter Jennings: A Reporter's Life* (PublicAffairs/Perseus, 2007)

Denizet-Lewis, Benoit. *America Anonymous* (Simon & Schuster, 2009)

Dodd, Douglas and Matthew B. Nerber *Generation Oxy* (Skyhorse Publishing, 2017)

Frank, Anne. *The Diary of a Young Girl* (Bantam, 1997)

Franklin, H. Bruce (editor). *Prison Writing of the 20th Century* (Penguin, 1998)

Ferguson, Craig. *Confessions of an Unlikely American* (HarperCollins, 2009)

Fitzgerald, F. Scott. *The Great Gatsby* (Scribner, 2004)

Gabor, Mate, M.D. *In the Realm of Hungry Ghosts: Close Encounters with Addiction* (North Atlantic Books, 2010)

Hamill, Pete. *A Drinking Life* (Back Bay Books, 1995)

Hepola, Sarah. *Remembering the Things I Drank to Forget* (Grand Central Publishing, 2015)

Holy Bible (Thomas Nelson Publishers)

Hunter, Stephen. *I, Ripper* (Simon & Schuster, 2015)

Kerman, Piper. *Orange is the New Black* (Spiegel & Grau, 2011)

Knapp, Caroline. *Drinking: A Love Story* (Dial Press, 1997)

Koehler-Pentacoff, Elizabeth. *The Missing Kennedy: Rosemary Kennedy and the Secret Bonds of Four Women* (Bancroft Press, 2015)

Lerner, Jimmy. *You Got Nothing Coming* (Broadway Books, 2003)

Moore, Allison with Nancy Woodruff. Shards: *A Young Vice Cop Investigates Her Darkest Case of Meth Addiction—Her Own* (Touchstone, 2014)

Nabokov, Vladimir. *Lolita.* (Vintage, 1989)

Nelson, Jill (editor), *Police Brutality* (Norton, 2000)

Oates, Joyce Carol (editor). *Prison Noir* (Akashic Books/Ontario Review, 2014)

Parsell, T.J. Fish: *A Memoir of a Boy in a Man's Prison* (Da Capo Press, 2007)

Santos, Michael. *Inside: Life Behind Bars in America* (St. Martins, 2007)

Sheff, Nic. *Tweak: Growing Up on Methamphetamines* (Atheneum, 2009)

Sheff, Nic. *We All Fall Down: Living with Addiction* (Little, Brown, 2011)

Steinberg, Avi. *Running the Books* (Random House, 2010)

Stickney, Brandon M. *All-American Monster: The Unauthorized Biography of Timothy McVeigh* (Prometheus Books, 1996)

Stickney, Brandon M. *The Amazing Seven Sutherland Sisters: A Biography of America's First Celebrity Models* (Niagara History Center, 2012)

Stromberg, Gary and Jane Merrill. *The Harder They Fall: Celebrities Tell Their Real-Life Stories of Addiction and Recovery* (Hazelden, 2005)

Tartt, Donna. *The Goldfinch* (Abacus, 2014)

Thompson, Hunter S. and Ralph Steadman. *The Curse of Lono* (Taschen, 1983)

Vargas, Elizabeth. *Between Breaths: A Memoir of Panic and Addiction* (Grand Central Publishing, 2016)

West, Cornel. *Race Matters* (Vintage, 2001)

Wiesel, Elie. *Night* (Hill & Wang, 2006)

ADDITIONAL REFERENCES

American Addictions Centers. "Group Therapy vs. Individual Therapy," undated, americanaddictioncenters.org

American Friends Service Committee Against Torture. "Survivors Speak: Prisoner Testimonies of Torture in United States Prisons and Jails," November 2014, afsc.org

Associated Press. "Young Adult Jail at Rikers to House All Inmates 18 to 21," September 4, 2015

Associated Press. "Why Suicide Rates Are So High Among Corrections Officers," January 9, 2018

Baum, Dan. "Legalize It All: How to Win the War on Drugs," *Harper's*, April 2016

Bengelsdorf, Herbert, "M.D. Mental Health Triage Rating Scale," Aspen Regional Health, New York, undated

Brown, J. Pat. and Beryl Lipton. "How Many People Die Each Year in the American Prison System?" muckrock.com, April 13, 2017

Bureau of Justice Statistics. "Drugs and Crime Facts," undated

citylab.com. "Jail to Homelessness Pipeline," August 2018

Collins, James. "The Weight of Evidence," *Time*, April 29, 1997

Committee Against Torture. "Survivors Speak: Prisoners Testimonies of Torture in United States Prisons and Jails," November 2014

Cornelius, Gary. "8 Ways to Destroy Your Correctional Officer Career," December 12, 2017, correctionsone.com

Federal Bureau of Prisons. "Offences," November 24, 2018, bop.gov

Forgotten Majority. "The Infamous Black Box," December 15, 2018, forgottenmajority.net

Human Rights Watch. "Callous and Cruel: Use of Force Against Inmates with Mental Health Disabilities in U.S. Jails and Prisons," May 12, 2015

Konda, Srinivas, MPH, et al., "U.S. Correctional Officers Killed or Injured on the Job," *Research Notes*, November/December 2013, ncbi.nlm.nih.gov

Lat, David. "How Tough-on-Crime Prosecutors Contribute to Mass Incarceration," April 8, 2019, *The New York Times*

Lennon, John J. "This Place is Crazy," *Esquire*, Pages 82 to 87 and 122 to 123. Summer 2018

Merod, Anna. "House Passes Most Significant Mental Health Reform Bill in Decades," July 17, 2006

Nachtwey, James. "The Opioid Diaries," *Time*, March 8, 2018

National Alliance on Mental Illness. "Jailing People with Mental Illness," undated

National Center for Health Statistics and Centers for Disease Control and Prevention. "Drug Statistics – National Institute on Drug Abuse," August 2018, drugabuse.gov

National Institute of Justice. "Recidivism," undated, nij.gov

National Institute on Drug Abuse. "Comorbidity: Substance Use Disorders and Other Mental Illnesses," August 2018, drugabuse.gov

NYS Department of Correctional Services, Training Academy, "Recognizing and Managing the Special Needs Inmate," undated, 34 pages, op.nysed.gov/surveys

Oritz, Erik. "Seven Inmates Killed at South Carolina Maximum-Security Prison After Hours of Fighting," NBC News, April 15, 2018

Park, Madison. "Trials, convictions rare for officers," CNN, October 3, 2018

PBS Frontline. "The New Asylums," May 10, 2005

Press, Eyal. "Madness," *The New Yorker*, May 2, 2016

Sawyer, Wendy, and Peter Wagner. "Mass Incarceration: The Whole Pie 2019," March 19, 2019

Spiegel, Renia. "Hear, O Israel, Save Us," *Smithsonian*, November 2018

Stewart, Ian. "Report: Americans Are Now More Likely to Die of An Opioid Overdose Than on the Road," NPR, January 14, 2019

State of New York. "Inmate Liaison Committee (ILC) Directive," October 5, 2017

State of New York. "The Comprehensive Alcohol and Substance Abuse Program," Department of Corrections and Community Supervision, 2011

Stier, Ken. "NYS Prison Budget Climbs, Despite Fewer Inmates," November 10, 2015, citylimits.org

Westacott, Emrys. "Jean-Paul Sartre's Story 'The Wall'", *ThoughtCo.*, April 8, 2018

Wood, Graeme. "How Gangs Took Over Prisons," *The Atlantic*, October 2014

Wilson, Rick. "The Growing Problems of the Prison System," American Friends Service Committee, November 27, 2012, afsc.org

Video

Boone, Delbert. FMS Productions. *Prevention. Relapse & Reentry*, undated.

PBS. "Omar & Pete," September 13, 2005

BOOK CLUB QUESTIONS

1. If you were in Brandon M. Stickney's position, how would you have handled being incarcerated for two years?

2. Do you think that you could ever become addicted to something?

3. Out of the five people that Stickney bonded with, who do you think you would have gotten along with the most? Why?

4. When Stickney shares information about the prison system that is different from what the government and politicians share, how do you feel?

5. Does the information that Stickney shares motivate you to learn more about the prison system? Would you consider joining protests against the system after reading this book?

6. If you were making a movie of this book, who would you cast?

7. Did you read Stickney's book All-American Monster, and, if so, how would you compare it to this book?

8. Was there anything you expected to happen when reading the book? Or was this the first time you ever read a book of this nature?

9. Were you surprised by the content of the book? Was there any content that you really disagreed with?

10. What did you think of the book's length? If it's too long, what would you cut? If too short, what would you add?

11. If you got the chance to ask the author of this book one question, what would it be?

12. If you could hear this same story from another person's point of view, who would you choose? Would you want to hear Stickney's parents' point of view? Would you want to hear one of the five men's point of view?

13. What new things did you learn after reading this book?

14. Is there anything that you still have questions about after reading the book?

15. What else have you read on this topic, and would you recommend these books to others?

16. Think about the other people in the book besides the author. How would you feel to have been depicted in this way?

17. What was your initial reaction to the book? Did it hook you immediately, or did it take some time to get into?

18. Would you be interested in knowing what happens to Stickney after he leaves prison? Do you want to know if he was able to live a sober lifestyle?

19. Did the book change your opinion or perspective about anything? Do you feel different now than you did before you read it?

20. What was your favorite or most memorable passage in the book? Why did it make an impression?

21. What is your impression of Stickney? Do you think that you would get along with him?

22. What is the book's greatest strength? Most serious flaw?

23. How much did you know about the prison system before you read this book? Did that change your perspective of the content?

24. Were you left wondering what happened to any of the five men after Stickney left?

25. Was the structure of the book helpful to your understanding of the material? If not, how do you think it could be structured?

ABOUT THE AUTHOR

Brandon M. Stickney is a biographer and documentarian. A native of Lockport, New York, with a B.A. from the University at Buffalo, he has appeared in *Time*, the Associated Press, *USA Today*, the *Los Angeles Times*, on A&E, the History Channel, NPR, and every major news network.

He is the author of *All-American Monster: The Unauthorized Biography of Timothy McVeigh* (Prometheus Books, 1996)—in print twenty-two years—and *The Amazing Seven Sutherland Sisters: A Biography of America's First Celebrity Models* (Niagara History Center, 2012). His first book was made into documentaries for A&E, Court TV, FilmRise, and truTV. His second book is a Travel Channel documentary for "Mysteries at the Museum." He is also the author of *The House the Beatles Built: A Memoir of My Time Working for Geoffrey Giuliano*.

Stickney's experience as a biographer, perspective on American incarceration, and his role in the underground world of opiate addiction make him uniquely qualified for this memoir of prison friendship, recovery, and societal reform.